CONVERSION
OF
COMPUTER SOFTWARE

To the men of Plugah Zayin.

וַיֹּאמֶר יְהֹוָה הֵן עַם אֶחָד וְשָׂפָה אַחַת לְכֻלָּם וְזֶה הַחִלָּם לַעֲשׂוֹת וְעַתָּה לֹא־יִבָּצֵר מֵהֶם כֹּל אֲשֶׁר יָזְמוּ לַעֲשׂוֹת:

(בראשית יא 6 ,)

Contents

Preface

The conversion of computer software is a task which most computer industry professionals approach with a mixture of fear and distaste. The decision to convert is usually the alternative of last resort, taken only when all other alternatives have been rejected. Managers hesitate to authorize conversions for fear of massive cost overruns and/or failure to meet schedules and performance objectives. Analysts and programmers usually approach conversion work with a clear lack of enthusiasm, as the work is often boring and repetitive and sometimes maddening.

Nevertheless, the need to convert software grows from year to year. The U.S. General Accounting Office issued a report in September 1977 stating that the federal government was spending more than $450 million to convert programs. Estimates of the worldwide annual cost of conversion is several billion dollars. Some surveys have estimated that the cost of conversion may run as high as 10% of the computing budget.

The purpose of this book is to give the reader an insight into the fundamental concepts of software conversion. The subject is considered from several different points of view:

1. The manager faced with a decision to convert or not to convert
2. The project manager faced with the task of organizing and managing a conversion project
3. The analyst and programmer involved in the details of conversion
4. The analyst and programmer assigned the task of developing conversion aids and tools

Not all subjects are of equal interest to all readers. For this reason the book has been organized so that the various chapters can be read independently. Each chapter includes an introduction and a summary to help the reader decide if the material in the chapter is relevant to his or her needs.

The first three chapters consider the subject from a broad point of view. The conversion process is considered in general terms in Chapter 1. Chapter 2 is devoted to the economics of conversion. Although the cost per line of a conversion varies considerably from case to case, there are a number of general rules that are applicable for all conversions. The management of a conversion project is discussed in Chapter 3. It should be emphasized that many of the well-known concepts regarding the management of software development projects are not completely applicable to conversion projects.

Chapter 4 considers the subject of program enhancements. Portability, performance, and maintainability are discussed in this chapter. The importance of this subject is often overlooked. When the primary objective of a conversion project is to move software from one system to another, a secondary objective can be to improve the software.

The next two chapters are devoted to technical solutions and strategies for conversion. Chapter 5 considers conversion software. Chapter 6 discusses conversion algorithms. The subject of conversion algorithms is really the technical cornerstone of a conversion project. Decisions related to the mapping of programs from one dialect or language to another have a profound influence on the performance of the resulting software.

The final chapter (Chapter 7) presents elements required in a language used for automatic converter development. The CONVERT language is used to illustrate the concepts developed in this chapter.

Throughout the book an attempt is made to use examples from real conversion projects. Examples have been taken from a variety of languages, including COBOL, FORTRAN, PL/1, BASIC, RPG, and Assembler languages. Other examples are related to data conversion and conversion of job control language programs.

Acknowledgements

I have been involved with software conversions since 1975. During this period my experiences with a number of people helped me formulate the opinions and concepts expressed throughout the book. Although I take full responsibility for the contents, I would like to acknowledge the roles played by some of these individuals.

My introduction to conversions resulted from a project initiated by Marshall Rafal of O.L.I. Systems and Kate Kalin of NCSS. We are still working together on a number of interesting projects. I spent several years involved in a variety of conversion projects with Ehud Huberman and Avi Peled, formerly of Shahat Ltd. They both contributed to my understanding of the conversion business.

My work with Alex Hill and Alan Reiter of Reiter Software Systems gave me insight into a number of topics related to the world of software. Through my contacts with Jeff Fenton, formerly of BSO Minisystems, and Bram de Hond of ARA Automation, I have had the opportunity to learn about the conversion marketplace in Europe. I would like to thank Jaap van der Korst of Philips for making it possible for me to spend several weeks at Plan Q seeing how a really big conversion project is managed.

I would like to acknowledge the useful material and insights I received from Nahum Rand of Rand Information Systems and Bob Dinkel of Dataware. Reference is made to this material in the book.

I have worked with a number of people developing conversion software and have learned from their experiences. In particular I would like to acknowledge Eric Hulsbosch, Barbara Lasky, Bernie Roizen, and Adam Rosenzweig.

Some of the material in this book is the result of my own research in the area of software conversions. I would like to thank the Samual Neeman Institute for Advanced Research in Science and Technology for their support of this effort.

The typing of the manuscript was performed by Miriam Beatson, Marion Gold, and Sheila Herskovits. I would like to acknowledge their help and offer my thanks.

I would also like to thank the Technion for all the help I have received throughout the period that I have been involved in this work. A number of my fellow Technion staff members have read sections of the book and have offered useful suggestions.

Finally, thanks to my family for their patience and understanding throughout the duration of this project.

John Wolberg
Haifa, Israel

CONVERSION
OF
COMPUTER SOFTWARE

1

The Conversion Process

1.1 INTRODUCTION

1.1.1 Terminology

The need or desire to move software from one environment to another is fundamental to computer usage. The move might be triggered by a new hardware configuration, a new operating system, or language and compiler changes. Three basic alternatives are usually considered whenever a move is contemplated:

1. *Emulation* is a process whereby the new environment is made to directly execute software that was written for the original environment.
2. *Conversion* is a process in which changes are made in the software so that the original system will execute properly in the new environment.
3. *Replacement* of software is the most radical choice. Alternative software is either developed or obtained for the new environment.

If emulation is possible, no software changes are required. If the conversion option is selected, the original software is used as the starting point from which the new software is developed. Replacement of software implies that the original software is discarded entirely. Replacement can be accomplished by the purchase or leasing of standard software or by a new development effort. We thus see that *conversion* is the middle ground between *emulation* and *replacement*.

When a decision has been made to convert the original software or develop new software, there are four basic strategies for completing the task:

1. *Translation* refers to the primarily automatic conversion of software.
2. *Recoding* refers to the manual conversion of software.
3. *Reprogramming* implies a software development effort which may include some system redesign but no significant functional redesign.
4. *Redesign* implies a software development effort which includes a functional redesign of the system.

Translation and recoding utilize the original software as the primary specification for the new system. Reprogramming and redesign yield software that bears very little resemblance to the original system. Reprogramming is usually a cheaper process than redesign because the old system does not have to be redesigned from a functional point of view.

Regarding terminology, in this book the *conversion* of software implies an important degree of translation and/or recoding. Some modules in the system might be reprogrammed and might even be redesigned; however, the bulk of the effort will be based on the original source code. Thus a distinction is made between systems that are converted, reprogrammed, or redesigned. In Chapter 2 we will see that this distinction has important economic implications.

1.1.2 Changes in the Computer Environment

The incentive for changing a particular computer environment is usually a combination of the following:

1. Reduced cost
2. Improved performance
3. Increased reliability
4. Increased capacity

In some situations the need for change can be caused by a problem such as discontinuation of support for a specific piece of hardware or software. Whatever the reason for change, there is a price associated with this line of action. A decision to change the existing environment (by either hardware or software modifications) must include an analysis of the impact the change will have on the existing application software systems.

For some situations the impact on the applications software will be nonexistent. For example, aquisition of additional disk drives rarely affects the existing software. Alternatively, some changes will have a major impact on the software. For example, replacement of one computer by another computer from a different manufacturer might require a major conversion, reprogramming, or redesign effort.

In analyses of the desirability of change, it is standard practice to list the benefits and costs associated with the new environment. The decision is then based on answers to several questions:

1. Will the new environment answer present and projected needs?
2. Are the estimated benefits associated with the change commensurate with the estimated costs in both hardware and software?
3. If a conversion, reprogramming, or redesign effort is required:
   a. Are suitable personnel available on an in-house basis?
   b. Can the project (or projects) be subcontracted?
   c. What are the estimated durations for the proposed projects?
   d. What computer resources will be required for completing the projects?
   e. What are the cost estimates for the proposed project (or projects)?

There is a degree of risk associated with undertaking major configuration changes. In particular, if the applications software is to be altered, estimates of effort, computer resource requirements, and project duration are subject to error. Gross *underestimates of required resources* to complete the software changes can result in large cost overruns and delays. Clearly, as the size of the software system increases, the risk associated with cost overruns and delays increases.

Another risk associated with changes in configuration is connected with the *predicted performance* of the applications software on the new system. If the old software is compatible with the new environment, a benchmark can be run to measure performance on the new system [1]. However, if a conversion, reprogramming, or redesign effort is required, the predicted performance cannot be totally verified as a phase of the feasibility study. Nevertheless, if the major demands on computer resources can be identified in the original software, some intelligent benchmarking can be used to reduce the probability of unpleasant surprises.

1.1.3 Methodology for Software Modification

Software can be modified by conversion or reprogramming. Some aspects of the methodology for affecting these types of changes are similar. If the software is to be completely redesigned, the methodology is similar to the well-known techniques for developing new software. Clearly, for both alternatives the methodologies are dependent on the system size.

Reasonable procedures for modifying small systems are not reasonable for large systems. For larger systems the degree of planning and coordination must be increased. The task of gathering, cataloging, and controlling the large volume of required material (e.g., programs, files, listings, flowcharts, manuals, etc.) becomes increasingly difficult. Testing procedures for large systems with many alternative paths through the system are clearly more complicated than the procedures required for smaller (and usually simpler) systems.

The actual modification process often complicates normal operations of a computer center. If the demand on computer resources is significant (when compared to total available resources), *scheduling problems* are encountered. For modification of large systems, the need for intensive testing can often significantly increase the normal work load. For critical software systems (i.e., systems that must remain in operation throughout the entire transition period), some degree of *parallel operation* must be anticipated as a part of the acceptance procedure. As a result of delays in software modification, the original budgeted time for parallel operation might be inadequate. If one is forced into the need to run two parallel computer installations for an extended period, large cost overruns are inevitable.

Many of the problems associated with software modification are the result of a lack of experience. Modifying existing software can be different from developing new software. Before undertaking a major software modification effort, it is extremely important to plan the effort intelligently and to be sure that the available personnel are capable of completing the modification successfully. A feasible alternative is to contract the work to a company specializing in the *conversion, migration,* or *transformation* of software. (The major companies providing software modification services often use different terms to describe their services. Conversion, migration, and transformation are probably the three most popular terms in use.)

1.1.4 Conversion versus Reprogramming

It has been noted that both conversion and reprogramming are methods for modifying software. There are similarities associated with these methods of *migration* (i.e., moving applications from one environment to another):

1. Both methods start with the same functional description of the application.
2. From the user's point of view, the software appears to be essentially the same before and after the migration. Whether the migration has been accomplished by conversion or reprogramming is of no interest to the end user.
3. For both methods, operating procedures associated with the application remain essentially the same before and after the migration.
4. For both methods, reports generated as part of the application remain essentially the same before and after the migration.
5. Since the software is only a black box (from the user's point of view) with defined system inputs and outputs, the testing procedures for conversion and reprogramming can be essentially the same.

Nevertheless, a basic difference exists between these two methods of software modification. Conversion technology utilizes the original software as the primary system documentation and starting point. Reprogramming is based only on the original functional description of the application, and the original software is essentially discarded.

The methodology for affecting a particular conversion can be described to a great extent algorithmically (e.g., when we see X, then do Y). Thus conversions can to a large degree be automated. Automation has several important effects on the conversion process:

1. The effort per line tends to decrease with an increasing number of lines. Since cost is usually proportional to effort, the cost per line also tends to decrease with an increasing number of lines.
2. Automation allows most of the conversion effort to be performed by lower-level personnel than are required for a reprogramming effort.
3. The conversion process is usually faster than comparable reprogramming efforts.

These differences lead to important cost advantages for conversions as compared to reprogramming as the size of the original system increases (see Section 2.4). The tendency is thus to convert rather than reprogram large systems when this option is possible. For some situations the conversion alternative is simply not feasible. For example, sensitive real-time applications programmed in an Assembler language and utilizing specific hardware features of the original system are usually reprogrammed if the move is to an entirely new environment. However, for most applications written in higher-level languages, the conversion option should be seriously considered before initiating a reprogramming effort.

1.2 SOFTWARE PORTABILITY

If software was truly portable, the need for conversions would be considerably reduced. The term *portable software* refers to software that can be moved from one computer environment to another with a minimum effort. Fenton defines portable software as software that can be moved after transformation using automatic converters [2]. The computer industry has long recognized the value of portable software; however, how one goes about achieving this goal is a debatable issue. An in-depth review of this subject is included in a book edited by Brown, *Software Portability* [3].

1.2.1 The Portability of Computer Programs

The most important step toward achieving portability of programs is to develop a standard language definition. The first attempt at language standardization was made by the American Standards Association [4]. Their X3.4.3 Committee was formed in 1962 to develop an American Standard FORTRAN and succeeded in issuing two standards in 1966 [5,6]. The first COBOL language standard was completed in 1968 [7].

COBOL is by far the most popular business-oriented programming language, and FORTRAN is the most popular scientific- and engineering-oriented language. Since both languages have been "standardized" for many years, it is useful to consider the impact of their standardization on language portability.

The standardization processes resulted in compromises between what the users wanted in the languages and what the manufacturers were then offering in their FORTRAN and COBOL compilers. There was no incentive for manufacturers to remove features from their compilers which went beyond the standard. In fact, a good marketing strategy was to include nonstandard features in the hope that users would use them and thus get locked into the manufacturers' hardware.

Thus in the late 1960s and early 1970s a variety of COBOL and FORTRAN compilers were released which claimed to be ANS Standard compilers but really were not. The standardization work did not end on publication of the relevant documents. A new COBOL standard was issued in 1974 [8] and a new FORTRAN standard was issued in 1978 [9]. Both standards attested to the fact that the original standards did not freeze the languages.

An analysis of two IBM COBOL compilers and one Univac compiler was reported by Fenton [2] and is summarized in Table 1.1.

TABLE 1.1   COBOL Reserved Words

	Compiler		
	IBM DOS/VS	IBM OS/VS	Univac OS/4
Total reserved words	337	428	311
Total of 300 ANS 74 COBOL reserved words	236	297	198
Percent ANS words missing	21	1	34
Percent reserved words added	43	44	57

These results illustrate the large differences between various compilers, between compilers and the standard language definitions, and even between two compilers issued by the same manufacturer.

Wide differences were also noted in FORTRAN minicomputer compilers [10]. White and Ripley surveyed 24 different minicomputer compilers plus IBM's FORTRAN IV-G and compared them to the ANSI FORTRAN 1966 standard. Ten of the compilers included some restrictions to the standard, but the restrictions were "minor" for four of the ten. All of the compilers included extensions to the standard and 23 of 25 included major extensions. Thus if one were to restrict programming to the standard FORTRAN, a reasonable level of portability could be obtained. However, usage of the extensions drastically reduces portability. The results of the survey are shown in Table 1.2.

TABLE 1.2A Number of Variations from ANSI Standard FORTRAN

Identification		Restrictions						Extensions					
Vendor	Compiler	Nil	Minor	Mod-erate	Mixed	Major	Total	Nil	Minor	Mod-erate	Mixed	Major	Total
Control Data	CYBER 18/MSOS5	0	6	0	1	0	7	0	5	5	0	1	11
Data General/Rolm	FIV	0	2	0	0	0	2	4	13	6	5	1	29
Digital Computer Controls	D-116 F74	0	0	0	0	0	0	1	10	8	3	1	23
Digital Equipment	OS/8	1	9	0	3	5	18	1	2	2	0	1	6
Digital Equipment	OS/8 FIV	0	1	0	0	0	1	3	4	3	3	1	14
Digital Equipment	PDP-9,15 FIV	0	0	0	1	0	1	1	4	5	3	2	15
Digital Equipment	RSX-11M FIV	0	0	0	0	0	0	4	10	10	5	2	31
Digital Equipment	RSX-11M FIV plus	0	0	0	0	0	0	3	11	11	8	2	35
Electronic Associates	PACER 1000 FIV	0	1	0	0	0	1	0	5	4	0	1	10
General Automation	SPC-16 FIV	0	0	0	0	0	0	1	13	4	5	2	25
Hewlett-Packard	HP-3000 II FIV	0	0	0	0	0	0	1	14	9	3	2	29
Honeywell	OS/700	0	7	0	3	3	13	1	14	7	3	2	27
IBM	1130/1800	0	1	0	3	0	4	1	3	2	2	1	9
IBM	System 7	0	0	0	0	0	0	0	15	6	4	2	27
Interdata	32-bit FVI	0	0	0	0	0	0	1	4	6	3	2	16
Interdata	16-bit FIV	0	0	0	0	0	0	1	3	4	2	2	12
Interdata	16/32-bit FV	0	0	0	0	0	0	1	6	6	4	2	19
Lockheed	LEC MAC 16	0	0	0	0	0	0	0	5	3	1	0	9
Lockheed	MAC 16	0	0	0	0	0	0	0	0	1	0	0	1
Modular Computer	Modcomp II	0	0	0	0	0	0	1	10	2	4	2	19
NCR	FIV All levels	0	1	0	0	0	1	0	7	2	3	1	13
Prime Computer	FIV	0	0	0	0	0	0	2	5	6	2	2	17
Varian	V70/620 FIV	0	0	0	0	1	1	0	8	6	3	1	18
Westinghouse	FIV	0	0	0	0	0	0	1	7	3	0	2	13
IBM	360/370 FIV-G	0	0	0	0	0	0	1	8	7	4	2	22
Total occurrences		1	28	0	11	9	49	29	186	128	70	37	450
Type of differences		1	12	0	4	6	23	8	21	11	18	2	60

Source: J. E. White and G. D. Ripley, "How Portable Are Minicomputer FORTRAN Programs?" *Datamation*, July 1977. Reprinted with permission of *Datamation*® Magazine, © by Technical Publishing Co., a Dun & Bradstreet company, 1977. All rights reserved.

TABLE 1.2B Sample of FORTRAN features by dialect.

| Identification | | Naming Conventions | Subscripting | I/O Handling | Special Statements | | |
Vendor	Compiler	Symbolic name (max length)	Number of subscripts in arrays	END-label and ERR-label READ (5, 10, END-100, ERR-50) x, y	ENCODE & DECODE	FIND	PRINT and READ format #, list
ANSI	66 Standard	6	3	no	no	no	no
Control Data	CYBER 18/MSOS5 FIV	6	3	no	yes	no	yes
Data General/Rolm	FIV	31	128*	yes	no	no	no
Digital Computer Controls	D-116 F74	24 (1st 6 used)	128*	no	yes	no	yes
Digital Equipment	OS/8	5	2	no	no	no	no
Digital Equipment	OS/8 FIV	6	7	no	no	no	no
Digital Equipment	PDP-9, 15 FIV	6	3	yes	yes	no	no
Digital Equipment	RSX-11M FIV	6	7	yes	yes	yes	yes
Digital Equipment	RSX-11M FIV Plus	6	7	yes	yes	yes	yes
Electronic Associates	PACER 1000 FIV	6	3	no	no	no	no
General Automation	SPC-16 FIV	6	∞	no	yes	yes	no
Hewlett-Packard	HP-3000 II FIV	15	255	yes	yes	no	no
Honeywell	OS/700	∞ (1st 6 used)	2047	yes**	no	no	no
IBM	1130/1800	5	3	no	no	yes	no
IBM	System 7	6	7	yes	no	yes	no
Interdata	32-bit FVI	6	3	yes	yes	no	no
Interdata	16-bit FIV	6	3	yes	no	no	no
Lockheed	16/32-bit FV	6	3	yes	yes	no	no
Lockheed	MAC 16	6	3	yes	no	no	no
Modular Computer	Modcomp II FIV	∞ (1st 6 used)	3	yes	no	yes	no
NCR	all levels FIV	∞ (1st 6 used)	∞	yes	yes	no	no
Prime Computer	FIV	6	7	yes	no	no	yes
Varian	V70/620 FIV	6	7	yes	yes	yes	no
Westinghouse	FIV	6	3	no	no	no	no
IBM	360/370 FIVG	6	7	yes	no	yes	yes

*a lower bound may be specified, such as ARRAY-10-20)
**"EOF used in place of END

When software has been designed with portability in mind, the complexity of any future conversion is reduced considerably. Several basic steps should be taken to improve portability:

1. Attempt to use only standard language features.
2. Avoid compiler or machine-dependent "tricks" used to save time or memory.
3. Document the program with the aid of comments.
4. Apply programming standards.

Nevertheless, some problems are inherent in the computer architecture and the data. The classical example of an architecturally dependent problem is the conversion of CDC FORTRAN programs to IBM FORTRAN. The FORTRAN IV-G compiler of IBM is based on 32- and 64-bit real numbers, whereas the CDC compilers utilize 60- and 120-bit real numbers. Clearly, floating-point calculations based on the CDC architecture will be made to greater precision than the same calculations on an IBM computer. For some applications (particularly those using large matrices) the added precision can be crucial!

An equally vexing problem exists in some COBOL conversions. When the two compilers are based on different collating sequences, the results of sorting nonnumeric lists will be different. It is clearly possible to program around this problem; however, one should appreciate that a large fraction of computer resources are spent in sorting and merging data (some estimates run as high as 25% of the total computer resources of the typical data processing installation). One should therefore be careful when attempting to solve the collation sequence problem. The solution should not result in a massive degradation of performance in the target system.

1.2.2 Portability of Data

When discussing software portability, one must also consider the portability of data. In particular, the growth of large *data base management systems* (DBMSs) has caused acute portability problems. When large amounts of data have been stored in a specific data base, it can be a major effort to convert the data to a form that is applicable to another DBMS. The user turns over the details of data storage and retrieval to the DBMS, and the DBMS is designed to organize the data in an efficient manner. However, efficient storage for one DBMS might be disastrous for another. Thus the portability of data is an extremely important subject when one considers the portability of software.

1.2.3 Summary

Portability is a worthwhile goal and steps can be taken to improve the portability of software. However, fundamental differences among various compilers, operating systems, and hardware make the goal of really portable software almost impossible to achieve. Even for old "standard" languages such as COBOL and FORTRAN, differences between compilers are still considerable. An attempt is being made by the U.S. Department of Defense to promote a language called Ada, which will truly yield portable software [11], yet the fruits of this and similar efforts will not be felt for some years to come. We are therefore left with a portability problem, and this problem often leads to software conversion.

1.3 THE DEVELOPMENT OF PROGRAMMING LANGUAGES

Some background in the general subject of programming languages is useful for an understanding of software conversion problems. A historical perspective of the development of programming yields an insight into the differences between various languages and language dialects. The process of converting programs requires an awareness of the differences in order to formulate a strategy for their resolution.

1.3.1 Current Language Usage

Before considering the developments leading to the proliferation of languages, it is useful to analyze the current usage of computer languages. Several surveys of language usage have been published and are summarized in Tables 1.3 to 1.5.

The results of all three studies confirm two well-known facts:

1. COBOL is by far the most popular programming language.
2. The use of Assembler languages is still significant.

The three surveys took place in the years 1972 to 1977 and clearly the situation has not remained static since then. Nevertheless, these two facts are equally valid in 1982.

The results tend to present a conflicting picture for RPG usage. The Datapro survey (Table 1.3) notes a fairly impressive RPG usage (20%), whereas Philippakis noted a decrease in RPG usage from 6% to 4% (Table 1.4). The EEC RPG usage was so low that it fell into the

TABLE 1.3   Datapro Survey: Percentage Usage
of Languages in 5813 Data Processing Centers[a]

Language	Percent Usage
COBOL	38
RPG	20
FORTRAN	12
Assembler	12
BASIC	7
PL/1	2
APL	1
Other	8
	100

[a]Each center responded on the basis of percent usage
for all languages and the percent usages were averaged
for all centers. Many centers used programs written in
more than one language.

Source: H. L. Gepner, "User Ratings of Software
Packages," *Datamation,* December 1977. Reprinted
with permission of *Datamation*®   Magazine, © by
Technical Publishing Co., a Dun & Bradstreet company, 1977. All rights reserved.

"other" category. The explanation for this apparent discrepancy can be
explained by language usage as a function of installation size. Installations using large computers (e.g., IBM 360/370/303x series) tend to use
COBOL, whereas smaller installations using small business computers
(e.g., IBM Systems 3 and 32) tend to use RPG. The Datapro survey
reached a much wider cross section of installations and included a larger
percentage of small installations than the other two surveys. Thus the
Datapro results showed a lower COBOL usage and a larger RPG usage.

The results regarding FORTRAN usage are conflicting. Large
installations doing primarily commercial data processing use very little
FORTRAN (as reflected in the EEC and Philippakis surveys). Installations doing primarily scientific and engineering work tend to be heavy
FORTRAN users. This category includes some installations with large
computers (e.g., CDC 6600 and 7600 series) and many minicomputer
installations (e.g., PDP 11/xx series). The Datapro survey included a
larger percentage of these types of installations.

The PL/1 results also require explanation. The main users of PL/1
are large IBM installations. Other hardware manufacturers offer PL/1
(e.g., CDC and Burroughs); however, the compilers are relatively new
and their usage is relatively modest. The increasing popularity of PL/1
at large IBM installations is reflected in the results of Philippakis (Table
1.4). The popularity of PL/1 in Europe is reflected in the EEC survey
results (Table 1.5). The low usage of PL/1 in the Datapro survey is a
result of the many smaller installations included in this survey.

TABLE 1.4   Programming Language Usage for the Years 1972 and 1977[a]

Language	1977			1972		
	Number of Sites	Average Percent Usage Where Used	Usage Index (%)	Number of Sites	Average Percent Usage Where Used	Usage Index (%)
Assembler	97	22	16	124	27	20
APL	4	14	0.4	1	1	0
BASIC	11	15	1	14	13	1
COBOL	119	70	63	138	70	59
FORTRAN	45	9	3	79	11	5
PL/1	26	32	6	26	28	4
RPG	23	25	4	49	20	6
Other	42	16	5	33	17	3

[a]This survey included 132 sites in 1977 and 164 in 1972. The usage index is defined as the average percent usage (where used) times the fraction of sites using the language. For example, the 63% value for COBOL in 1977 is computed as follows: 70% × 119/132.

Source: A. S. Philippakis, "A Popularity Contest for Languages," *Datamation*, December 1977. Reprinted with permission of *Datamation*® Magazine, © by Technical Publishing Co., a Dun & Bradstreet company, 1977. All rights reserved.

TABLE 1.5   EEC (European Economic Community) Survey of about 100 Data Processing Centers by the Software House CAP-SOGETI[a]

Language	Percent Usage
COBOL	56
Assembler	22
PL/1	12
FORTRAN	7
Other	3
	100

[a]The survey was performed in 1975 and was admittedly biased toward larger commercial installations.

Source: P. J. Brown, "EEC Work on Portability," in *Software Portability*, Cambridge University Press, New York, 1977, Chap. VIII.B.

A discussion of current language usage would be incomplete without recognition of the current trend toward *nonprocedural languages*. Traditional languages such as COBOL and FORTRAN are called *procedural languages*. The programmer of a procedural language instructs the computer *how to do* a given task, whereas the programmer of a nonprocedural language merely defines *what has to be done*. Languages falling within the nonprecedural class include vendor proprietary software products such as MARK IV, NOMAD, and RAMIS. Many of the nonprocedural languages are designed to operate in a DBMS environment. Although current usage of nonprocedural languages is still relatively small, usage has grown considerably in recent years. McCracken predicts that by the mid-1980s more than half of all computer time will be spent running applications programs constructed with nonprocedural-oriented languages [12].

1.3.2 Historical Perspective of Programming Languages

An excellent review of the history of programming languages through the late 1960s is included in Jean Sammet's book; *Programming Languages: History and Fundamentals* [4]. The proceedings of the ACM SIGPLAN History of Programming Languages Conference [13] is an important source of information, with particular emphasis on the technical factors that influenced the development of a selected group of important languages. The group of languages was limited to those that were in use by 1967, still in use in 1977, and had a considerable influence on the field of computing. The criteria for choosing the languages included usage, influence on language design, overall impact on the environment, novelty, and uniqueness.

If one were to generalize about the basic trend in computer language development over the past several decades, the main conclusion is that languages tend more and more toward simplification of programming from the user's point of view. The evidence supporting this conclusion can be summarized in three separate developments:

1. The development of higher-and-higher-level languages which include features unavailable in older languages and their dialects (e.g., APL and PL/1 compared to FORTRAN for engineering and scientific applications, Pascal and PL/1 compared to COBOL for commercial applications).

2. The development of data base management systems for simplifying a wide variety of commercial applications (e.g., ADABAS, IDMS, IMS, TOTAL).

3. The development of special-purpose languages for simplifying

specific problem areas (e.g., APT for programming numerically controlled machine tools, LISP for list processing, and SNOBOL for text processing).

As a result of this trend toward programming simplicity, new applications can be developed in a much more cost effective manner than was possible a decade ago. To appreciate where we are at today, it is useful to reflect back on the early history of programming languages.

The early papers (circa 1946) of Goldstine and von Neumann [14] influenced the development of both computer hardware and software to such an extent that some of their basic design principles are still relevant today:

1. Numerically coded instructions and addresses
2. A uniformly addressed linear store
3. A single accumulator
4. Data stored in binary form
5. Programs and data treated in the same manner (allowing creation and modification of programs)

The point that these early giants of the computer industry seemed to miss was that programming at the machine language level would prove to be progressively less feasible as the power of computers (and thus complexity of applications) grew. However, the die had been cast— and to this day, higher-level-language compilers are usually built around existing computer architecture. If the need for higher-level languages had been recognized from the beginning of the computer age, the design of languages and the development of computer architecture could have been complementary. Much of the existing chaos in the industry might have been avoided.

To appreciate the need for a higher-level language, one need only glance at a machine language instruction [4]:

011011   000000   000000   000000   000001   000000

Writing entire programs (sequence of instructions) in such a cumbersome form proved to be impractical, so the earliest improvements in machine languages allowed one to use mnemonic codes and decimal notation to represent instructions. For example, the equivalent form of the foregoing binary machine language instruction might be

CLA   0   0   0   64

Thus, through a progression of improvements, machine languages evolved from a purely binary form to a form with a higher and higher degree of symbolic notation and abstraction. The concept of a *programming language* was the natural outgrowth of this process.

Sammet discusses the problem of defining what is and what is not a programming language. She concludes that a programming language is *a set of characters and rules for combining them which have the following characteristics:*

1. The user can write a program without knowing much—if anything —about the physical characteristics of the machine on which the program is to be run.
2. The language must have some significant amount of machine independence.
3. There should be no need for the user to write any sequence of machine code. Normally, more than one machine instruction is created for each statement in the programming language.
4. The language must have a notation which is somewhat closer to the specific problem being solved than is normal machine code.

Prior to 1957 a number of automatic coding systems had already been developed which satisfied these criteria to some degree. Sammet lists the American systems in approximate chronological order:

1. Short code (Univac)
2. Speedcoding (IBM 701)
3. Laning and Zieler System (Whirlwind)
4. A-2 and A-3 (Univac)
5. BACAIC (IBM 701)
6. PRINT (IBM 705)

By 1959 the list included more than 100 languages (or automatic programming systems) for use on more than 20 computers.

Thus, prior to 1960, the scene had been set: A wide variety of different languages had been developed for varying purposes and for use on different computers. Even within the same company, different groups worked on different languages without any serious attempt at coordination. One could hardly expect that this situation could have been avoided. A number of companies were making strenuous efforts to enter the computer field and useful software was a prerequisite to selling hardware. There was a tremendous incentive to provide languages that would complement the existing hardware. There was very little incentive to attempt to see where the industry was going, develop language standards for the computers of the future, and then proceed in an orderly fashion.

In May 1962, the industry attempted to standardize one language.[1] American Standards Association Committee X3.4.3 was formed to develop a FORTRAN language standard. The FORmula TRANslating system, FORTRAN, was originally developed by the Programming Research Group of the Applied Science Division of IBM. The first instruction manual was issued in 1956 [15]. IBM continued to develop FORTRAN and in June 1958 released their new version: FORTRAN II. The most important new features in this version of the language were the subroutine concept (i.e., the SUBROUTINE, FUNCTION, CALL, and RETURN statements) and the COMMON statement. The END statement was also added to allow independent compilation of the main program and the subroutines. The other manufacturers realized the importance of FORTRAN and a number of FORTRAN compilers were released in the early 1960s.

The ALTAC system (developed for the Philco 2000) was an extended version of FORTRAN II and was released in 1960. Univac released their first FORTRAN compiler in 1961. By 1963 almost all manufacturers had released a FORTRAN compiler or had committed themselves to producing some version of FORTRAN. At that time there was no standard on which one could proceed, so each manufacturer worked to the best of its ability. Work started on a standard FORTRAN in 1962, but the standard was not accepted until 1966.

One might assume that once an agreed-upon FORTRAN standard was available, the differences between the various versions of the language would decrease with time. However, the opposite seems to have happened. FORTRAN 66 is a very limited language, particularly in such areas as input/output, data structures, and character string manipulation. Many manufacturers (with the notable exception of IBM), started adding features to strengthen their version of FORTRAN. The 1970s have seen the remarkable rise of the minicomputers, each mini usually accompanied by a FORTRAN compiler. The number of restrictions and extensions for the various minicomputer FORTRAN compilers as compared to the standard (see Table 1.2) is considerable and is further proof that a language standard is only the first step in promoting portable software [10].

The second major language to be standardized was COBOL (COmmon Business-Oriented Language). The development of COBOL differed significantly from the development of FORTRAN. A meeting of users, manufacturers, and academic representatives was held at the University of Pennsylvania Computing Center in April 1959 to discuss the possibility of developing a common business language. As a result

---

[1] The subject of *language standardization* is treated in detail in a recent book by Hill and Meek [16].

of the meeting, a second meeting was sponsored by the U.S. Department of Defense at which several committees were set up to proceed with the concept [4]. The unique feature of the project was that the committees included representatives of six manufacturers (Burroughs, IBM, Minneapolis-Honeywell, RCA, Remington-Rand, and Sylvania). The development of COBOL was initiated as an industry-wide project. One might have expected that the resulting COBOL versions would exhibit a much higher degree of portability than FORTRAN (which was clearly an IBM-conceived language). The differences among the COBOLs of today are approximately as numerous as the differences among the FORTRANs, even though the COBOL standard is newer. (The first ANSI COBOL standard was accepted in 1968 and the revised ANSI COBOL standard was accepted in 1974.) Comparisons of various COBOL compilers are included in papers by Fisher [17] and Fenton [2]. Both authors note considerable differences.

Besides FORTRAN and COBOL, a number of other languages conceived and developed in the 1960s are in widespread use today. The list of languages discussed in the ACM SIGPLAN History of Programming Languages Conference [13] includes the following: ALGOL60, APL, APT, BASIC, COBOL, FORTRAN, GPSS, JOSS, JOVIAL, LISP, PL/1, SIMULA, and SNOBOL. Very few languages developed in the 1970s have yet to achieve widespread usage. (The post-1970 languages falling into this catagory are Pascal and the major DBMS languages). Paradoxically, Assembler languages (which are really the first step beyond machine language programming) are still used extensively.

A question often asked is the following: With all the incredible advances in computer software technology, why do such clearly cumbersome languages as COBOL, RPG, Assembler, and FORTRAN still dominate the world of computer software? Three reasons seem to provide the best explanation for this phenomenon:

1. The most widely used languages, such as COBOL, RPG, and FORTRAN, offer the best opportunities for portability.
2. Approximately two-thirds of all software activity is involved with program maintenance; thus languages tend to be self-perpetuating. If, for example, the programming staff of a particular installation is required to be thoroughly familar with COBOL in order to maintain the existing COBOL programs, there is a certain incentive for continuing to program in this language.
3. Language maturity is often characterized by several side benefits, such as efficient compilers which are relatively bug-free, and extensive libraries of utility-type routines.

To summarize, the area of programming languages has proven to be much less prone to change than the area of computer hardware. The popular languages of the 1960s still dominate the scene. Many of the less popular languages of the 1960s have faded from use, and newer languages geared to more recent technological advances are becoming more important. The differences between various versions of the same language are serious impediments to software portability. Dialect differences are still considerable in the two major languages that were originally standardized in the 1970s: COBOL and FORTRAN.

The use of nonprocedural languages is growing but their use is still only a small factor when one considers the entire scene. The dream of really portable software is still far from becoming a reality and the need for conversions will be with us for many years.

1.4 PROGRAM CONVERSIONS

A complete conversion consists of conversion of all components of a software system, including programs, data, job control statements, and so on. However, the conversion of computer programs is usually the most challenging phase of the project. Within the confines of a particular computer language one can utilize a wide variety of different statement types. The difficulties encountered in converting a program are dependent on the manner in which the program is written. Programs in the same language and of the same length might require totally different levels of effort for conversion. The variety inherent in program conversions is usually greater than the variety one finds in other phases of a conversion project (e.g., data and job control files).

When considering program conversions we normally refer to a *source state* and a *target state*. The description of each state includes several elements: the programming language and version (i.e., dialect), the compiler used to generate the object programs, the machine configuration, and the operating system. The source and target states may differ in one or more of these elements. All program conversions fall into one of three categories:

1. The target is to be a different version of the same source language (e.g., CDC FORTRAN Version 2.3 to IBM FORTRAN IV-G).
2. The target language is different from the source language (e.g., RPG II to ANS-COBOL).
3. The source and the target states both utilize the same version of a given language (e.g., any language reformatter or source code optimizer).

These three alternatives are summarized in Table 1.6. A relative *ease-of-conversion* rating is also included in the table. A rating of *easy* implies that the differences between the source and target states are easily defined and that the conversion can be specified algorithmically. For such conversion one can expect to acquire or develop automatic converters that will be close to 100% effective.

A rating of *difficult* implies that the mapping between the source and target states is more complex. Algorithms can be defined to do many of the required tasks; however, some tasks will require visual examination of the source code and manual change. Automatic converters can be used to assist in the conversion; however, even after a pass through the converter, a significant amount of manual effort will be required to complete the task.

A rating of *very difficult* implies that very little help can be expected from automatic converters because most of the source-to-target mapping cannot be described algorithmically. For such cases, the conversion often degenerates into a line-by-line rewrite of the source programs. It is sometimes useful first to convert the source programs into an intermediate language (often called a meta-language). The conversion from the meta-language to the target language is (hopefully) simpler than a direct conversion from the source language.

TABLE 1.6   Different Types of Program Conversions

| Type | Source | | Target | | Ease of Conversion |
	Language	Version	Language	Version	
1: Intra-language	L1	V1	L1	V2	Easy to difficult
2: Inter-language	L1		L2		Difficult to very difficult
3: Same compiler	L1	V1	L1	V1	Usually easy

1.4.1 Type 1: Intralanguage Conversion

As denoted in Table 1.6, intralanguage conversions imply conversions from one dialect of a given language (i.e., version VI of language L1) to another dialect of the same language (i.e., version V2 of language L1). The ease-of-conversion rating for these types of conversions can vary from easy to difficult. The conversion tends to be easy if version V2 is a more powerful version of L1 than V1. If V2 includes V1 as a subset, the conversion might be trivial. For example, there are many versions of FORTRAN that are compatible with the 1966 FORTRAN IV standard but yet include many expanded features (e.g., CDC FORTRAN). The G version of IBM FORTRAN IV is closer to the 1966 FORTRAN IV standard, so conversions from IBM FORTRAN IV-G to CDC FORTRAN are usually easy.

The alternative situation (i.e., V1 is more powerful than V2) results in more difficult conversions. For example, conversions from CDC FORTRAN to IBM FORTRAN IV-G can be difficult if the programs include some of the more exotic CDC FORTRAN features. This concept can be illustrated by the ENCODE and DECODE statements of CDC FORTRAN. These statements are like WRITE and READ statements but no peripheral equipment is involved. They are in-core WRITE and READ statements (e.g., from one variable location to another). An example from the CDC FORTRAN Reference Manual (6000 Version 2.3) demonstrates ENCODE:

```
    DIMENSION A(2), B(2), ALPHA (4)
    A(1) = 'ABCDEFGHIJ'
    A(2) = 'KLMNO'
    B(1) = 'PQRSTUVWXY'
    B(2) = 'Z12345'
    ENCODE (20,1, ALPHA) A,B
  1 FORMAT (A10,A5/A10,A6)
```

The ENCODE statement means that records of 20 characters are to be written from the variables A and B to the variable ALPHA according to FORMAT 1. For this case, A, B, and ALPHA are vectors. The result of this ENCODE is the following (where the character "b" denotes a blank):

First record		Second record	
ABCDEFGHIJ	KLMNObbbbb	PQRSTUVWXY	Z12345bbbb
word 1	word 2	word 3	word 4
ALPHA(1)	ALPHA (2)	ALPHA(3)	ALPHA(4)

It should be noted that 6000 series CDC computers are word-oriented machines, each word containing 10 BCD characters (or 60-bit numbers).

The conversion of CDC FORTRAN programs to IBM FORTRAN IV-G is complicated if ENCODE and DECODE are used. There are several machine architectural differences that are important:

1. IBM uses EBCDIC code (an 8-bit-per-character code) and CDC uses BCD code (a 6-bit-per-character code).

2. Single-precision IBM variables are 4 bytes per variable and double-precision variables are 8 bytes per variable. CDC single-precision variables are 10 bytes per variable.

There are several important language differences:

1. IBM FORTRAN does not include ENCODE or DECODE (or a reasonable equivalent).
2. IBM FORTRAN does not allow direct assignment of character strings [e.g., A(1) = 'ABCDEFGHIJ'].

If the usage of characters throughout the CDC programs is strictly for report or character data generation, the differences between EBCDIC code and BCD code are unimportant. (It hardly matters how the letter A is stored internally if all we are interested in is its appearance on a printed report.) If, however, the numerical equivalent of a character variable is used (e.g., in a SORT routine), then the differences between EBCDIC and BCD might cause differences in the final results (which might or might not be important).

The difference between 4 and 10 characters per variable can be important if the program logic requires addressing to particular elements within a vector that is being used to store character data. However, if the whole vector is being used as a single character string, the logic is usually straightforward.

The lack of ENCODE and DECODE can be overcome by writing equivalent routines (either in FORTRAN or in Assembler). In fact, many IBM installations using FORTRAN for nonnumeric applications have available library routines which are equivalent or can be used to accomplish the same tasks. (An excellent introduction to nonnumeric computations in an IBM 360/370 FORTRAN environment is included in a book by Brillinger and Cohen [18].)

The assignment of character strings is probably the most trivial of all the problems listed above. The simplest solution is to use the FORTRAN DATA statement. However, if a particular variable is going to be assigned and reassigned to the values of a variety of character strings, a more elegant approach is to write an alternative routine (let us call it MOVE).

An IBM equivalent form of the CDC FORTRAN program segment included above might be the following:

```
DIMENSION A(5), B(5), ALPHA(10)
CALL MOVE (A, 1,'ABCDEFGHIJ')
CALL MOVE (A,11, 'KLMNO')
CALL MOVE (B,1, 'PQRSTUVWXY')
```

```
CALL MOVE (B, 11, 'Z12345')
CALL ENCODE (20, 1, ALPHA, A,B)
1  FORMAT (A10,A5/A10,A6)
```

Note that the number of elements per array has been increased by a factor of 2.5 so that the number of characters per array is the same in the converted program. (If 2.5 times the number of elements is not an integer number, one would simply have to increase the dimension of the array to the next integer number.)

It should be emphasized that some intralanguage problems are inherent in machine differences and not language differences. Continuing with the CDC to IBM FORTRAN example, the long word length of CDC variables is particularly advantageous for some numeric calculations. The advantage becomes crucial when high-precision calculations are required. Increasingly in many engineering and scientific programs the calculations involve manipulation of large matrices of numbers (e.g., in finite-element calculations used in engineering design). Often one must carry intermediate calculations to extreme accuracy (let us say 20 decimal places for floating-point numbers) to get acceptable final results (let us say three-decimal-place accuracy). Using DOUBLE PRECISION numbers in IBM FORTRAN IV-G, the maximum accuracy that could be obtained is eight decimal places, which is insufficient for this example. The alternative conversion strategies are the following:

1. Utilize an IBM FORTRAN compiler that permits greater precision (e.g., the IBM FORTRAN IV-H-Extended compiler).
2. Develop a software approach to the problem. For example, remainders of arithmetic operations could be stored and then used in subsequent calculations.

Such an approach would require a redesign of the arithmetic functions used in the programs. Besides requiring the services of a competent mathematician on the conversion team, the resulting programs might be difficult to understand (and thus to maintain) and there might be performance degradation problems.

To summarize intralanguage conversions, the following conclusions are generally applicable:

1. If V2 is more powerful than V1, the conversion is usually easy.
2. If V1 is more powerful than V2, the situation can be difficult. However,
   a. If we examine the actual usage of V1, the situation might be less complicated than one might expect from a comparison of the two language reference manuals.

b. Automatic converters geared to the differences between the two versions but limited to the important differences noted in the source (i.e., V1) programs can probably be developed which complete the bulk of the conversion.

c. Even if the source (i.e., V1) programs are written using the full power of V1, conversion strategies can usually be developed to permit a large degree of automatic conversion. The resulting programs might be difficult to understand (and maintain) and might suffer from significant performance degradation. For such cases, one might want to consider a certain amount of reprogramming as opposed to conversion, particularly for the program modules using a large amount of the system resources (i.e., CPU time, input/output).

A growing area of interest in intra-language conversion is from one microcomputer BASIC to another. More and more software is being written for the *personal computer* market and much of this software is written in BASIC. I recently reviewed a book by Helms which compares a variety of popular BASICS [19]: Apple II Applesoft, Atari 400/800, Commodore PET, IBM Advanced Personal Computer, Radio Shack Level II, Radio Shack Extended Color, and Texas Instruments 99/4. The book includes useful information for facilitating conversions among these dialects of BASIC.

1.4.2 Type 2: Interlanguage Conversion

Conversion from one language to another (i.e., L1 to L2) is usually the most difficult type of program conversion. Conversions of this type range from difficult to very difficult. A variety of automatic converters exist for various language combinations, however, one should not expect the converters to be 100% effective. A partial list of commercially available interlanguage converters is included in Table 1.7.

Many suppliers claim a high percentage conversion rate for their automatic converters (e.g., greater than 95%). Indeed, for some simple source programs the automatic conversion might be 100% effective (i.e., the resulting code compiles error-free and executes properly with test data). However, for some cases, even though the automatic converter succeeds in achieving a high percentage conversion, the semantics associated with the source programs cause severe problems even though the syntactical problems are easily resolved. Clearly, programs originally developed with portability in mind will be more apt to pass through a converter with a minimum of problems.

When a program has been written using clever tricks based on language and compiler idiosyncracies, the execution of a target program

TABLE 1.7 Some Commercially Available Interlanguage Converters

Source Language	Target Language	Supplier	Comments
PLAN	COBOL	Olympic Systems, Pittsburgh, Pa.	ICL 1900 series PLAN programs to ANS COBOL
Autocoder	COBOL	Dataware, Tonawanda, N.Y.	7070 or 7074 Autocoder to ANS COBOL (DOS or OS)
PL/1	COBOL	Dataware	IBM PL/1 to ANS COBOL (both PL/1 and COBOL can be OS or DOS)
Easycoder Easytran	COBOL	Dataware	Honeywell Easycoder and Easytran to ANS COBOL (DOS or OS)
RPG	PL/1	Dataware	RPG or RPG II (IBM System 3, MOD 20, 360/370 DOS/OS, or Univac 9200 and 9300) to IBM PL/1 (DOS or OS)
FORTRAN IV	PL/1	O.L.I. Systems New York, N.Y.	FORTRAN IV to PL/1
PL/2	FORTRAN	O.L.I. Systems	PL/1 to FORTRAN IV aid
RPG	COBOL	Dataware	IBM DOS/OS RPG, System 3 RPG II, Univac 9300 RPG, H200 RPG to ANS COBOL to run on IBM 360/370 processors using DOS or OS
RPG	COBOL	Philips, Eindhoven, the Netherlands	RPG programs from IBM, Siemens, or Univac to ANS COBOL

TABLE 1.7 (cont.)

Source Language	Target Language	Supplier	Comments
Assembler	COBOL	Dataware	IBM 360/370 (DOS to OS) or MOD 20 BAL to IBM ANS COBOL (DOS or OS)
1400 OBJECT	COBOL	C-S Computer Systems, New York, N.Y.	1401/40/60 OBJECT decks to any COBOL
RPG	COBOL	DASD, Milwaukee, Wisc.	Most RPGs to ANS COBOL
DIBOL	COBOL	DASD	DEC DIBOL to most COBOLs
NEAT 3	COBOL	DASD	NCR NEAT 3 to most COBOLs
NEAT 3	COBOL	Univac	NCR NEAT 3 to Univac COBOL
NEAT 3	COBOL	Honeywell	NCR NEAT 3 to Honeywell COBOL
Assembler	COBOL	Hopper	Burroughs B300/B500 Assembler to COBOL
Easycoder	COBOL	Honeywell	Honeywell Easycoder to COBOL
PL/1	COBOL	Univac	PL/1 to COBOL
PLAN	Assembler	Univac	ICL 1900 PLAN to Univac Assembler
FORTRAN	COBOL	F. Lenker & Assoc., Raleigh, N.C.	FORTRAN to COBOL

can lead to erroneous results even though the program is syntactically correct. For some situations, automatic converters can be designed to scan for dangerous semantical usage and issue suitable warnings. Once a warning has been issued, the next step is to examine the code to ascertain if changes must be made.

In general, if L1 is less powerful than L2, one can usually design for a relatively high level of automatic conversion. One would expect that the most important functions of L1 could easily be reproduced in L2. When L1 is more powerful than L2, the situation is reversed. Usually, some important functions in L1 have no simple equivalent in L2. For such cases, automatic converters are less effective. However, for programs written in L1 but not utilizing the full power of L1, the program convertibility to L2 is greater.

1.4.3 Type 3: Same-Compiler Conversions

The simplest type of conversions are for programs for which the source and target states are the same. There are several types of conversions that fall within this category:

1. Conversions to make programs conform to standards
2. Conversions to improve performance
3. Conversions to a new system concept (e.g., a new file access method) within the framework of a particular compiler

For such cases the conversions are usually easy. One can expect to accomplish most if not all of the conversion automatically.

As an example of conversions for which the source and target states are the same, let us consider the general topic of *program standardization*. The reasons for transforming programs to a standard form include the following:

1. Facilitate maintenance
2. Facilitate conversion (and/or portability)

(It is easier to convert programs written in a standard form than programs written according to each programmer's whim.)

Clearly, the standards imposed on the programmer are language and installation dependent. Nevertheless, for most languages and installations there is a fairly high degree of similarity between various standards. The elements of style that form the basis of a standard include many universal concepts. Van Tassel [20] discusses a number of topics which are normally included in programming standards:

1. Comments
2. Blank lines
3. Blank spaces
4. Identification and sequence numbering
5. Selection of variable names
6. File names
7. Standard abbreviations
8. Splitting words
9. Punctuation
10. Placement of statements
11. Alphabetizing lists
12. Parentheses
13. Paragraphing
14. Selection of paragraph names

Consider, for example, the following COBOL program segment discussed by Brown [21]:

```
IF COST IS EQUAL TO ZERO MOVE ZERO TO PAGE-A, MOVE 1 TO NEW-LINE,
ELSE PERFORM MAX-SIZE, IF COST IS GREATER THAN ZERO PERFORM
ZERO-COST, ELSE PERFORM BIG-COST.
```

A COBOL standard might require this segment to be written as follows:

```
IF COST = 0
    THEN MOVE 0 TO PAGE-A
        MOVE 1 TO NEW-LINE
    ELSE PERFORM MAX-SIZE
        IF COST > 0
            THEN PERFORM ZERO-COST
            ELSE PERFORM BIG-COST.
```

The logical structure of this segment is now much clearer than in the original form.

As a second example, consider the following PL/I program segment:

```
A = B+C;  DO  I = 1 TO N;  D(I) = I;  END;
```

If we assume that our standard requires single statements per line, indention of DO loops, and blank spaces around operators, the converted code would appear as follows:

```
A = B + C;
DO I = 1 TO N;
   D(I) = I;
END;
```

A FORTRAN example illustrates the advantages of alphabetizing lists. Consider the following COMMON block:

```
COMMON X,Y,A,B,D,
+C, JOHN, JOE, ETA, VEL
+BINARY
```

After standardization the COMMON block might appear as follows:

```
   COMMON A,    B,    BINARY, C,    D,
1           ETA, JOE, JOHN,     VEL, X,
2           Y
```

The revised form of this COMMON block makes it easier to locate variables. However, a familiarity with FORTRAN should make a programmer apprehensive about such a change. Unless the COMMON block is exactly the same in all subroutines and function routines, alphabetizing COMMON blocks can lead to extremely subtle logical errors. This example illustrates that good programming techniques might not necessarily be applicable to standarization of existing programs!

1.5 COMPLETE SYSTEM CONVERSIONS

Conversion of a complete system can be subdivided into a number of phases:

1. Planning
2. Data preparation
3. Conversion
4. Testing
5. Implementation

The percentage of total cost associated with each phase is clearly variable. In Chapter 2 some general rules of thumb are discussed; however, one should be aware that there are considerable differences among different types of conversions.

In this section data bases of 9 and 31 completed conversion projects are analyzed. The data represent the experience of Rand Information Systems (RIS) in large system conversions [22]. It should be appreciated that RIS has been specializing in conversions since 1968. During that period they have developed a methodology and a variety of conversion tools and aids [23]. One can therefore expect that their effort (measured in person-hours or person-months) and their project duration (measured in months) would be lower than if the same tasks were performed in-house using personnel relatively inexperienced in large system conversions.

The RIS data base of nine completed conversion projects is summarized in Table 1.8. If we assume 173.2 person-hours per person-month,[1] the project effort ranges from 59.1 to 343.8 person-months. The project duration ranges from 7 to 32 months. Most of the mainframe manufacturers are represented in the data base (Burroughs, CDC, GE, Honeywell, ICL, IBM, and Univac). A variety of languages are represented; however, the emphasis is on COBOL. This result is not surprising. As noted in Section 1.4 (see Tables 1.4 and 1.5), more than 50% of the usage on mainframe computers is for COBOL programs.

A second RIS data base of 38 projects includes duration information for 31 projects but no information regarding person-months of effort. These data are summarized in Table 1.9. It is interesting to note the variety of source-to-target combinations. It should also be noted that the nine projects included in Table 1.8 are also included in Table 1.9.

The data are shown graphically in Figures 1.1 and 1.2. There is considerable scatter in the data, so a straight line seems to be the most reasonable model for representing the functional relationships. A straight line on a log-log plot is an equation of the form

$$y = a_1 L^{a_2} \tag{1.1}$$

where y is the dependent variable [i.e., E (effort) or D (duration)], and L is the independent variable (thousands of lines to be converted). The parameters a_1 and a_2 were determined using the method of least squares. Values of a_1 and a_2 are dependent on the method used to weight the data [24].

The weighting used for the data in Figure 1.1 was

$$w_i = \frac{1}{E_i} \tag{1.2}$$

This equation implies that greater weight was given to the points with smaller values of E. This is reasonable because the variance in the data increases with increasing E. To a nonstatistician, what exactly does this mean? If we were to repeat a particular conversion project many times

[1] Boehm suggests a value of 152 hours per person-month [25].

TABLE 1.8 Rand Experience in Large Conversions

Number of Programs	Number of Statements	Source Environment	Target Environment	Duration (Months)	Person-Hours
1673	2000K	Honeywell COBOL, FORTRAN, BASIC	Burroughs B7700 COBOL, FORTRAN, BASIC, DMS	23	35,146
1620	1300K	IBM 360 COBOL, FORTRAN, IDMS	Univac COBOL, FORTRAN, DMS	18	59,376
1500	500K	IBM 370 COBOL	Burroughs B6700 COBOL	12	35,532
729	571K	IBM 370 COBOL, FORTRAN	Honeywell 60/66 COBOL, FORTRAN	24	24,657
382	308K	ICL 1900 COBOL, FORTRAN	IBM 370 COBOL, FORTRAN	12	12,384
344	311K	IBM 7074, 1401 Autocoder	IBM 370 PL/1	18	38,987
213	32K	Burroughs 6700 COBOL	IBM 370 PL/1	7	10,236
200	179K	Univac Series 70 ALC, Honeywell 60/66 COBOL	Honeywell 60/66 COBOL, IBM 370 COBOL	32	37,014
157	160K	GE 415 MAP, COBOL, CDC 6600 COBOL	Univac 1100 COBOL	10	5,819

TABLE 1.9   Rand Experience in Large Conversions

Number of Programs	Number of Statements	Source Environment	Target Environment	Duration (Months)	Average Statements/ Program
1673	2000K	Honeywell COBOL, FORTRAN, BASIC	Burroughs B7700 COBOL, FORTRAN, BASIC, DMS	23	1195
1620	1300K	IBM 360 COBOL, FORTRAN, IDMS	Univac COBOL, 1100 FORTRAN, DMS	18	802
1600	410K	Variety Honeywell IBM, Univac, CDC COBOL, FORTRAN, Assembler	IBM 370 COBOL, FORTRAN	14	256
1500	500K	IBM 370 COBOL	Burroughs B6700 COBOL	12	333
1500	2000K	IBM 7080 Autocoder	IBM 370 COBOL, IMS	Various contracts	1333
729	571K	IBM 370 COBOL, FORTRAN	Honeywell 60/66 COBOL, FORTRAN	24	783
711	1100K	Univac 1100 COBOL FORTRAN	IBM 370 COBOL, FORTRAN	14	1547
680	700K	Honeywell H2060 COBOL	CII/HB 64/60 COBOL	20	1029
553	240K	CDC 6400 COBOL, FORTRAN	IBM 370 COBOL, FORTRAN	13	434
505	625K	Burroughs B4700 COBOL	CII/HB 66/40 COBOL	20	1238
450	300K	Philips P1000 COBOL	Univac 1100 COBOL	14	667
410	585K	Variety IBM COBOL, FORTRAN	IBM 370 COBOL, FORTRAN	11	1427

Number of Programs	Number of Statements	Source Environment	Target Environment	Duration (Months)	Average Statements/Program
382	308K	ICL 1900 COBOL, FORTRAN	IBM 370 COBOL, FORTRAN	12	806
375	133K	ICL 1900 PLAN, COBOL, IBM 370 ALC, COBOL	ICL 2970 COBOL	18	355
359	142K	Univac 1100 COBOL	IBM 370 COBOL	8	396
344	311K	IBM 7074, 1401 Autocoder	IBM 370 PL/1	18	904
298	233K	Honeywell 2040 COBOL	IBM 370 COBOL	10	782
285	164K	NCR 200 COBOL, NEAT	IBM 370 COBOL	6	575
237	204K	Univac III SALT	Honeywell 6000 COBOL	18	861
227	200K	ICL 1900 COBOL	IBM 370 COBOL	18	881
213	32K	Burroughs 6700 COBOL	IBM 370 PL/1	7	150
200	179K	Univac Series 70 ALC, Honeywell 60/66 COBOL	Honeywell 60/66 COBOL, IBM 370 COBOL	32	895
190	98K	ICC 1900 COBOL, PLAN	Univac 1100 COBOL	8	516
184	88K	NCR 315 NEAT, COBOL	IBM 370 COBOL	9	478
180	160K	IBM 370 COBOL	Honeywell 60/66 COBOL	12	889
180	136K	Honeywell Series 200 Easycoder	Honeywell 6000, IBM 370 COBOL, IMS	Various contracts	756

TABLE 1.9 (continued)

Number of Programs	Number of Statements	Source Environment	Target Environment	Duration (Months)	Average Statements/Program
170	155K	ICL 1900 COBOL	ICL 2970 COBOL	12	912
161	466K	IBM 7080 Autocoder, 360 RPG	IBM 370 COBOL	Various contracts	2894
160	227K	Honeywell 8200 ARGUS	IBM 370 COBOL	12	1419
157	160K	GE415 MAP, COBOL, CDC 6600 COBOL	Univac 1100 COBOL	10	1019
144	180K	ICL 1900 COBOL, PLAN	Univac 1100 COBOL	8	1250
141	69K	IBM 1401 Autocoder	IBM 370 COBOL	6	489
139	—	IBM 7070, 1401 Autocoder, COBOL	IBM 370 COBOL	Various contracts	—
127	67K	Honeywell Series 200 Easycoder	IBM 370 COBOL	Various contracts	528
117	93K	ICL 1900 COBOL, PLAN	Univac 1100 COBOL, DMS	7	795
117	—	IBM 370 DOS	IBM 370 OS	6	—
114	100K	ICL 1900 PLAN, COBOL	Univac 1100 COBOL	18	887
102	175K	Univac Series 70 (RCA 501 EZCODE)	IBM 370 COBOL	Various contracts	1716

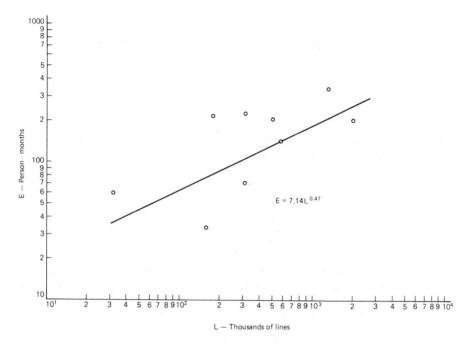

Figure 1.1 Relationship between person-months and lines of code (data from Table 1.8).

(but all independently), we would expect an increasing spread in the effort (i.e., person-hours) for increasing size of the project. The weighting used for the data in Figure 1.2 was $w = 1$ (i.e., constant weight for all points).

The resulting least-squares equations are

$$E = 7.14L^{0.47} \tag{1.3}$$

and

$$D = 4.1L^{0.22} \tag{1.4}$$

The method of least squares also yields uncertainty estimates for the parameters. The uncertainties associated with 7.14 and 0.47 in Equation (1.3) were 8.81 and 0.19, respectively. The uncertainty estimates associated with 4.1 and 0.22 in Equation (1.4) were 1.74 and 0.07, respectively.

Some very interesting conclusions can be obtained by examining the results:

1. The data included in Table 1.8 yield an exponent of 0.47 ± 0.19. This entire range (i.e., 0.28 to 0.66) is well below 1 and implies

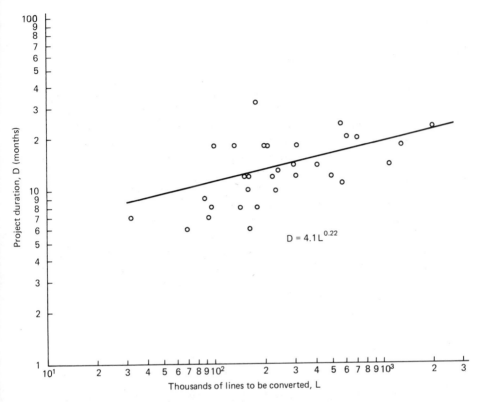

Figure 1.2 Relationship between project duration and lines of code (data from Table 1.9).

that conversion projects are affected by the economy of scale. For example, if L is doubled, the expected value of E increases by a factor of $2^{0.47} = 1.385$. If the value of effort per line is 1 for a conversion of length L, the equation implies that effort per line would be $1.385/2 = 0.69$ for a conversion of length $2L$ (i.e., a savings of 31% per line).

2. The exponent obtained for project duration is small (i.e., 0.22 ± 0.07) and implies that project duration is relatively insensitive to the size L of the conversion. This conclusion requires some explanation. Clearly, if the number of people on the conversion team remains constant, the duration would increase significantly with L. However, by adding members to the team the total project duration can be held to within objective limits. This point is corroborated by Oliver [1]: "Manpower and time are not generally interchangeable in a software production project, but within bounds of good taste, they are in a conversion project."

3. The equations developed in this section can be used to estimate relative efforts when comparing redesign, reprogramming, and conversion. Such a comparison is made in Section 2.4.

REFERENCES

1. Oliver P., "Software Conversion and Benchmarking," *Software World*, Vol. 10, No. 3, pp. 2-11, 1979.

2. Fenton, J. S., "Portability—The Practical Problem," *Proceedings of the ON-LINE Conference: Pragmatic Programming and Sensible Software*, Chameleon Press, 1978.

3. Brown, P. J., ed., *Software Portability*, Cambridge University Press, New York, 1977.

4. Sammet, J. E., *Programming Languages: History and Fundamentals*, Prentice-Hall, Englewood Cliffs, N.J., 1969.

5. *U.S.A. Standard FORTRAN*, American National Standards Institute (ANSI), USAS X3.9-1966, New York, 1966.

6. *U.S.A. Standard Basic FORTRAN*, American National Standards Institute (ANSI), USAS X3.10-1966, New York, 1966.

7. *U.S.A. Standard COBOL*, American National Standards Institute (ANSI), USAS X3.23-1968, New York, 1968.

8. *ANS Standard COBOL*, American National Standards Institute (ANSI), USAS X3.23-1974, New York, 1974.

9. *ANS Standard FORTRAN*, American National Standards Institute (ANSI), ANSI X3.9-1978, New York, 1978.

10. White, J. W., and G. D. Ripley, "How Portable Are Minicomputer FORTRAN Programs?" *Datamation*, July 1977.

11. Wegner, P., "Programming with ADA: An Introduction by Means of Graduated Examples," *SIGPLAN Notices*, Vol. 14, No. 12, pp. 1-46, December 1979.

12. McCracken, D. D., "The Changing Face of Applications Programming," *Datamation*, November 15, 1978, pp. 25-30.

13. ACM SIGPLAN History of Programming Languages Conference, *SIGPLAN Notices*, Vol. 13, No. 8, August 1978.

14. Goldstine, H., and J. von Neumann, "Planning and Coding Problems for an Electronic Computing Instrument," in *Collected Words of J. von Neumann*, ed. A. Taub, Pergamon Press, Elmsford, N.Y., 1963.

15. *Programmers Reference Manual, The FORTRAN Automatic Coding System for the IBM 704 EDPM*, IBM Corp., October 15, 1956.

16. Hill, I. D., and B. L. Meek, *Programming Language Standardisation*, Ellis Horwood, London/Wiley, New York, 1980.

17. Fisher, D. L., "Portable COBOL: Facts and Fiction," *Proceedings of the ON-LINE Conference: Pragmatic Programming and Sensible Software*, Chameleon Press, 1978.

18. Brillinger, P. C., and D. J. Cohen, *Introduction to Data Structures and Non-numeric Computations*, Prentice-Hall, Englewood Cliffs, N.J., 1972.

19. Helms, H. L., *The BASIC Book: A Cross Referenced Guide to the BASIC Language*, McGraw Hill, New York, 1983.

20. Van Tassel, D., *Program Style, Design, Efficiency, Debugging and Testing*, Prentice-Hall, Englewood Cliffs, N.J., 1974.

21. Brown, G. D., *Advanced ANS COBOL with Structured Programming*, Wiley-Interscience, New York, 1977.

22. Rand, N., Rand Information Systems, private communication, August 1980.

23. Rand Information Systems, "Conversion Special Report: Changing to New Technology," National Symposium on Computer System Enhancement, Washington, D.C., November 1979.

24. Wolberg, J. R., *Prediction Analysis*, Van Nostrand Reinhold, New York, 1967.

25. Boehm, B. W., *Software Engineering Economics*, Prentice-Hall, Englewood Cliffs, N.J., 1981.

Conversion Economics

2.1 INTRODUCTION

The decision to convert is invariably an economic decision. A set of circumstances requires a change in the basic computing system. For some situations existing software will not be compatible with the new system. The three alternative lines of action are to convert the software, replace the software, or discard the software. A choice among these alternatives is usually made by considering the economic implications of the various lines of action.

To make intelligent decisions, one requires a methodology for estimating the costs, personnel requirements, and time required for the various alternatives. One method of estimation is to use correlations based on past experience. Estimation equations are discussed in Sections 2.2 to 2.4.

If a decision has been made to convert, for most conversions (except the most trivial), some attempt will be made to partially automate the process. Clearly, an investment is required in conversion aids and tools, so one is confronted with an optimization problem. By investing more in automation, one reduces the manual effort required in a conversion. But clearly, one reaches a point where the savings are no longer commensurate with the additional investment. This optimization problem is analyzed in Sections 2.5 and 2.6.

The number of paramount importance when attempting to estimate conversion costs is the cost per line. Clearly, if we had a value for the conversion cost per line of source code, a simple multiplication yields the total cost of the conversion. Some numbers are available and can be used to give rough estimates. An analysis of some available data is presented in Section 2.7.

2.2 CONVERSION ESTIMATION EQUATIONS

The first step in estimating the cost of a conversion project is to use the equation developed in Section 1.5 [i.e., Equation (1.3)]. This equation yields an estimate for E (person-months) as a function of L (thousands of lines of code). By using an average cost per hour or cost per month, the total cost of conversion can be computed. For example, RIS used a figure of $30 per hour to make cost estimations [1].

There is, of course, an additional cost for computer usage that must be included in any estimate of the total cost of a conversion project. However, this cost is dependent on the specific arrangements for computer usage for each project. For example, computer time might be supplied free of charge for the purposes of conversion by the vendor of the target machine. Alternatively, one might have to buy time at commercial rates. If an in-house computer is used, the usage charge can be set at any level decided upon by management. An extremely rough estimate for average computer usage for a conversion project is that computer usage cost is equal to personnel cost.

The cost per statement (exclusive of computer usage) is computed in Table 2.1 for the nine RIS conversion projects summarized in Table 1.8. The cost per statement values range from $0.53 to $9.59 (based on $30 per hour). Equation (1.3) yields a value of E for any value of L based on these nine projects. Examining Figure 1.1 we see that the nine data points are widely scattered about the least-squares line. The two most widely scattered points are at $L = 160$ and $L = 179$. These points are 57% below and 155% above the line, respectively. If we take these values as very rough upper and lower limits, the estimation that is obtained using Equation (1.3) is accurate to a factor of 2 to 3. If we arbitrarily choose a value of 2.5, we can assume the following limits:

$$\frac{E_c}{2.5} < E < 2.5 \times E_c \qquad (2.1)$$

where E is the expected value of effort (person-months) for a given conversion project of length L (thousands of lines) and E_c is the value of E computed using Equation (1.3) (i.e., $E = 7.14L^{0.47}$).

A more accurate method of estimation is to use a value obtained from a similar conversion but scaled using the 0.47 exponent:

$$E = E_i \left(\frac{L}{L_i}\right)^{0.47} \tag{2.2}$$

For example, assume that we wish to convert a 300,000-line system written in IBM 370 COBOL to Burroughs B6700 COBOL. An examination of Table 1.8 shows that the third entry in the table is for this particular type of conversion. The values of E_3 and L_3 are 35,532 and 500, respectively. Substituting these values into Equation (2.2), we calculate an expected value for E:

$$E = 35,532 \left(\frac{300}{500}\right)^{0.47} = 27,948 \text{ hours}$$

Based on a cost per hour rate of \$30, the estimated cost per statement is

$$\text{cost per statement} = \$30 \times 27,948/300,000 = \$2.79$$

As expected, this cost per statement is greater than the cost for the 500,000-line conversion (as shown in Table 2.1).

TABLE 2.1   Cost per Statement for RIS Conversion Projects

Project	Number of Programs	Thousands of Statements	Person-Hours	Hours/Program	Statements/Hour	Cost/Statement[a]
1	1,673	2,000	35,146	21	57	\$0.53
2	1,620	1,300	59,376	37	22	1.37
3	1,500	500	35,532	24	14	2.13
4	729	571	24,657	34	23	1.30
5	382	308	12,384	32	25	1.21
6	344	311	38,987	113	8	3.76
7	213	32	10,236	48	3	9.59
8	200	179	37,014	185	5	6.20
9	157	160	5,819	37	27	1.09

[a]Based on a rate of \$30 per hour. Note that this cost does not include computer usage.

Instinctively, it is more accurate to use Equation (2.2) rather than (1.3); however, this can be done only if one can find relevant data. Even if the exact conversion of interest is not included in Table 1.8, we can sometimes use the existing data to advantage. For example, we see that the cost per statement is high for interlanguage conversions (note projects 6 and 7 in Table 2.1). Thus if the conversion is to be from one language to another (not merely from one version to another version of the same language), we might use Equation (2.2) and the data from project 6 or 7 or an average. Similarly, for projects with multiple source and target machines, the data from project 8 might be relevant.

An estimation equation for project duration was presented in Section 1.5 [i.e., Equation (1.4)]. An equation analogous to (2.2) can be used for scaling from existing data:

$$D = D_i \left(\frac{L}{L_i}\right)^{0.22} \tag{2.3}$$

For example, for the case discussed above (i.e., a 300,000-line conversion from IBM 370 COBOL to Burroughs B6700 COBOL), the values of D_3 and L_3 are 12 months and 500,000 lines, respectively (see Table 1.8). Substituting these values into Equation (2.3), we calculate an expected value for D:

$$D = 12 \left(\frac{300}{500}\right)^{0.22} = 10.7 \text{ months}$$

The value of D computed using Equation (1.4) is

$$D = 4.1 \times 300^{0.22} = 14.0 \text{ months}$$

The value of 10.7 months is a more reasonable estimate for the project duration because it is based on data from a similar project. The value of 14 months is based on the overall correlation of all the RIS data.

2.3 REPROGRAMMING AND REDESIGN ESTIMATION EQUATIONS

The alternative to the conversion of software is the replacement of software. Two replacement options are *reprogramming* and *redesign*. Oliver makes the following distinction [2]:

1. *Reprogramming* may entail a system redesign (e.g., batch to on-line) but no significant functional redesign. The process is manual and not based on a line-by-line translation of the original system.
2. *Redesign* involves functional redesign and is therefore akin to new development.

Oliver considers both reprogramming and redesign to fall within the realm of conversion technology; however, I prefer to consider them as alternatives to conversion. They are both manual options and are governed by the rules of general software development. (In my terminology the conversion option implies that some degree of automation is possible because the new code will be based to a large extent on the original code.)

The distinction between reprogramming and redesign is not clear. At what point do the functional changes become "significant"? Clearly, reprogramming implies a smaller effort than redesign, however, it is difficult to place quantitative criteria on the degree of savings. For the purposes of the following analysis, the savings is arbitrarily assumed to be 50%. To develop equations similar to (1.3) and (1.4), the following assumptions are made:

1. *Redesign* of an existing system requires an effort comparable to the development of a new system of the same size.
2. *Reprogramming* of an existing system requires an effort equal to one-half the effort required for redesign.

Several correlations are available for new system development projects. Walston and Felix analyzed a data base of 60 completed software development projects with delivered source lines ranging from 4000 to 467,000 [3]. The programming effort ranged from 12 to 11,758 months. The overall correlation is

$$E = 5.2L^{0.91} \tag{2.4}$$

An assumption that redesign is equivalent to new system development thus leads us to the following relationship:

$$E_{rd} = 5.2L^{0.91} \tag{2.5}$$

where E_{rd} is the effort in person-months required to redesign a system of L thousands of lines.[1] Our assumption that reprogramming requires approximately one-half the effort of redesign yields the following relationship:

$$E_{rp} = 2.6L^{0.91} \tag{2.6}$$

where E_{rp} is the effort in person-months to reprogram a system of L thousands of lines.

Walston and Felix partitioned their data base into several classes of programs and noted that the exponent for L was in all cases nearly 1. Thus the development of new systems (and redesigning or reprogramming of old systems) is not appreciably helped by a scaling effect. Doubling the value of L will on average increase E by a factor of $2^{0.91} = 1.88$. This increase is significantly greater than the increase in E one would expect from a conversion project. [From Equation (1.3) we note an increase in E by a factor of $2^{0.47} = 1.39$ if L is doubled.]

Schneider analyzed data prepared by the Rome Air Development Center (RADC) consisting of 400 software projects [4]. He used a more sophisticated model which includes N (the number of programs)

[1] Boehm [9] suggests the correlation $E = 2.4L^{1.05}$.

as well as L. The suggested overall correlation for programs written in higher-level languages is

$$E = 28 \times N\left(\frac{L}{N}\right)^{1.83} \tag{2.7}$$

The ratio L/N is the average size of a program divided by 1000 and is relatively constant. Thus Schneider's results suggest that E is approximately proportional to N, which is approximately proportional to L. The close-to-linear relationship noted by Walston and Felix is thus verified by Schneider.

Using Equations (2.4) and (2.7), we can recalculate E for the nine points included in Table 2.1. The results are shown in Table 2.2. Analyzing the results leads one to the immediate conclusion that conversions are much cheaper than new system development. For the same values of L, Equation (2.4) yields values that range from 2.1 to 25.8 times the conversion project efforts. The ratio increases as L (the project size) increases. The results obtained using Equation (2.7) and the same values of L and N yield values that range from 7.4 to 320 times the conversion project efforts.

It is interesting to compare the results from Equations (2.4) and (2.7), as shown in Table 2.2. The results from (2.7) are consistently higher (from a factor of 3.6 to a factor of 12.3 higher). The large differences are at first glance suprising because both correlations are for new system development. The most probable explanation is the difference in complexity among the two data bases. Although Schneider does not describe the nature of the systems included in the RADC

TABLE 2.2   Comparison of Conversion Effort and New System Development Effort

| Project | L | N | Conversion | | New Development | |
			Actual[a]	Eq. (1.3)	Eq. (2.4)	Eq. (2.7)
1	2,000	1,673	203	254	5,247	64,945
2	1,300	1,620	343	208	3,546	30,323
3	500	1,500	205	132	1,486	9,222
4	571	729	142	141	1,677	14,571
5	308	382	71.5	105	956	7,947
6	311	344	225	106	965	8,381
7	32	213	59.1	36.4	122	436
8	179	200	215	81.8	584	4,805
9	160	157	33.6	77.6	527	4,512

[a]Computed from person-hours in Table 2.1 divided by 173.2 hours per month.

study, one can assume that many of the systems were highly sophisticated (and indeed, the results indicate a very high level of effort per line of code). One might expect that the RADC study includes a large number of real-time applications fine tuned for performance for a given hardware configuration and operating system. Such systems are rarely converted. If the system for some reason must be moved to a new environment, it would most probably be redesigned. Thus for purposes of comparison with conversion effort, the Walston and Felix correlation [i.e., Equation (2.4)] is probably more relevant than Equation (2.7).

2.4 COMPARING CONVERSION, REDESIGN, AND REPROGRAMMING

The results from Sections 1.5, 2.2, and 2.3 can be used to develop equations for computing the relative efforts required to redesign, reprogram, or convert a given system [5]. The relevant equations are summarized in Table 2.3. The equations are shown graphically in Figure 2.1.

TABLE 2.3   Correlations for Redesign, Reprogramming, and Conversion

	Equation Number	Equation
Redesign	(2.5)	$E_{rd} = 5.2 L^{0.91}$
Reprogramming	(2.6)	$E_{rp} = 2.6 L^{0.91}$
Conversion	(1.3)	$E_c = 7.14 L^{0.47}$

From the graph we see that if it is decided to convert a system rather than redesign or reprogram the system, there should be a significant savings in effort for systems of several tens of thousands of lines of code. The proportional savings increases as L increases.

It should be understood that for smaller systems conversion might also be the cheapest option; however, the analysis was based on the RIS data (see Table 1.8) and the smallest system in the data base was 32,000 lines. Thus the RIS data are not applicable for making conclusions regarding smaller conversions. The author is familiar with conversion projects for systems with fewer than 10,000 lines which were completed in a matter of days. The speed of the projects can be explained by the availability of automatic converters, which accomplished over 90% of all necessary changes automatically. For smaller conversions for which automatic converters are unavailable, it is not obvious which option is the cheapest and fastest.

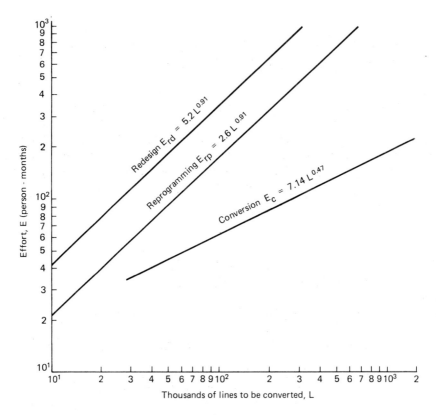

Figure 2.1   Redesign, reprogramming, and conversion efforts.

Ratios for redesign and reprogramming compared to conversion efforts can be obtained by dividing Equations (2.5) and (2.6) by (1.3):

$$\frac{E_{rd}}{E_c} = 0.728 L^{0.44} \tag{2.8}$$

$$\frac{E_{rp}}{E_c} = 0.364 L^{0.44} \tag{2.9}$$

(Note that we have assumed that $E_{rp}/E_{rd} = 0.5$.) Similar equations can be developed for project duration. Walston and Felix include a correlation for a project duration D (person-months) as a function of L (thousands of lines) for new system development:

$$D = 4.1 L^{0.36} \tag{2.10}$$

If we assume that the duration for redesign is the same as new system development, and (very arbitrarily) assume that duration for reprogram-

[1] Boehm [9] suggests a similar equation: $D = 3.48 L^{0.40}$.

ming is 80% of the new system development, we obtain the following two equations:

$$D_{rd} = 4.1L^{0.36} \tag{2.11}$$

and

$$D_{rp} = 3.3L^{0.36} \tag{2.12}$$

Using Equation (1.4) for project duration of conversion projects, we obtain the following ratios:

$$\frac{D_{rd}}{D_c} = 1.0L^{0.14} \tag{2.13}$$

$$\frac{D_{rp}}{D_c} = 0.8L^{0.14} \tag{2.14}$$

In Table 2.4 four projects of varying L are compared. We note that estimated effort for redesign increases from 3.25 to 15.2 times the effort for conversion as the project size increases from 30,000 to 1,000,000 lines. The estimated project duration will also increase, but we note that the increase is much less than the increase in effort.

TABLE 2.4   Comparing Projects of Various Sizes by Effort and Duration for Redesign, Reprogramming, and Conversion[a]

	Effort Ratio		Duration Ratio	
L	E_{rd}/E_c	E_{rp}/E_c	D_{rd}/D_c	D_{rp}/D_c
30	3.25	1.63	1.61	1.29
100	5.52	2.76	1.91	1.15
300	8.95	4.48	2.22	1.78
1000	15.2	7.61	2.63	2.10

[a]The subscript rd refers to redesign, rp to reprogramming, and c to conversion.

2.5 OPTIMIZING A CONVERSION PROJECT

The term *optimization* has different meanings in different situations. However, regardless of how we define optimization, the fundamental concept is that some objective must be minimized or maximized. When applied to the conversion problem, the usual objective is to minimize cost. We can reduce the manual effort associated with a conversion by investing in conversion tools and aids; however, we reach a point where the additional cost cannot be justified on the basis of the potential saving. The following analysis yields insight into the trade-off between the automatic and manual portions of the conversion.

A conversion project can be subdivided into five phases. Although the percentage of cost spent for each phase varies from conversion to conversion, the values shown in Table 2.5 are representative. Brandon suggests a slightly different set of values [6] (i.e., 15% for language translation, 25% for data preparation, 50% for testing, and 10% for installation); however, the differences are not important. What is important to note is that more than 50% of the cost of a conversion project is associated with conversion and testing of the source code. All the costs in Table 2.5 can be included in one of three categories [7]:

1. *Automatic cost*, C_a. This category includes the cost for purchasing and/or developing conversion software (i.e., converters and/or conversion aids) and the cost associated with running the conversion software. A fraction of the phase 3 (i.e., conversion) cost can be attributed to C_a.

2. *Manual cost* C_m. This category includes the remainder of the phase 3 (i.e., conversion) cost and the phase 4 (i.e., testing) cost. This work requires programmer intervention and interpretation; however, some of the tasks can be simplified using additional conversion software (e.g., file comparison software).

3. *Fixed cost* C_f. This category includes those cost items that do not vary regardless of the level of automation used in the conversion phase. The costs for phases 1, 2, and 5 (i.e., planning, data preparation, and implementation) are included in C_f. Conversion software can be used to simplify various tasks included in C_f (e.g., management planning tools, data preparation tools, etc.); however, the cost C_f is independent of C_a.

TABLE 2.5   Representative Cost Percentages for the Various Phases in a Conversion Project

Phase	Description	Cost Percentage
1	Planning	5
2	Data preparation	10
3	Conversion	25
4	Testing	45
5	Implementation	15
		100

The total cost of the project C_t is the sum of the three costs described above:

$$C_t = C_a + C_m + C_f \qquad (2.15)$$

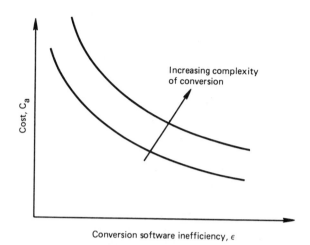

Figure 2.2 Automatic cost of conversion C_a as a function of the conversion software inefficiency ϵ.

Let us define a parameter ϵ as the *inefficiency* of the conversion software. (The parameter ϵ might, for example, be the fraction of lines of code that must be manually altered after the code has been processed by the conversion software.) A value of $\epsilon = 0$ means that the software performs perfectly (i.e., the resulting software is completely error-free if the source code is also error-free). For some conversions it is possible to develop perfect conversion software, but in general, the cost C_a becomes very large as ϵ approaches zero. We can see this phenomenon qualitatively in Figure 2.2.

The manual cost of conversion C_m is also a function of ϵ; however, it increases as ϵ increases (see Figure 2.3). Even if ϵ is zero, some cost

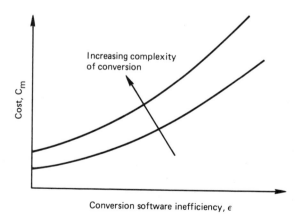

Figure 2.3 Manual cost of conversion C_m as a function of the conversion software inefficiency ϵ.

must be allocated to testing (if only to prove that the automatic conversion procedures have been executed properly). As ϵ increases, we can expect a greater number of problems to be associated with the code generated in the automatic phase. The greater the number of problems (i.e., bugs) included in the converted code, the greater the cost C_m.

For a given conversion we can plot the three cost components and the total cost C_t as functions of ϵ and we see in Figure 2.4 that an optimum value of ϵ (i.e., ϵ_{opt}) is obtained. The implication of Figure 2.4 is clear: There is an optimum level of automation associated with a given conversion project. Investing in conversion software reduces C_t until ϵ_{opt} has been achieved. Beyond this point additional investment results in an increase in C_t.

We can carry our analysis one step further by considering the influence of the size of the conversion (i.e., L thousands of lines) on the various cost components. Clearly, all components (including C_f) increase as functions of L; however, only C_a and C_m are affected by ϵ. The cost components are shown in Figure 2.5 for two values of ϵ (where ϵ_1 is greater than ϵ_2). The important point to note in Figure 2.5 is that C_m increases more rapidly than C_a as L increases. The explanation for this phenomenon is simple: The initial investment in conversion software is independent of the size of the conversion, whereas the manual effort is size dependent. The implication of Figure 2.5 is subtle: the optimum value of ϵ_{opt} decreases as L increases (see Figure 2.6). Re-

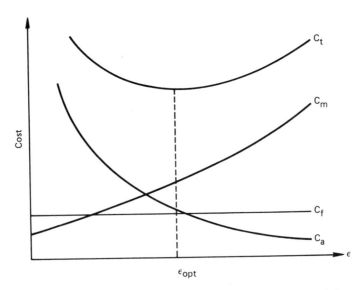

Figure 2.4 Cost components and total cost C_t as functions of the conversion software inefficiency ϵ.

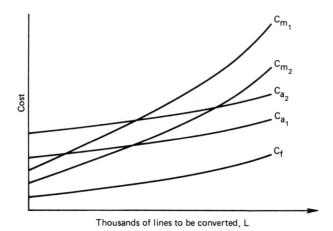

Figure 2.5   Cost components as functions of L (thousands of lines) for two levels of conversion software (ϵ_1 and ϵ_2). ϵ_1 is greater than ϵ_2, which means that level 2 uses better conversion software.

stating this conclusion in practical terms: As the size of the conversion increases, it is worthwhile to increase the investment in conversion software.

The conclusions from Figure 2.2 through 2.6 can be summarized as follows:

1. Conversion software of varying quality can be obtained or developed for a given conversion. A measure of the quality is ϵ, the *conversion software inefficiency*. Perfect software has a value of ϵ equal to zero.

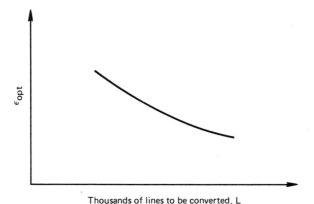

Figure 2.6   Influence of the size of the conversion on the optimum value of converter inefficiency ϵ. (Decreasing ϵ_{opt} is obtained by increasing the investment in conversion software.)

2. For a given conversion there is an optimum value of ϵ. If ϵ is less than the optimum, the investment in conversion software is excessive. If ϵ is greater than the optimum, the investment in conversion software is inadequate and money is being wasted in the manual effort associated with conversion and testing.

3. As the size of the conversion increases, the optimum value of ϵ decreases. Thus it becomes increasingly worthwhile to develop or obtain high-performance conversion software.

2.6 A MATHEMATICAL MODEL FOR CONVERSION OPTIMIZATION

The analysis presented in Section 2.5 regarding optimization of a conversion project is entirely qualitative. The primary conclusion of the analysis is that there is an optimum level of automation associated with any conversion project. It is cost-effective to invest in conversion software up to a point, but beyond this point, the additional cost is greater than the saving associated with the improved software.

When we attempt to quantify the analysis we are faced with some basic problems:

1. How do we actually measure the converter inefficiency ϵ?
2. How do we obtain the functional dependence of C_a and C_m on ϵ? (See Figures 2.2 and 2.3.)
3. How do we obtain the functional dependence of C_a, C_m, and C_f on L? (See Figure 2.5.)

If we assume that ϵ is the fraction of lines of code that remain to be manually altered upon completion of processing by the conversion software, how do we relate the various costs to ϵ? Clearly, ϵ must be an average value, and will vary considerably from program to program. To complicate matters further, for two programs of the same size and the same number of lines that remain to be altered manually, the cost associated with completing the conversion is not necessarily the same. These problems are typical of the problems associated with mathematical modeling. Our procedure will be to assume an idealized model which we know is not entirely accurate. We will then use the model in an attempt to gain some insight into the optimization problem. Clearly, interpretation of the results should be tempered by our awareness of the assumptions made in developing the model.[1]

---

[1] For those readers who have a basic abhorrence of mathematics, the remainder of this section can be skipped without any loss of continuity.

Let us assume the following model for C_a:

$$C_a = C_{a_1} + C_{a_2}N + C_{a_3}L \qquad (2.16)$$

where C_{a_1} is the cost for developing or obtaining the conversion software, C_{a_2} is the initial cost for running the software per program, and C_{a_3} is the incremental running cost per thousand lines of code. The parameter N is the number of programs and L is the total number of lines (in thousands of lines). Equation (2.16) is based on the assumption that the cost of running conversion software varies approximately linearly with the number of lines of code. This linear relationship has been observed for a variety of converters [8]. The cost coefficients C_{a_2} and C_{a_3} are based primarily on three factors:

1. The complexity of the conversion.
2. The quality of the conversion software (e.g., the parameter ϵ is a measure of quality).
3. The computer costs for the machine on which the software is to be used.

If one is purchasing a conversion service based on existing conversion software, the cost coefficients should be relatively easy to obtain. However, if one is undertaking the development of the necessary software, it is difficult to estimate these cost coefficients. For lack of a better approach, for such cases one can base cost estimates on results for comparable conversion software.

Let us assume the following models for C_{a_1}, C_{a_2} and C_{a_3}:

$$C_{a_i} = \frac{K_{a_i}}{\epsilon^{\alpha_i}} \qquad (2.17)$$

where the K_{a_i}'s and the α_i's are constants. To simplify the analysis, let us assume that α_1, α_2, and α_3 are all equal to the same value α:

$$C_{a_i} = \frac{K_{a_i}}{\epsilon^{\alpha}} \qquad (2.18)$$

It is reasonable to use a value of α greater than zero, which therefore causes C_a to approach infinity as ϵ approaches zero (see Figure 2.2).

Let us assume the following model for C_m:

$$C_m = C_{m_1}N + C_{m_2}L + C_{m_3}\epsilon^{\beta}L^{\gamma}N^{\delta} \qquad (2.19)$$

where C_{m_1} is the initial cost per program for running the testing phase, C_{m_2} is the incremental cost per thousand lines for running the testing phase (for the case where there are no errors in the code generated by the conversion software), and C_{m_3} is the coefficient for the final term, which is a measure of the cost associated with errors generated by the conversion software. The parameters β, γ, and δ are all positive coefficients. If $\epsilon = 0$, there are no errors and the last term goes to zero.

Let us assume the following model for C_f:

$$C_f = C_{f_1} N^\eta L^\nu \tag{2.20}$$

where C_{f_1} is a constant and η and ν are positive constant coefficients. This model implies that C_f will be different for two conversions of the same L but different values of N. This implication is certainly reasonable.

We can derive an equation for C_t (the total cost) as a function of ϵ, L, and N by substituting (2.16), (2.18), (2.19), and (2.20) into (2.15):

$$C_t = \epsilon^{-\alpha}(K_{a_1} + NK_{a_2} + LK_{a_3}) \\ + NC_{m_1} + LC_{m_2} + C_{m_3} \epsilon^\beta L^\gamma N^\delta + C_{f_1} N^\eta L^\nu \tag{2.21}$$

To find the value of ϵ_{opt}, we must set the derivative $\partial C_t / \partial \epsilon$ to zero and solve for ϵ:

$$\frac{\partial C_t}{\partial \epsilon} = -\alpha \epsilon^{-\alpha-1}(K_{a_1} + NK_{a_2} + LK_{a_3}) \\ + \beta \epsilon^{\beta-1} C_{m_3} L^\gamma N^\delta = 0 \tag{2.22}$$

$$K_{a_1} + NK_{a_2} + LK_{a_3} = \frac{\beta}{\alpha} \epsilon^{\alpha+\beta} C_{m_3} L^\gamma N^\delta \tag{2.23}$$

$$\epsilon_{opt} = \left(\frac{K_{a_1} + NK_{a_2} + LK_{a_3}}{\frac{\beta}{\alpha} C_{m_3} L^\gamma N^\delta} \right)^{1/(\alpha+\beta)} \tag{2.24}$$

To simplify the analysis, let us assume that all the coefficients (i.e., α, β, γ and δ) are equal to 1. Equation (2.24) reduces to the following:

$$\epsilon_{opt} = \sqrt{\frac{K_{a_1} + NK_{a_2} + LK_{a_3}}{C_{m_3} LN}} \tag{2.25}$$

Let us assume that L/N is approximately constant (i.e., all program modules are approximately the same size) [4]; we obtain the following equation from Equation (2.25):

$$\epsilon_{opt} = \frac{\sqrt{K_{a_1}/N + K_{a_2} + K_{a_3}(L/N)}}{\sqrt{C_{m_3} L}} \tag{2.26}$$

For large values of N, the term K_{a_1}/N approaches zero and

$$\epsilon_{opt} \rightarrow \frac{\sqrt{[K_{a_2} + K_{a_3}(L/N)]/C_{m_3}}}{\sqrt{L}} = \frac{\text{constant}}{\sqrt{L}} \tag{2.27}$$

This behavior agrees with the qualitative result suggested in Figure 2.6. That is, as L increases, ϵ_{opt} decreases.

An alternative assumption can be made: L remains constant but N increases (i.e., we are comparing systems of varying program module size). For such situations, as N becomes large,

$$\epsilon_{opt} = \frac{\sqrt{(K_{a_1}/L + K_{a_3})/C_{m3}}}{\sqrt{N}} + \frac{\sqrt{K_{a_2}/C_{m3}}}{\sqrt{L}} \rightarrow \frac{\sqrt{K_{a_2}/C_{m3}}}{\sqrt{L}} \qquad (2.28)$$

In other words, for systems of the same L but differing N, the model suggests that the investment in conversion software should be greater for the system with the larger value of N. However, for large values of N, ϵ_{opt} approaches a minimum value.

It is interesting to compare the level of investment for conversion software for two conversions of the same type but differing values of N and L. Let us make the following assumptions:

1. Equation (2.25) yields an acceptable value for ϵ_{opt}.
2. The average program module size is independent of N (the number of programs). That is, L/N is approximately constant.
3. The value of N is large.

For such situations Equation (2.27) is valid and we thus obtain the following ratio:

$$\frac{\epsilon_{opt_1}}{\epsilon_{opt_2}} \rightarrow \sqrt{\frac{L_2}{L_1}} = \sqrt{\frac{N_2}{N_1}} \qquad (2.29)$$

We see that the ratio of values for ϵ_{opt} approaches the square root of the inverse ratio of the size of the conversions (measured in total lines or number of programs). If, for example, $L_2 = 2L_1$, then $\epsilon_{opt_2} = \epsilon_{opt_1}/\sqrt{2}$. We can use Equation (2.18) to estimate the relative investment in conversion software for the two optimum cases:

$$\frac{(C_{a_1})_2}{(C_{a_1})_1} = \left(\frac{\epsilon_{opt_1}}{\epsilon_{opt_2}}\right)^{\alpha} = 2^{\alpha/2} \qquad (2.30)$$

Equation (2.25) was derived by assuming that α is equal to 1, so our relative investment in conversion software should be $2^{1/2} = 1.41$. In other words, increasing the size of the conversion by a factor of 2 implies an increase in the optimum investment in conversion software of about 40%.

An interesting variation in the optimization problem is the reuse of existing conversion software. Clearly, if the cost of developing or obtaining conversion software (i.e., C_{a_1}) is totally applied to a given conversion project, the value for C_{a_1} for a second project of the same type would be zero if the software is reused. If we assume that Equation (2.18) is valid, we see that C_{a_1} is proportional to K_{a_1} and that K_{a_1} appears in Equation (2.24) (i.e., the equation used to compute ϵ_{opt}). By reducing K_{a_1}, we reduce ϵ_{opt}, so even if L and N are the same, the optimum value of ϵ is reduced for the second project. The implication is clear: If conversion software is to be reused, it is worthwhile to budget some funds for upgrading the software. Upgrading the software can accomplish two different objectives:

1. Improve the software from the point of view of function (i.e., reduce ϵ).
2. Improve the software from the point of view of performance (i.e., reduce K_{a_2} and K_{a_3}).

2.7 CONVERSION COST PER LINE

For some situations a feasible method for converting programs is to contract for a service on a per line basis. For smaller systems the bulk of the effort is associated with the conversion and testing of programs. (There might be some additional effort required for conversion of data and job control.) For larger systems the program conversion effort is a smaller percentage of the total job.

Most services will offer two prices. The lower price is for *clean compile* and the higher price is for *full implementation*. The clean compile service brings programs to a level where they pass through the target compiler error-free. The full implementation price includes testing of programs until the program output is correct for each test case agreed upon. Typically, the price for full implementation is two to three times the price for clean compile.

A number of companies offer such services and therefore prices tend to be comparable. A price list from Dataware, Inc., is shown in Table 2.6. This list includes a fairly large selection of conversions with the emphasis on COBOL. Since COBOL is by far the most popular programming language (see Tables 1.3–1.5 in Section 1.3), it is not surprising that fixed price per line services tend to concentrate on COBOL.

It should be emphasized that the prices shown in Table 2.6 include computer charges. If we compare the prices the Table 2.6 to the cost per statement for the RIS data shown in Table 2.1 (Section 2.2), we see that the RIS prices are generally higher even though computer costs are *not* included in the RIS data. The explanation for this apparent paradox is that the RIS data are for complete system conversions, whereas the Dataware prices are for program conversions.

TABLE 2.6   Dataware Prices as of May 1, 1980

From	To	Clean Compile		Full Implementation	
		Per Line	Per Program	Per Line	Per Program
FORTRAN	FORTRAN	$0.40	$40	$0.80	$80
COBOL	COBOL	0.40	40	0.80	80
RPG/RPG II	COBOL	0.50	40	1.25	80
RPG/RPG II	PL/1	0.75	40	1.50	80
Autocoder	COBOL	1.25	40	2.50	80
PL/1	COBOL	1.50	40	3.00	80
Easycoder/Easytran	COBOL	1.25	40	2.50	80
IBM Assembler	COBOL	1.50	40	3.00	80

Source: Dataware, Inc., Tonawanda, N.Y.

One interesting point to note about the data in Table 2.6 is that the prices include a charge per program as well as a charge per line. For example, a COBOL-to-COBOL conversion of 200 lines would cost 200 × $0.80 + $80 = $240 for full implementation. Conversion of two 100-line programs would cost 200 × $0.80 + 2 × $80 = $320. The difference is certainly reasonable. It costs more to convert and test two programs of 100 lines than one program of 200 lines.

It is interesting to use the model developed in Section 2.6 to predict the cost of conversion per line. We have already noted that conversions are affected by the economy of scale. That is, as L increases, the cost per line (measured by C_t/L) decreases. We can use the model to explain why in fact this happens. If we divide Equation (2.21) by L, we obtain

$$\frac{C_t}{L} = \epsilon^{-\alpha} \left(\frac{K_{a_1}}{L} + \frac{N}{L} K_{a_2} + K_{a_3} \right)$$
$$+ \frac{N}{L} C_{m_1} + C_{m_2} + C_{m_3} \epsilon_\beta L^{\gamma-1} N^\delta + C_{f_1} N^\eta L^{\nu-1} \tag{2.31}$$

If we assume that L/N (i.e., the average size of the individual modules) is approximately constant, then our equation becomes

$$\frac{C_t}{L} = \frac{Q_1}{L} + Q_2 L^{\gamma-1} + Q_3 L^{\nu-1} + Q_4 \tag{2.32}$$

The equations for the Q_i's can be obtained by comparing (2.31) and (2.32). The value of C_t/L will decrease with increasing L if $\gamma \leqslant 1$ and $\nu \leqslant 1$. Since observations confirm the fact that C_t/L decreases as L

increases, these conditions for γ and ν are apparently reasonable. Equation (2.32) also yields a lower limit for C_t/L for large values of L:

$$\frac{C_t}{L} \rightarrow Q_4 = \epsilon^{-\alpha} \left(\frac{N}{L} K_{a_2} + K_{a_3} \right) + \frac{N}{L} C_{m_1} + C_{m_2} \qquad (2.33)$$

This equation is a contradiction to the simple formula developed in Section 1.5 but is more reasonable. In Equation (1.3) an exponential relationship between E (which is partially analogous to C_t) and L was assumed. For cases where the exponent is less than 1, $C_t/L \rightarrow 0$ as $L \rightarrow \infty$, which is clearly unreasonable.

2.8 SUMMARY

In this chapter equations were developed for estimating the relative effort (or cost) associated with conversion, reprogramming, and redesign of computer software. In Section 2.4 it was shown that in general, the larger the system, the lower the ratio of conversion to redesign or reprogramming effort. The basis for this conclusion is the fact that conversions can be automated (to some degree) and are therefore affected by the economy of scale. A similar conclusion was noted for project duration; however, the relative improvement was not as dramatic.

In Section 2.5 it was noted that there is an optimum level for investment in conversion tools and aids. As the size of the conversion project increases, clearly this investment should be increased. The arguments developed in Section 2.5 were primarily qualitative. A mathematical model for optimization was described in Section 2.6. Although a number of simplifying assumptions were used to develop the model, some interesting conclusions were obtained from the model.

In Section 2.7 program conversion costs per line were discussed. For some situations it is feasible to contract for conversions on a per line (plus per program) basis. Some computer software companies offer this type of service and one can usually choose between a *clean compile* or a *full implementation* option. (Typically, full implementation costs two to three times as much as clean compile.) It was emphasized that this type of service is different than a total system conversion. For example, the end user still must convert data and job control files, in addition to completing the installation and final system testing. The difference becomes increasingly important as the total system size increases.

The general subject of cost estimation for conversion projects has received increasing attention. The U.S. Federal Conversion Support Center (FCSC) has recently published a document comparing various conversion cost estimating techniques [10]. Boehm states that although the FCSC model has not been fully calibrated and validated, its estimates appear to be reasonable and consistent [9]. Boehm also discusses a technique for estimating an equivalent number of delivered source instructions (EDSI) for conversion projects. Once the EDSI has been calculated, the effort E is estimated using normal program development estimation methods. This approach seems to be quite reasonable for primarily manual conversions (i.e., conversions with a large reprogramming component).

As an example, Boehm considers a 50,000 line FORTRAN program being converted from a UNIVAC 1110 to an IBM 3033. The computed EDSI is 10,500 lines and using his basic model for new program development effort ($E=2.4L^{1.05}$) with L equal to 10.5, a value of E equal to 28 person-months is obtained. This value is significantly less than the 45 person-months computed using Equation (1.3) with L equal to 50. The Boehm estimate should be more accurate because it is based upon an analysis of the problems associated with the specific FORTRAN conversion. Equation (1.3) is an estimate based on a correlation of data from a variety of conversion projects. We can expect to see continuing improvements in the methods for estimating conversion effort and duration as additional data become available.

REFERENCES

1. Rand, N., Rand Information Systems, private communication, August 1980.
2. Oliver, P., "Software Conversion and Benchmarking," *Software World*, Vol. 10, No. 3, pp. 2-11, 1979.
3. Walston, C. E., and C. P. Felix, "A Method of Programming Measurement and Estimation," *IBM Systems Journal*, Vol. 17, No. 1, pp. 54-73, 1977.
4. Schneider, V., "Prediction of Software Effort and Project Duration—Four New Formulas," *SIGPLAN Notices*, Vol. 13, No. 6, pp. 49-59, 1978.
5. Wolberg, J. R., "Comparing the Cost of Software Conversion to the Cost of Reprogramming," *SIGPLAN Notices*, Vol. 16, No. 4, pp. 104-110, April 1981.
6. Brandon, D. H., "Commercial Software," in *Software Portability*, Cambridge University Press, New York, 1977, Chap. VI.D.
7. Wolberg, J. R., "Conversion Tools and the CONVERT Language," *BSO Conversion Symposium Proceedings*, April 1980, pp. IV-1 to IV-9.
8. Wolberg, J. R. and M. Rafal, "The Development and Use of Automatic Converters for Software Conversions," *Proceedings of the ONLINE Conference: Pragmatic Programming and Sensible Software*, Chameleon Press, 1978, pp. 77-92.
9. Boehm, B. W., *Software Engineering Economics*, Prentice-Hall, 1981.
10. Houtz, C., and T. Buschbach, Review and Analysis of Conversion Cost-Estimating Techniques, GSA Federal Conversion Support Center Report No. GSA/FCSC-81/001, Falls Church, VA., March 1981.

Management of a Conversion Project

3.1 INTRODUCTION

There is an increasing awareness that modern management methods are applicable to the wonderful world of software. In the early 1970s the software community started seriously to address the subject of managing software development and maintenance. Boehm wrote a paper in *Datamation*, which received wide attention: "Software and Its Impact: A Quantitative Assessment" [1]. The paper was based on a study by the U.S. Air Force Systems Command and the message was loud and clear: *Software is big business.* A considerable amount of quantitative information was included to support Boehm's conclusions and observations.[1]

The Boehm article popularized a number of concepts that have become part of the *common wisdom* of the software industry:

1. *The increasing ratio of the cost of software to hardware.*
2. *The virtual incompressibility of the software development cycle with respect to elapsed time.* (Boehm referred to an article by Brooks regarding this concept [2]. Since then Brooks has expanded this point in his book, *The Mythical Man-Month* [3]. This book is a classic and should be read by every software manager!)

---

[1] This material has been updated and summarized in Boehm's recent book, *Software Engineering Economics*, Prentice-Hall, 1981.

3. *The increasing software productivity* (measured in machine instructions per person-month) *due to language development.*
4. *The impact of hardware constraints on software productivity.*
5. *The importance of budgeting sufficient time for analysis and design and then program integration and testing.* (Boehm pointed out that too much attention was being directed toward program coding and auditing and not enough to the other major activities of software projects.)
6. *The impossibility of testing all possible logical paths through most computer programs.*

In conclusion, Boehm quoted from Lord Kelvin: *"When you can measure what you are speaking about and express it in numbers, you know something about it; but when you cannot measure it, when you cannot express it in numbers, your knowledge is of a meager and unsatisfactory kind: it may be the beginning of knowledge, but you have scarcely, in your thoughts, advanced to the stage of science."*

In recent years a large number of articles and conferences have considered in increasing detail many concepts related to software management. *Business Week* brought mass attention to the problem of creating computer software in a September 1980 cover story: "Missing Computer Software" [4]. Several books have been written which summarize the current *state of the art.* (It is still not clear whether software development has achieved Lord Kelvin's status of being a science or if it is still an art form.) Jensen and Tonies have covered a number of important topics in their book, *Software Engineering* [5]. Gunther has written *Management Methodology for Software Product Engineering* [6]. Metzger discusses the programming development cycle in *Managing a Programming Project* [7]. These books include extensive bibliographies regarding the relevant literature through the late 1970s.

In this chapter we focus our attention on a limited segment of the software management scene: managing the conversion of software. Most of the concepts and methods of general applicability are also relevant to conversion projects. However, there are differences and in the following sections we explore some of these differences.

3.2 AN OVERVIEW OF CONVERSION MANAGEMENT

An important (but not well known) fact about conversions is that they tend to have more management than technical problems. An explanation for this phenomenon is included in a Rand Information Systems (RIS) report [8]: "From the point at which test data and source material are collected to the point at which the converted programs are installed in the new environment, there are approximately 12 discrete tasks which have to be managed. So, *for a conversion of 1000 programs, nearly 12000 tasks have to be managed*. It would not be so bad if these tasks were independent, but, in fact, they are interdependent and the progress of one task can greatly affect the progress of other concurrent and later tasks."

The RIS report goes on to describe the problems associated with the control of the large volume of materials in a conversion: "To take a single program from the source environment to the target environment, there will be, on the average, five or six data sets which include the source material, a couple of input files, a couple of output files and perhaps the master file. So for *1000 programs, approximately 6000 data sets may have to be managed*. In addition, there are record definitions and record layouts, system flowcharts and documentation on how the program is used (such as the original job control files, operator console log sheets or run books). The control of these materials is critical to an organization's ability to manage the conversion according to the time and resources that have been allocated for it."

When one considers other problems such as the sequencing and scheduling of the various phases of the conversion, the impact of the conversion load on the affected data center, enforcement of uniform quality standards for the programs being converted, the need for some degree of parallel testing and operation, and the effect of the conversion on the morale of the technical staff, one can easily see that the manager of a conversion project is faced with a challenging task indeed! There are a variety of approaches to coping with the problems associated with a major conversion and some of the alternatives are discussed in Section 3.3.

Oliver compares the management of conversion projects to other software production projects [9] : "A conversion project is only slightly different from any other software production project with respect to its management. Careful planning is required, the project must be initiated, and once initiated it must be controlled. Finally, there is a completion phase. If there is a significant difference between the management of a conversion project and the management of a production project it is one of emphasis: a conversion project requires (and allows for) more discipline and stricter adherence to procedures. If properly executed, a conversion is very much an assembly-line type of operation, where *the total effort is broken down into well-defined tasks which are more dependent upon experience and strict adherence to procedures than on innovation and ingenuity* for their successful completion. This is true partly because of the high degree to which the conversion process can be automated. It should also be noted that many of the ground-rules for software production do not apply to conversions. For example, *manpower and time are not generally interchangeable in a software production project, but within bounds of good taste, they are in a conversion project."*

The interchangeability of personnel and time are best illustrated using a graph similar to that popularized by Brooks to illustrate his concept of total elapsed time versus number of people on a software project [3]. Brooks observed that adding personnel to typical software projects will eventually result in increased time to project completion! In Figure 3.1 a hypothetical project C illustrates this type of situation. Project C can theoretically be completed in 24 months by one person. By increasing the staff to eight, the completion time is reduced in 17 months, but beyond nine the reduction is negligible. Once the staff is increased beyond 13, we start to see delays in the project completion date caused by too many people working on the project. *Adding an extra person at this point is like throwing fuel on a fire; it will only cause added slippage in the completion date.*

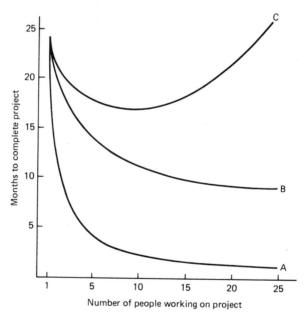

Figure 3.1 Months to complete a project versus the number of people working on the project. Project A is representative of a project exhibiting complete interchangeability of personnel and time. Project B is representative of a typical conversion project, and project C is representative of a software development project with complex interrelationships between subtasks.

Analyzing our hypothetical project C from the point of view of cost, we see that we should clearly use only one person. The cost for one person is based on 24 person-months, whereas the cost using eight people is based on $17 \times 8 = 136$ person-months! However, logic based on development cost measured in person-months is not the only consideration. For example, by reducing the development cycle from 24 months to 17 months, the use of the new system might result in a net saving far beyond the cost of an additional 112 (i.e., 136 - 24) person-months.

This argument is illustrated by Brooks in an example based on the development of IBM OS/360. The system required about 5000 person-years between 1963 and 1966 to develop. The number of people working on the project was over 1000 at the peak. He postulated a 10-person team of really top people replacing the bulky 1000-person team. He assumed a productivity improvement of a factor of 7 per person (because of their high caliber). He assumed an additional factor-of-7 improvement due to a vastly reduced communication problem resulting from the smaller staff. The required number of years to complete the project using the 10-person team would thus be $5000/(10 \times 7 \times 7) = 10$. Brooks then asks the obvious question: *"Will the product be interesting 10 years after its initial design? Or will it have been made obsolete by the rapidly developing software technology?* The dilemma is a cruel one. For efficiency and conceptual integrity, one prefers a few good minds doing design and construction. Yet for large systems one wants a way to bring considerable manpower to bear, so that the product can make a timely appearance. How can these two needs be reconciled?"

The opposite situation is noted in project A—a project with complete interchangeability of personnel and time. For example, the project can be completed in 24 months by one person, or in one month by 24 persons. One must leave the computer industry to find examples of projects fitting this model. Some agricultural projects (such as picking oranges) exhibit this type of behavior. For example, by doubling the number of pickers we can approximately halve the time required to pick a grove clean. Building a dam using coolie labor is another type of project exhibiting interchangeability of personnel and time.

Conversion projects often exhibit behavior represented by project B in Figure 3.1. This project is the middle ground between A and C. We can partition the conversion into a large number of small independent tasks so that we are not plagued by complex interrelationships between the various tasks. The tasks are interdependent from the point of view of scheduling; however, each task can be performed independently. A number of reasons account for the lack of total interchangeability in time and personnel:

1. Certain tasks can only be started after other tasks have been completed.

2. The number of tasks that can be worked on at a given time is limited by the available resources. For example, if the tasks are performed on an interactive basis, the number of terminals available for the project will limit the rate at which the tasks can be completed. Even if the project is performed in a batch mode, the number of jobs that can be processed in a given unit of time is limited.

3. Scheduling can be affected by critical delivery dates of hardware and software.

4. Some phases of the project (e.g., project planning and the development of conversion software) exhibit project C-type behavior and cannot be completed in less time than the associated minimums.

For these reasons, a conversion project is usually characterized by a minimum duration for completion. By adding personnel we can approach this minimum, but basic limitations do not allow us to complete the job in less time. Clearly, this minimum varies from project to project and some analysis is required to estimate the *critical path* for each conversion project. For our hypothetical project B in Figure 3.1, the minimum is nine months.

When confronted with the Brooks *months versus personnel* curve (i.e., project C of Figure 3.1) for the first time, the typical reaction includes a degree of skepticism. Esterling has developed a model for software personnel costs which is extremely helpful in explaining the effect of *interactions* on software productivity [10]. The results are summarized in Figure 3.2 as a function of n. The parameter n is defined as "the number of *interacting* people on the project. Interacting people are the persons working directly on the project (Indians, not chiefs). Supervisors are included only if they are full-time contributing members of the team." It should be clear that much of the "lost time" comes from legitimate demands of the project (e.g., coordination, definition of interfaces, design and coding walkthroughs, integration of systems, etc.). Nevertheless, the conclusion from Figure 3.2 is clear: *Increasing the number of interacting people on a software project leads to a decreasing productivity per person.*

It might not be obvious why a conversion project does not fit this model. To explain the difference, consider two project C tasks: Each task is to write a small module that will be integrated into a larger system. If, for example, the modules will share common variables or if the output from one module is the input to the second module, there is an

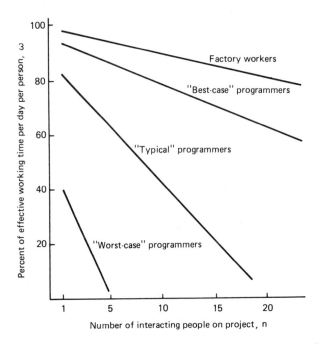

Figure 3.2 Percent of effective working time versus the number of interacting people on a software development project. Note: This model is particularly applicable to projects like project C shown in Figure 3.1. (From B. Esterling, "Software Manpower Costs: A Model," *Datamation*, March 1980, pp. 164-170. Reprinted with permission of *Datamation®* Magazine, © by Technical Publishing Co., a Dun & Bradstreet company, 1980. All rights reserved.)

inescapable need for coordination. Alternatively, consider two project B tasks: Each task is to convert a small module within a larger system. There is no need for coordination. The functional specifications of the source must only be reproduced in the target. There is no need to change inputs, outputs, or the usage of data in common storage. One person can be assigned to each task in project B and work independently. Thus project B can be considered as consisting of a number of tasks most of which can be characterized by a value of *n* equal to 1. Assigning an additional person to a conversion team should not influence the time required to complete these individual tasks.

3.3 PRECONVERSION TASKS

Regardless of where a conversion is ultimately performed and who actually does the job, there are a number of tasks which should begin when the need for a conversion is recognized. There are a number of reasons for initiating a conversion. For example:

1. *A basic hardware change* (e.g., replacement of the installation mainframe)

2. *A change in operating system*

3. *Acquisition of software* developed for a different environment

4. *A decision to convert an application from one mode of operation to another* (e.g., batch to on-line)

Once the need for change has been recognized, Pachaury lists a number of tasks that should be undertaken [11]:

1. *Analyze the current work load.* Typical questions that should be answered include:
   a. What are the current data processing costs, broken down by major components (hardware, supplies, operations, systems, programming, etc.)?
   b. Which programming languages and standards are used?
   c. How many programs are in each application area?
   d. How many programs are adequately documented?
   e. How many data files are involved?
   f. What are the usage statistics for the various programs and applications?
   g. For transaction-oriented systems, what are the current transaction rates?
   h. Who are the suppliers of any acquired software packages in current use?
   i. What areas of a company's operation will be affected by the conversion?

2. *Predict the growth rate in data processing needs:*
   a. At what rate will the on-line files grow?
   b. What new applications will have to be handled in the new environment?
   c. Is there an anticipated growth in transaction rate for transaction-oriented systems?

3. On the basis of actual usage and predicted growth, *estimate the computing work load and capacity required for the environment.* It is clearly a preconversion task to consider the target environment from the point of view of its capacity to do the required data processing. It would be *extremely discouraging* (to say the least) to complete a major conversion only to discover that the target environment is hopelessly short of capacity to handle the full work load!

4. *Evaluate the available options in making major changes in data processing methods.* The types of options to consider might include conversion from batch to on-line processing, use of a DBMS

(data base management system), use of telecommunications for data transmission, and adoption of new systems and programming standards.

Much of the information obtained by answering these questions will be useful once conversion planning is initiated. However, we see that this information is also necessary for a more fundamental task: deciding whether or not to authorize a change, and if so, selecting the components (both hardware and software) that will be used in the target environment.

The RIS report discussed in Section 3.2 offers advice regarding the planning for change [8]. They suggest that an organization should consider two different areas: one philosophical and the other technical. The philosophical issues are fundamental to the way the organization visualizes the data processing function. For example, should there be a centralized data processing unit with a network to branch offices or should the computer capability be distributed? Should the distributed approach be integrated with a centralized data base, or should each office be independent?

After the philosophical alternatives have been resolved, the technical alternatives must be reviewed. Basic issues include:

1. The type of hardware (e.g., mainframes, minis, or even micros)
2. The communications network (e.g., private lines or public carriers)
3. Peripherals such as data-entry devices, terminals, tape and disk drives, and telecommunications equipment.
4. Software, including operating systems, data communication and data management systems, programming languages, utilities, and related software, such as text editors, report generators, data inquiry, and word-processing packages

The RIS report summarizes this early planning stage as follows: "In light of the number of available choices, how can an organization build a program for implementing the changes? *First, it must know where it is today and where it wants to be tomorrow.*"

3.4 MANAGEMENT ALTERNATIVES

The preconversion tasks and analysis should be performed by a small group of experts with high-level management guidance and interaction. The impact of a fundamental change in the data processing operation of an organization can be monumental, so top management should certainly be involved in the decision-making process. Management should not hesitate to seek advice from experts both inside and outside the organization. Once a direction has been chosen, it becomes increasingly more painful to alter the course!

After the target environment has been defined, the conversion process can be initiated. Once again management is faced with a variety of alternatives. The major choice is between *in-house conversions and conversions performed by outside contractors.* However, there are a wide variety of organizational alternatives within these broad categories. For example, if the conversion is to be performed in-house, the following is a partial list of methods that I have seen used:

1. *A team of conversion specialists is formed to assist the various applications groups convert their systems.*
2. *The organization provides a management team to supervise the conversion effort; however, staffing is primarily through high-level subcontractors.*
3. *The conversions are performed by the applications programming staff.*

The first alternative has been used with considerable success by the Philips organization. The Philips conversion team is called Plan Q and is discussed in Section 3.7. The second alternative is being used by the research laboratories of a large European oil company. The advantage of this approach is that the applications programmers (who are primarily scientists and engineers) do not have to be diverted from their main areas of activity. The subcontractors have been hired for the duration of the project. It makes considerable sense to perform conversions using temporary staff if conversions are not seen as an ongoing activity. The third alternative is used most often for moderately small conversions. However, if the conversion will require many person-months of effort, management faces a morale problem if this alternative is chosen. Many applications programmers are willing to spend a few months on a conversion; however, if he or she is asked to spend six months to a year on the project, the reaction might be extremely negative.

Many of the problems associated with in-house conversions can be eliminated if an organization uses the services of an outside contractor specializing in conversion projects. This approach is becoming increasingly popular, especially for large conversions. Snyders mentions a number of companies that provide this type of service [12]. The advantage of using an outside service include the following:

1. The experience of the outside contractor improves the probability that the project will be completed on time and within budget.

2. The demands on the organization's programming staff are dramatically reduced. (Some coordination will be required; however, the bulk of the effort is performed by the contractor's staff.)
3. If the contracting firm uses its own computing facilities, the impact on the organization's computing center is reduced. A large conversion requires a lot of machine time and other resources, and this factor must be considered in the conversion planning phase.

As usual, the choice to perform the conversion in-house or to go outside is primarily an economic decision. Management must first address the most basic issue: *Is the probability of success for both alternatives high?* If the answer for either alternative is *no*, then the choice is simple—we would obviously choose the only remaining alternative. However, if both alternatives are judged to have a high probability of success, a number of other factors should be considered:

1. Will the target environment (i.e., hardware, operating system, etc.) be available in-house for the conversion?
2. Is the capacity of the target machine large enough to allow the additional load required by the conversion?
3. Are staff available for the conversion?
4. If the answer to question 3 is negative, can temporary staff be hired for the duration of the conversion?
5. Does the organization have *available* personnel with the skill and experience required to successfully manage the conversion project?
6. How do the cost estimates compare for an in-house conversion versus the use of an outside contractor?

These are major issues that will affect management's decision. However, it should be clear that even if the services of an outside contractor are obtained, the organization's involvement with the project is certainly not finished. Coordination between the contractor and the organization is necessary in many phases of the conversion, including data preparation, testing, and implementation. In addition, it is in everyone's interest that the organization should receive progress reports and should have some approval function at major milestones of the project.

An overall approach to change based on conversion is a method described in the RIS report as *incremental migration* [8]. The report suggests that it is sometimes advantageous to enhance the applications incrementally rather than relying on one large project to alter completely *all* the organization's data processing systems. This approach is shown schematically in Figure 3.3. The project is initiated by a straight conversion of all the applications to the target environment. On this first

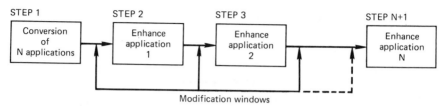

STEP 1

| Conversion of N applications |

STEP 2

| Enhance application 1 |

STEP 3

| Enhance application 2 |

STEP N+1

| Enhance application N |

Modification windows

Figure 3.3   Incremental migration steps showing modification windows. (From Rand Information Systems, "Conversion Special Report: Changing to New Technology," National Symposium on Computer Systems Enhancement, 1979.)

step of the project no attempt is made to enhance the applications. The emphasis is to bring the applications into production in the target environment. Then, one by one, the individual applications are enhanced. Upon completion of enhancement and testing, the old version of each application is replaced by the newer enhanced version. After each step has been completed, management has an opportunity to reevaluate the overall plan and introduce modifications where necessary. The major incentive for adopting incremental migration is that the advantages of the new environment can start to be realized upon completion of the conversion step. The entire process of revising all applications can be spread over a period of years with feedback from each enhancement affecting the following steps. The basic conversion step can be completed rapidly compared to a redesign of all the major applications systems.

3.5 CONVERSION PLANNING

The planning phase of a conversion project can be a matter of days or months, depending on the size of the project. The percentage of the total effort directed toward planning is dependent on a number of factors, including how one defines the planning function. In Table 2.5 a representative value of 5% was arbitrarily chosen for the initial planning phase. However, if one includes planning associated with the other activities, the total planning effort might represent a more significant portion of the total effort.

Brooks suggests that planning a software task should require about one-third of the total effort [3]! He states that this amount of effort is required to produce a detailed and solid specification but not enough to include research or exploration of totally new techniques. In a *Datamation* article by Lehman an average value of 12½% of the time available to a project manager and staff is spent on planning (and replanning) [13].

Lehman breaks down the planning functions as follows:

Planning Function	Time (%)
Developing an overall project management plan	22
Developing control procedures	19
Staff planning	18
Organizational planning	16
Quality assurance planning	12
Administrative planning	8
Other	5
	100

How applicable these numbers are to conversion planning is debatable. However, it is an accepted premise that conversion projects are simpler than comparable software development projects. (Otherwise, we might as well redesign software if there is no incentive to convert!) This simplification is felt in the reduced level of interdependence of the various tasks in the project. Some reduction in the percent of effort directed toward planning is therefore reasonable when we compare convesion planning and the planning of software development projects.

The usual starting point for conversion planning is the *requirement analysis* [8,9]. RIS states that the development of a successful work plan (which is really what planning is all about!) is dependent *above all else* on a current statement of requirements. "The simplest way to define a conversion requirement is to prepare an inventory. One of the ways to start is with a manual inventory of the number of programs and files. The libraries should be dumped and the library listings compared with the manual inventory. After resolving differences, additional details should be included such as the number of statements in the various programming languages, file organization methods, the total number of record types and the number of record types having non-character data. Special considerations such as input/output software written in-house should also be reviewed"[8].

The next major step in the planning process is to develop a *conversion guide*. This guide should identify the differences between the source and target environments and suggest an approach for resolution of each difference. Figure 3.4 is an example of an entry in a conversion guide, prepared by F International Limited for a European customer planning a large XDS SIGMA 7 EXTENDED FORTRAN IV-to-IBM FORTRAN IV conversion. Clearly, the conversion guide (or guides) should cover all aspects of the conversion, including the conversion of programs, data, and so on.

Before making major decisions based on the conclusions of the conversion guide, some effort should be directed toward testing its

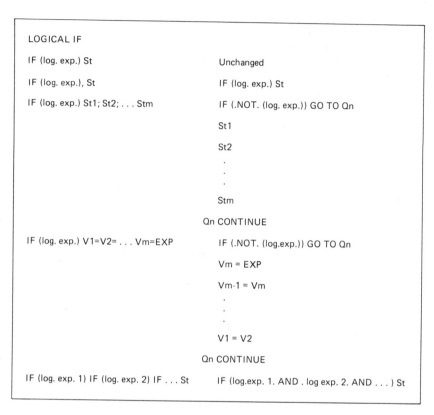

LOGICAL IF

IF (log. exp.) St	Unchanged
IF (log. exp.), St	IF (log. exp.) St
IF (log. exp.) St1; St2; . . . Stm	IF (.NOT. (log. exp.)) GO TO Qn
	St1
	St2
	.
	.
	.
	Stm
	Qn CONTINUE
IF (log. exp.) V1=V2= . . . Vm=EXP	IF (.NOT. (log.exp.)) GO TO Qn
	Vm = EXP
	Vm-1 = Vm
	.
	.
	.
	V1 = V2
	Qn CONTINUE
IF (log. exp. 1) IF (log. exp. 2) IF . . . St	IF (log.exp. 1. AND . log exp. 2. AND . . .) St

Figure 3.4   Typical example of an entry in a conversion guide. (From "Conversion of Programs from XDS SIGMA 7 EXTENDED FORTRAN IV to IBM FORTRAN IV," *Conversion Guide*, F International Ltd., Buckinghamshire, England.)

major premises. Based on the methods suggested in the guide, will the conversion be successful? One method of testing the quality of the guide is to apply it (probably on a manual basis) to some representative programs. If the guide has already been used in a previous conversion project, one can clearly be optimistic about its reliability.

Based on the requirements analysis and the conversion guide, the planning team can next direct attention toward actual *conversion methods*. For example, which aspects of the conversion will be performed manually, and which aspects will be performed using conversion tools and aids? If converters are to be developed in-house (or on a contractual basis), which items in the conversion guide should be included in the converter specification statements? Some items might actually be converted, others might merely result in FLAG messages. These decisions are part of the planning function.

The next planning step is to *estimate required resources*. The major resources are personnel and machine time. Based on the conversion requirements and the methods chosen to accomplish the conversion, estimates must be made of such parameters as *lines per person-hour* and *CPU seconds per line*. Estimation techniques are discussed in Section 3.6; however, it is worthwhile mentioning that estimating productivity is a crucial step in the planning of a conversion project. If the lines per person-hour are grossly overestimated, we can expect a severe slippage in the project schedule. If we grossly underestimate the machine requirements per line, we can enter into a situation where the conversion work load runs into stiff competition with the computer production load. RIS notes that "this single issue of the conflict between the conversion load and the production load on the new machine may in itself be cause for a conversion to slip 50 to 100 percent" [8].

The final planning step is to develop a *realistic schedule*. Clearly, this schedule will only be as good as the estimate of the required resources. The schedule should take into consideration such obvious factors as the delivery dates for new hardware (and perhaps software), and the leasing arrangements on the current system. Is it a simple matter to extend the lease on the current system, or are there severe cost penalties for holding on to the machine beyond the lease expiration date? Referring back to project B in Figure 3.1, it is important not to attempt to complete the project in less time than the lower limit of the curve. RIS warns against an unrealistic completion date: "The key is not to get trapped into attempting a long job in a short period of time because someone has made an emotional decision that the conversion will be done in N months" [8].

The scheduling effort should result in some document such as a Gantt chart which can be used by the project manager to follow the progress of the project from stage to stage. A typical Gantt chart is shown in Figure 3.5. Note that the Gantt chart includes a pilot conversion which is extremely useful in determining if the resource estimates and conversion procedures are accurate. For large conversions a pilot conversion (typically including some of the representative subsystems) should be considered as mandatory.

In summary, the major steps in planning a conversion project are as follows:

1. *Requirements analysis*
2. Development of a *conversion guide*
3. Statement of *conversion methods*
4. *Resources estimation*
5. *Scheduling*

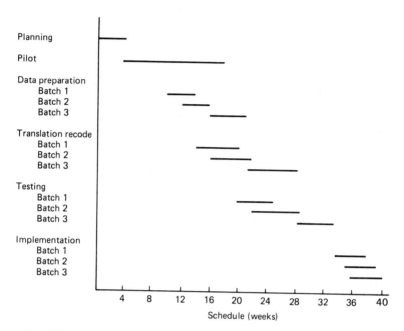

Figure 3.5 Gantt chart showing a conversion schedule. (From Rand Information Systems, "Conversion Special Report: Changing to New Technology," National Symposium on Computer Systems Enhancement, 1979.)

Proper planning with adequate attention to these various steps should increase the probability of completing the conversion on schedule and within budget.

3.6 ESTIMATION TECHNIQUES

Frederick Brooks has some choice remarks to make about software estimating: "Observe that for the programmer, as for the chef, the urgency of the patron may govern the scheduled completion of the task, but it cannot govern the actual completion. An omelette, promised in two minutes, may appear to be progressing nicely. But when it has not set in two minutes, the customer has two choices—wait or eat it raw. Software customers have had the same choices. The cook has another choice; he can turn up the heat. The result is often an omelette nothing can save—burned in one part, raw in another" [3].

Miscalculations based on unreasonable estimates are probably the major reason why some conversion projects exceed the budget and miss the scheduled completion date. In Sections 1.5 and 2.2 some equations were developed for estimating project person-months (E) and project duration (D) as functions of the number of thousands of lines of code (L) to be converted. These equations were developed from an RIS data base of completed conversion projects, and their applicability to a specific situation should be considered carefully. My inclination is to use equations of this sort to yield an initial "ballpark" estimate of the conversion effort and duration. *However, before trying to develop a schedule and budget, I strongly suggest seeking more reliable data upon which to base an estimate of required resources.*[1]

Oliver cautions against the use of linear relationships to develop resource requirements [9]. The effect of program size on conversion time and cost is illustrated by the following example: "A competent programmer supported by a set of software tools can convert 500 lines of COBOL source code per day. This suggests that a 10,000 line program could be converted in 20 days whereas experience shows that some 36 days would in fact be required and that this number could go up to 104 days if the conversion is from an assembler language with complex file structures and large volume files."

The variables affecting conversion productivity include the following:

1. The *source and target differences.* If the two systems are very similar, one can expect a high productivity (i.e., lines per person-hour or lines per person-day). The opposite is unfortunately also true!

2. The *level of usage of the most troublesome statements.* Some statements in the source language require considerable effort to convert. However, if these statements are used rarely, their impact on average productivity will be small.

3. The *skill of the programmer.* Many of the papers and books referenced in this chapter include evidence to show the large differences in programmer productivity for software development projects. For example, Brooks uses a factor of 7 to differentiate between the productivity of average programmers and high-level specialists [3]. In conversion work, the required level of ingenuity is less and the degree of standardization is greater, so we can expect a smaller productivity range between the worst and best programmers on the team. Oliver suggests ranges of 300 to 500 lines per day for COBOL-to-COBOL and FORTRAN-to-FORTRAN conversions, which is nearly a factor of 2 [9]. Although not as dramatic as the

---

[1] Houtz and Buschbach review some conversion cost estimating techniques in a recent FCSC report [15].

differences for software development projects, a factor of 2 in productivity can have a huge impact on the conversion schedule.

4. The *learning curve.* Conversion work tends to be repetitive, so one can expect an increase in productivity through a learning period. RIS suggests that the difference between new and experienced programmers (with respect to a particular conversion) can be as large as a factor of 6 in productivity [8]. Thus one can expect slippage in the schedule for projects plagued by a high turnover of personnel.

5. The *availability of hardware.* Conversion work requires a high level of computer acitivity. Regardless of how talented the staff is in conversions, if the machine is not available, the job will not get done.

When one considers all these variables, it becomes obvious that the estimation of required resources is a tricky matter. For large conversions, the usual procedure is to run a pilot project to obtain productivity estimates under "real" conditions. The Gantt chart shown in Figure 3.5 shows the pilot conversion as a separate function from planning. However, one can consider the pilot conversion as a verification step for the planning and scheduling of the total project. The pilot will give the project manager an opportunity to spot weaknesses in the assumptions used to develop the resource estimations. The planning and scheduling can be revised accordingly with a minimum of damage to the organization. The pilot can also be used for checking and improving procedures and tools that will be used throughout the project. Finally, it is also helpful in convincing management and the members of the project team that the job really can be done.

It is worthwhile to compare the productivity ranges mentioned above with numbers obtained using the formula developed in Section 1.5:

$$E = 7.14L^{0.47} \tag{1.3}$$

If we assume an average of 22 working days per month, we can develop the following formula for *productivity* (P) measured in *lines per day:*

$$P = \frac{1000 \times L}{22 \times E} = \frac{1000 \times L}{22 \times 7.14 \times L^{0.47}} = 6.37L^{0.53} \tag{3.1}$$

We can use Equation (3.1) to predict productivity for different-size projects. Results are summarized in Table 3.1. We note that the productivity range suggested by Oliver (300 to 500 lines per day) is applicable only to very large projects (i.e., between 1 million and 10 million lines of code). The explanation for this apparent discrepancy is quite straightforward. The RIS data used to develop Equation (1.3) include the total

TABLE 3.1   Productivity[a] P and Person-Months[b] E as a Function of the Total Number of Lines to be Converted.

Number of Lines	L	P (lines/day)	E (person-months)
100,000	100	73	62
1,000,000	1000	248	184
10,000,000	10000	840	542

[a]Estimated using Eqn. 3.1
[b]Estimated using Eqn. 1.3

project hours, not just the programmer hours. *One would therefore be making a grievous error if productivity measured in programmer hours only were used to develop a project budget.* The productivity rate predicted by Equation (3.1) should be treated as an estimate of total productivity with all project hours included (i.e., planning, data preparation, conversion, testing, implementation, documentation, etc.)

Another interesting thought occurs when considering the numbers shown in Table 3.1. Is it really possible to get the very high levels of productivity predicted for large projects? Doesn't the programmer productivity (e.g., 300 to 500 lines per day for COBOL-to-COBOL or FORTRAN-to-FORTRAN conversions) provide some sort of upper limit? We will have an opportunity to consider this question in the following section in our discussion related to Plan Q—probably the largest conversion project ever undertaken.

3.7 MANAGING A VERY LARGE CONVERSION: PLAN Q[1]

Plan Q is the name used by Philips for their Concern Migration Center. As a case study, Plan Q is by no means typical; it is probably the largest conversion project ever undertaken. Nevertheless, it is well worth considering because a number of innovative concepts have been developed at Plan Q. In this section we discuss some of these concepts and consider their relevance to other conversion projects.

Perhaps the most interesting concept implemented at Plan Q is their "factory-like" approach to conversions. Jaap van der Korst, the manager of Plan Q since its inception in 1967, describes the operation as a *conversion factory*. One hears such terms as "flow of the goods" and "factory manager," which seem quite remote from the usual terminology one expects in a software development environment. And yet it

[1] Plan Q, Concern Migration Center, Philips Gloeilampfabrieken, Eindhoren, The Netherlands.

works! The most noteworthy aspect of Plan Q is that they successfully convert programs *on schedule* and *within budget*. When one compares this fact with the typical time and cost overruns that we have come to expect in software development projects, we are led to an important conclusion: *There are fundamental differences between conversions and development projects.* Management can exploit these differences to complete conversion projects on a much more orderly basis than what has unfortunately become the software industry norm.

3.7.1 Background

Plan Q was initiated by Philips in 1967 as a central site to help the company introduce the Philips P1000 line of computers to their 32 separate computer centers. The reasons for a centralized approach included the following:

1. Concentration of effort would result in a buildup of conversion know-how.
2. The cost to the individual centers would be reduced by decreasing the hardware overlap period and the freeze period for new applications.
3. The scale of the project would justify development of very high quality tools and aids.
4. The problem of staffing one center with experienced personnel would be much simpler than finding additional short-term assistance at the individual centers. (The applications programming staff of the various centers were typically quite busy with planned development projects.)

The original concept was to organize Plan Q as a support facility. Three P1000 series computers were available and the permanent staff included about 30 people. The permanent staff consisted of systems programmers, technical consultants, and administrative and operations personnel. At any given time about 30 "clients" from the centers would be at Plan Q working on their conversions with the help of the permanent staff.

In 1977, Philips decided to cease production of middle-sized and large computers. It was decided to replace the 56 P1000 series computers at the 32 centers (in seven European countries) by IBM or IBM-compatible hardware and IBM software. By this time the inventory of programs that had to be replaced had grown to 40,000! At an average of 1000 lines per program, this meant that 40 million lines of code had to be replaced. A meeting of the center managers in early 1978 led to a decision to continue using a centralized approach. Clearly, the experience gained in the earlier conversions by Plan Q was a major reason for once again opting for a centralized approach.

There were, however, some new concepts initiated for the P1000-to-IBM conversions. About 10,000 of the 40,000 programs were DB/DC (i.e., data base/data communications) applications. Because many of these applications used special Philips software which had no IBM-compatible equivalent, the DB/DC applications required a large degree of redesign and reprogramming. It was decided to leave the responsibility for replacing these applications with the individual centers. The remaining programs were primarily *batch applications* written mainly in COBOL in a standardized Philips style. The conversion of these programs was to be performed at Plan Q by Plan Q personnel. Representatives from the centers would be involved in *preparation* and *implementation*, but not *conversion*.

The master migration plan extends from June 1978 to December 1982. The Plan Q phase of the project was essentially completed by December 1981 and the DB/DC applications are scheduled for completion by December 1982. The conversions are organized on a center-by-center basis, with several centers being converted simultaneously. The scheduled time per center varies from three months to almost two years, depending on the number of programs per center. At the time of my last visit to Plan Q (October 1981), more than 90% of the programs had already been converted. The conversions were being completed on schedule and a number of the P1000 computers had already been replaced. Using the powerful tools developed throughout the project, they are now continuing to do conversion work for third parties.

3.7.2 Statistical Information

Plan Q has developed a very sophisticated data base of information related to the conversion tasks. As a result they can estimate productivity and develop accurate schedules. The statistics allow us to get a very detailed picture regarding the nature of a "typical" Philips batch application:

1. *Applications.* The average application consists of about 11 job steps.
2. *Job steps.* About half of the job steps are utilities (e.g., SORTs) and 9.7 out of 11 are conditional.
3. *Programs.* The average program consists of about 1000 lines of COBOL.

4. *Job control.* The ratio of JCL statements to COBOL statements for a particular application is between 0.04 and 0.08.

5. *Files.* The average number of SELECTs (i.e., files) per program is 3.6 and 2.9 of them are SEQUENTIAL.

6. *Depth of structure.* The average program uses 38.2 GO TOs and 23.4 PERFORMs. Modern techniques of structured programming suggest a higher ratio of PERFORMs to GO TOs. (Some purists would like to see GO TOs eliminated completely.)

7. *COBOL conversions.* The conversion of COBOL programs is performed at close to a 100% level automatically.

8. *JCL conversions.* The JCLs are converted at about 60 to 95% levels automatically. The average JCL deck expands from 107 to 142 statements as a result of the conversion.

9. *Staffing.* The average number of people working at Plan Q for the P1000-to-IBM conversions was 55 during the peak period of the project.

An *average* COBOL program is defined as a 1000-statement program. There are an average of 1.73 *elements* per program. (An element is defined as a COBOL program, a JCL deck, a macro, a data set, etc.) The *factory hours* required to convert an element is on the average 0.92 without testing or 3.06 with testing. Total Plan Q hours per factory hour is 1.38. Thus with testing the total time to convert an average COBOL program is:

$$1.73 \, \frac{\text{elements}}{\text{program}} \times 3.06 \, \frac{\text{factory hours}}{\text{element}} \times 1.38 \, \frac{\text{Plan Q hour}}{\text{factory hour}}$$

$$= 7.3 \, \frac{\text{Plan Q hours}}{\text{program}}$$

We can convert this value to lines per eight-hour day:

$$P = \frac{1000 \text{ lines}}{7.3 \text{ hours}} \times \frac{8 \text{ hours}}{\text{day}} = 1096 \, \frac{\text{lines}}{\text{day}}$$

Let us now compare this number to P_c, a value obtained using Equation (3.1) for $L = 30,000$:

$$P_c = 6.37 \times 30,000^{0.53} = 1503 \, \frac{\text{lines}}{\text{day}}$$

Since the largest project included in the RIS database was 2 million lines (i.e., $L = 2000$), it is quite surprising how close the computed productivity (i.e., P_c) is to the actual measured productivity P.

One might question this high productivity from the point of view of the programmer. If a top programmer can convert 500 lines per day of COBOL to COBOL, how is it possible that total productivity, including the total staff hours and the entire mix of conversions (e.g., JCLs as well as COBOL), can exceed this 500-line-per-day limit? The explanation must be related to the quality of the *conversion tools and aids.* In a very large project, one can make the necessary investment required to automate the process to the maximum possible degree. Plan Q has developed high-quality conversion tools and thus achieves levels of productivity far in excess of the levels usually encountered in COBOL-to-COBOL conversions.

One other interesting fact should be mentioned. The involvement of personnel from the various computer centers requires on the average eight hours per average program. This involvement includes assistance in data preparation and implementation plus consultancy when required. *This statistic is particularly relevant when one plans to subcontract a conversion job.* The budget should include some allowance on the part of the customer for work with the contractor. Someone on the customer's staff should have the responsibility of coordinating this effort and should have sufficient free time (or help) to do the job properly.

3.7.3 Testing Philosophy

The Plan Q testing philosophy is significantly different from the philosophy followed in typical software development projects. The usual approach is first to test the individual modules and then to test the entire system. The Plan Q approach is first to complete the conversion of the modules and then to test the entire system. Only if problems are encountered do they go down to the level of the individual programs (or other types of elements).

Experience has shown that with their high level of automation, once a COBOL program has achieved *clean compile* status, it usually performs error-free. Most testing problems are encountered at the job control level and thus the emphasis is on the overall system. Nevertheless, testing represents 2.14 out of 3.06 factory hours to convert an average element. These numbers imply that 70% of the factory effort is directed toward testing. If one notes that the average number of elements per program is 1.73 and total hours per program are 7.3, then testing represents 1.73 × 2.14/7.3 or 40% of the total effort. This high level of testing is typical of conversion work. (In Table 2.6 we note that the Dataware prices for *full implementation* are twice the prices for *clean compile* conversions.)

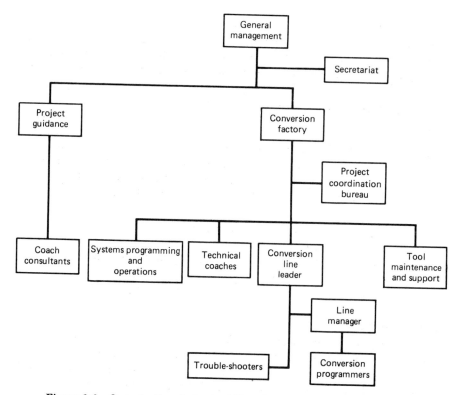

Figure 3.6 Organizational chart of Plan Q. (From A. J. van der Korst, *Plan Q and Migration*, IDL-MIG-70/9407, 1979.)

3.7.4 Project Organization and Management

An organizational chart of Plan Q is shown in Figure 3.6. The central function of Plan Q is the *conversion factory*, which is under the direct supervision of a *factory manager*. The manager is responsible for the work progress in the factory. He manages the following groups:

1. *Project coordination bureau.* This group handles the "flow of goods" for the factory. Their task starts when the incoming material arrives at Plan Q, through monitoring work-in-progress and providing figures for post-calculations. They are also responsible for supplying the "finished goods" to the clients.
2. *Tool maintenance and support.* This group develops conversion tools and supports the users of these tools.

3. *Conversion line.* In the factory there are several lines, each managed by a line manager. Technical assistance is given by the trouble-shooters while site programmers and/or other specialists are available for consultation.

4. *Technical coaches.* The main function of the coaches is to interface with the sites. They support the sites (i.e., the various centers) during the *migration proposal* preparation phase. Help is given in preparing inventories and batches for conversion. The technical coaches also support the sites during implementation of the application systems.

5. *Systems programming and operations.* This group is involved in implementing the conversion tools into the operating systems and giving advice regarding available systems software.

The second group reporting directly to the general management is the *project guidance group.* The members of this group (i.e., the *coach consultants*) initiate the necessary organizational work at the sites. The coach consultant for a particular project is the Plan Q project leader, who has the responsibility for seeing that the conversion progresses according to plan. Coordination between the site and the factory is maintained through the coach consultant.

The obvious question one might ask when considering Figure 3.6 is the relevance of this organizational chart to a more modest conversion project. I believe that the relevance is the recognition of the importance of the various functions included in the chart. Plan Q places emphasis on coordination, monitoring, preparation of the material to be converted, and troubleshooting. These types of tasks are quite normal in a factory type of environment, but less common in a software environment. To a large measure, the success of Plan Q can be attributed to their emphasis on control.

3.7.5 Management Control Tools

Plan Q utilizes a control system called CCS (Conversion Control System) for managing conversion projects [14]. In the document abstract, CCS is described as having been developed to enable Plan Q to apply a *factory-like* approach to conversions. Its main purpose is to allow coordination and automation of the technical actions that occur during conversion. In many ways it is similar to production control systems used to control other types of factories.

The system comprises a set of files and user-written commands (and command processors). A variety of tasks can be automated using CCS:

1. *Copy* source elements from user input tapes to disk files
2. *Submitting* a conversion job stream
3. *Creating and updating files* for project status information
4. *Retrieval and editing* of converted source elements
5. *Syntax checking, compilation, and link editing* of converted source elements
6. *Backing up and restoring* of the projects disk spaces
7. *Inquiring* as to the project status, source elements, and backups
8. *Reporting* problems
9. *Protecting* against concurrent updating and unauthorized use
10. *Communicating* between conversion team members and with the computer operation

The CCS system runs under the IBM operating system VM/CMS and has been developed as a user extension of CMS. The members of a conversion team use CCS as an interface between their "user machines" and the master machine. All communications between the various virtual machines are handled by CCS users through a variety of simple commands. A single user command calls a sophisticated program which performs the required task in a well-defined and tested manner. By having such a system, it is possible to institute standard procedures which simplify the entire process and avoid many costly errors. A summary of CCS commands is shown in Table 3.2.

Another important management tool is the Plan Q data base, which includes the relevant information regarding the conversion process. The statistics discussed in Section 3.7.2 were obtained using information in the data base. Other tools access the data base to generate reports that are useful for planning and scheduling.

A system called PHIMASS (Philips Migration Assistance Support System) is used for inventory purposes. This tool is used to help develop the migration policy document and the migration proposal. These documents are used to develop the plan and schedule for each conversion.

As noted in the Plan Q documents and confirmed in the RIS Conversion Report [8], control is essential for managing large conversion projects. To hope to accomplish this function without sophisticated management tools is wishful thinking. There are just too many tasks that have to be accomplished to rely on a manual system. Managers

TABLE 3.2 Summary of CCS Commands

Command	Class[a]	Description
BACKUP	A	Dumps the contents of all CMS disks in use by a conversion team onto tape
CLEAN	A	Removes converted source elements from CMS after shipment
COLLECT	A	Copies converted source elements from the master virtual machine back to CMS
CONVERT	A	Copies source elements from tape onto the CMS disk, registers them, and generates and submits a conversion job stream
GETLIST	G	Reads and displays a job stream output list from the virtual card reader
HELP	G	Gives on-line information about CCS commands
PROCESS	C	Manages modification of source elements
REPORT	G	Displays information about: Backups Current problems where assistance is needed Outstanding converted source elements Status of the conversion project Status of a specific source element Status of all source elements
RESTORE	G	Restores individual source elements
SHIP	A	Loads selected source elements and load modules onto tape for shipment to the conversion site
SIGNAL	G	Signals that a source element is ready to be tested, passed the tests, or gives problems
SUBMIT	G	Submits a job stream to a virtual machine
UPDSTAT	A	Processes internal transactions to modify the project status file

[a]Class A means that the command can be used only by the team administrator; a C command can be used by a conversion programmer, and G are general commands.
Source: J. E. M. Zwart, *Plan Q Conversion Control System CSS*, UDV-AP-C780031, Philips, Eindhoven, The Netherlands, March 1978.

embarking on large conversions should pay particular attention to developing or obtaining suitable software for controlling the project.

3.8 SUMMARY

An increasing amount of information related to managing software projects is becoming available. However, when one considers the more specific area of managing software conversions, there is very little information available. And yet, there are fundamental differences. In this chapter we have attempted to highlight the differences as well as the similarities.

We have also attempted to bring information contained in relatively hard to obtain sources to the reader's attention. Some of the information is quantitative in nature and the reader is cautioned against using the numbers blindly. However, there is something very comforting about seeing someone else's numbers! When one has nothing else to use, they form a reasonable starting point for ballpark estimates.

Clearly, no attempt has been made to present a "management approach" that is valid for all situations. Such an animal just does not exist. However, by bringing to the reader's attention some of the ideas and concepts used by others, we hope to help the reader formulate a plan that will contribute to the success of his or her conversion project.

REFERENCES

1. Boehm, B., "Software and Its Impact: A Quantitative Assessment," *Datamation*, May 1973, pp. 48-59.

2. Brooks, F., "Why Is Software Late?" *Data Management*, August 1971.

3. Brooks, F., *The Mythical Man-Month (Essays on Software Engineering)*, Addison-Wesley, Reading, Mass., 1978.

4. "Missing Computer Software," *Business Week*, September 1, 1980, pp. 46-53.

5. Jensen, R., and C. Tonies, *Software Engineering*, Prentice-Hall, Englewood Cliffs, N.J., 1979.

6. Gunther, R., *Management Methodology for Software Product Engineering*, Wiley-Interscience, New York, 1978.

7. Metzger, P. W., *Managing a Programming Project*, 2nd ed., Prentice-Hall, Englewood Cliffs, N.J., 1981.

8. Rand Information Systems, "Conversion Special Report: Changing to New Technology," National Symposium on Computer Systems Enhancement, 1979.

9. Oliver, P., "Software Conversion and Benchmarking," *Software World*, Vol. 10, No. 3, pp. 2-11, 1979.

10. Esterling, B., "Software Manpower Costs: A Model," *Datamation*, March 1980, pp. 164-170.

11. Pachaury, V., "System Conversion—Problems and Approaches," *Data Processing*, May 1977, pp. 21-23.

12. Snyders, J., "Conversion Packages and Services," *Computer Decisions*, March 1982, 35-50.

13. Lehman, J., "How Software Projects Are Really Managed," *Datamation*, January 1979, pp. 119-129.

14. Zwart, J. E. M., *Plan Q Conversion Control System CCS*, UDV-AP-C780031, Phillips, Eindhoven, The Netherlands, March 1978.

15. Houtz, C. and T. Buschbach, "Review and Analysis of Conversion Cost-Estimating Techniques," GSA Federal Conversion Support Center Report No. GSA/FCSC-81/001, Falls Church, Va., March 1981.

4

Program Enhancements:
Portability, Performance,
and Maintainability

4.1 INTRODUCTION

The main objective of program conversions is to move the original programs to a target environment. However, secondary objectives might include enhancement of the target code. For example, we might require that the resulting programs meet some predetermined performance requirements. In addition, some effort might be directed toward enhancing the maintainability of the resulting programs.

Program enhancement is thus seen to be a natural activity within the overall realm of a conversion project. The enhancement of code can be accomplished at two different points:

1. Prior to conversion
2. Upon completion of the conversion

These two options should *not* be considered as alternatives. The main objective of the preconversion enhancement effort is to improve program portability. The objective of postconversion enhancement is to improve the quality of the resulting programs in the target environment.

Most of the techniques described in the following sections are presented using examples. Almost all of the examples are limited to COBOL, FORTRAN, and PL/1, for several reasons:

1. Most readers are familiar with at least one of these languages.
2. The majority of conversion projects involve at least one of these languages.
3. These languages include sufficient variety so that simple examples can be used to illustrate each point.

It should be emphasized, however, that the concepts and techniques described in this chapter are also relevant to most other languages (e.g., ALGOL, BASIC, Pascal, etc.)

4.2 ENHANCING PORTABILITY

The key to enhancing portability is *program standardization.* Program standardization is defined as a process that introduces changes in the program source code, but these changes do *not* affect the object code. Programs written in a standard manner are easier to convert than nonstandard programs.[1] Clearly, the optimum time for imposing program standardization is at the program development stage. However, in conversion projects, programs are usually received long after the development stage has been completed. A typical scenario is that a system (i.e., programs, data, job control files, etc.) has been developed and has been in production in a particular environment. The task at hand is to move the system to a new environment.

As an early step in the conversion process, the source code can be subjected to a degree of standardization. The purpose of this effort is to simplify the conversion process (i.e., enhance portability). Clearly, any interaction with the original software introduces an element of risk. Have the modifications associated with our standardization effort created any new bugs in the resulting code? For this reason it is recommended that preconversion standardization be accomplished with the aid of software tools. All tasks that one would normally want to accomplish at this stage can be defined in an algorithmic manner and can therefore be programmed. If the tools are well tested and of high quality, the associated risk in their usage should be small.

Clearly, the goals of standardization are language dependent and even project dependent. It is important to know how the next stage in

---

[1] There is a fundamental difference between conversion software and compilers. In conversion software the source code undergoes a series of gradual modifications based on pattern recognition techniques. Compilers use parsing techniques to break down the source code. Once the code has passed through the parser it is no longer used.

the project (i.e., program conversions), is to be accomplished. Will the conversion effort utilize software tools, and if so, in what form do the tools expect to receive the input code? If, for example, the original programs are standardized as a first stage within the conversion software, preconversion standardization is clearly redundant. Whether standardization is conceived as a separate task or as a first pass within a larger conversion package, there are a variety of topics that should be considered regardless of the programming language:

1. Statement alignment
2. Blank spaces
3. Sequence numbering
4. Spelling
5. Punctuation
6. Command syntax
7. Continued lines
8. Subunit identification
9. Placement of comments
10. Flagging special problems

4.2.1 Statement Alignment

Proper alignment of statements (in any language) can simplify the conversion task. The following rules are applicable for most situations:

1. Each statement should start on a new line.
2. Each statement type should start at the same column on the line.
3. All statement labels should be positioned according to a well-defined rule (e.g., on a separate line or starting at a given column on the line).
4. Indentation to show the program structure should only be introduced just prior to the manual phase of the conversion. As input to an automatic converter, unindented code is easier to handle.
5. Treat conditional statements (e.g., IF NAME = JOHN MOVE LAST TO FIRST.) as two separate statements.
6. Whatever rules one chooses to realign the statements, be sure that the resulting program will compile in exactly the same manner as before. (It would be self-defeating to introduce changes that affect the object code at this early stage.)

As an example, let us propose some rules for realigning a COBOL Procedure Division. Let us assume the following scheme:

1. All paragraph names start in column 8.
2. All other statements start in column 12.
3. All continued lines start in column 13.
4. Conditional statements are treated as two separate statements.
5. Phrases such as ELSE and AT END are included on a separate line starting in column 12.

Consider the following program segment:

```
XY_START.
        READ IN1_FILE INTO INPUT_REC
            AT END GO TO XY_END.
        IF NAME=JOHN MOVE LAST TO FIRST,
            ELSE MOVE LAST TO NEXT.
        PERFORM XY_LOOP VARYING X FROM 1 BY 1
            UNTIL (X>N) OR (NAME=JOHN).
        IN N=M MOVE 10 TO X, ELSE MOVE 12 TO X,
            ADD 2 TO Y.
```

The realigned code would be:

```
XY_START.
        READ IN1_FILE INTO INPUT_REC
        AT END
        GO TO XY_END.
        IF NAME=JOHN
        MOVE LAST TO FIRST,
        ELSE
        MOVE LAST TO NEXT,
        PERFORM XY_LOOP VARYING X FROM 1 BY 1
            UNTIL (X>N) OR (NAME=JOHN).
        IF N=M
        MOVE 10 TO X,
        ELSE
        MOVE 12 TO X,
        ADD 2 TO Y.
```

The important question is: Have we accomplished anything? We have taken a program segment that exhibited some degree of structure and have broken it down into an unstructured collection of statements.

However, the realigned code has a major advantage: If we are developing an automatic converter based on the realigned code, our pattern searching is considerably simplified. For example, assume that the converter must perform an operation on all MOVE statements. The MOVEs can now be easily located (i.e., lines with a nonasterisk in column 7, a blank in column 8, and the string 'MOVE ' starting in column 12). Using the original code, a search for MOVE statements would require scanning entire lines!

A second example illustrates the need for caution in developing standardization software. Assume that our original programs are written in PL/1 and that we must align the programs so that all statements start on a new line. For example, the following line of code:

```
A=B+C;  STR='JOHN';  J=K;
```

would be realigned as follows:

```
A=B+C;
STR='JOHN';
J=K;
```

At first glance it appears to be a trivial matter to write a program to accomplish this task. However, one would have to take the following possibility into consideration:

```
A=B+C;  STR='JOHN;';  J=K;
```

The semicolon within the literal 'JOHN;' is clearly not intended to be an end-of-statement mark. The conversion of this line of code should be

```
A=B+C;
STR='JOHN;';
J=K;
```

and *not*

```
A=B+C;
STR='JOHN;
';
J=K;
```

The point made by this example should be loud and clear: Imposing standards using software tools is risk-free only if the software is error-free. Poor-quality software can cause both syntactical and semantical problems. How one measures the quality of software tools is another matter. However, usage of tools yields some feeling regarding their reliability.

4.2.2 Blank Spaces

Blank spaces are used in many languages as delimiters and are included in the syntactical rules of the language (e.g., COBOL and PL/1). Usually, however, the rules include the phrase "at least one blank". Not only would the code look strange without blanks, the compiler would be unable to translate many statements. As an example, consider the following COBOL statement:

```
IF AMOVE=BTO MOVE CTO TO DMOVE.
```

Without blanks, the statement appears as follows:

```
IFAMOVE=BTOMOVECTOTODMOVE.
```

It would be extremely difficult to write a compiler capable of unscrambling this collection of letters!

Other languages are based on syntactical rules that allow the programmer to eliminate all blanks. The best known example is FORTRAN. Translating the foregoing COBOL statement to FORTRAN yields

```
IF (AMOVE .EQ. BTO) DMOVE=CTO
```

which is just as valid without blanks:

```
IF(AMOVE.EQ.BTO)DMOVE=CTO
```

The following line of FORTRAN,

```
DO 100 I=1,N
```

is less comprehensible if the blanks are removed:

```
DO100I=1,N
```

Nevertheless, the compiler has no problems recognizing this statement as a DO loop.

Clearly, program portability is enhanced if a standard policy is adopted regarding usage of blanks. Pattern recognition at the code conversion stage is simplified if we search for "a blank followed by X" rather than "one or more blanks followed by X." The most straightforward rule for blank standardization is: *Remove all unnecessary blanks*. For all languages, blanks within *literals* and *comments* must be considered as necessary and are therefore left alone. For syntax requiring *one or more blanks*, the recommended policy is to replace all instances of multiple blanks by single blanks. For syntax where blanks are optional, the blanks should be removed.

As an example, consider the following lines of FORTRAN code:

```
      DO 10 I=1,N
      WRITE(6,100)  A(I),B(I)
  100 FORMAT(1H  , ' A=', F10,3, '   B=',F10.3)
   10 CONTINUE
```

After blank removal the code would appear as follows:

```
      DO10I=1,N
      WRITE(6,100A(I),B(I)
  100 FORMAT(H ,' A=',F10.3,'   B=',F10.3)
   10 CONTINUE
```

Note that the blank within the Hollerith field (i.e., 1H) and within the literals (i.e., ' A=' and ' B=') were not removed because they are necessary. In addition, the blank between the statement labels and the statements are also left untouched because they are meaningful.

In COBOL, blank removal is more complicated. Consider the following statement:

```
      COMPUTE  TO  =  (T * (A  +  B))  +  XYZ.
```

The statement would appear as follows after blank removal:

```
      COMPUTE TO = (T * (A + B)) + XYZ.
```

In COBOL there must be at least one blank around each operator (e.g., =, +, and * in the statement above), no blanks to the right of a left parenthesis or to the left of a right parenthesis, and at least one blank to the left of a left parenthesis and to the right of a right parenthesis.

4.2.3 Sequence Numbering

Most languages allow for sequence numbering of programs. Typically, columns 73 to 80 are reserved for some sort of identification code. If the code includes a number that changes from line to line, this number is called the *sequence number*.

The value of sequence numbers was most apparent when programs were stored as decks of cards. If an operator or programmer (or cleaning person or stray cat) caused a deck to drop on the floor, the sequence numbers were there to save the day. Today, most programs are stored on disks and tapes and the value of sequence numbers has become less apparent. However, they can be quite useful for documentation and inventory purposes and it is recommended that the standardization process include a sequence numbering phase. A reasonable policy is to start numbering the first line as 10 (or 100) and then add 10 (or 100) to each subsequent line. The use of steps greater than 1 allows inclusion of additional lines of code without changing the original sequence numbers.

A reasonable question is: Why add lines and yet maintain the original sequence numbers? Would it not be better to renumber the modified program after lines have been added? The value of maintaining the original numbers is that the correspondence between the original code and the modified code can easily be detected by an examination of the sequence numbers. It would be an easy matter to generate a report that prints the original code and next to it the modified code if the sequence numbering has been maintained. Such a report can be quite helpful in the manual phases of a conversion project.

As an example, consider the following lines of FORTRAN code:

```
        DO 100 I=1,N                        XYZ00050
        IF(A.EQ.B) 20,30                    XYZ00060
    20  C='XYZ'                             XYZ00070
        GO TO 100                           XYZ00080
    30  D=STR+'XYZ'                         XYZ00090
        REWIND INFILE                       XYZ00100
   100  CONTINUE                            XYZ00110
```

The converted code (to another dialect of FORTRAN) might be the following:

```
        DO 100 I=1,N                        XYZ00050
        IF(A.EQ.B) GO TO 20                 XYZ00060
        GO TO 30                            XYZ00061
    20  CALL MOVE(C,1,'XYZ ',1,4)           XYZ00070
        GO TO 100                           XYZ00080
    30  CALL STRIN$(D,1,STR,1,'XYZ ',4,2)   XYZ00090
        NUNIT$=NF$1(INFILE)                 XYZ00100
        REWIND NUNIT$                       XYZ00101
   100  CONTINUE                            XYZ00110
```

Maintaining the original sequence numbers allows us to easily generate the following comparative report:

```
    DO 100 I=1,N              DO 100 I=1,N                    XYZ00050
    IF(A.EQ.B) 20,30          IF(A.EQ.B) GO TO 20             XYZ00060
                              GO TO 30                        XYZ00061
 20 C='XYZ'              20   CALL MOVE (C,1,'XYZ ',1,4)      XYZ00070
    GO TO 100                 GO TO 100                       XYZ00080
 30 D=STR+'XYZ'          30   CALL STRIN$(D,1,STR,1,'XYZ ',4,2)   XYZ00090
    REWIND INFILE             NUNIT$=NF$1(INFILE)             XYZ00100
                              REWIND NUNIT$                   XYZ00101
100 CONTINUE             100  CONTINUE                        XYZ00110
```

Note the placement of the line REWIND INFILE and the equivalent two lines of modified code. The routine for changing sequence numbers must also be programmed to handle cases where added code is placed *above* a given line as well as *below* the line.

Another useful purpose of sequence numbering is for conversion planning. Printing the original code after standardization (including sequence numbering) allows us to determine at a glance the total number of lines in the program. This number can then be used to estimate the time required for conversion and can be helpful in organizing a conversion schedule.

4.2.4 Spelling

A typical feature of many languages is the use of alternative forms for spelling *keywords* or *reserved words*. For example, the PL/1 keywords DECLARE, PROCEDURE, and INITIAL can be abbreviated as DCL, PROC, and INIT. The COBOL reserved words COMPUTATIONAL -1 and PICTURE can be written in their shortened forms COMP-1 and PIC. The FORTRAN phrase GO TO can be replaced by GOTO.

The most reasonable policy regarding spelling is to *always use one form* of a keyword or reserved word when several alternatives are available. Once again the rationale behind this rule is clear: Usage of a unique form for each word simplifies pattern recognition and therefore enhances portability. As an example, consider the following segment of a PL/1 procedure:

```
XYZ: PROC(A,B,N); DCL A(*);
     DECLARE (ITEM(80),I) BIN FIXED;
     DO I=1 TO N;
        ITEM(I)=A(I);
     END;
```

Upon realignment, the code might appear as follows:

```
XYZ:
    PROC(A,B,N);
    DCL A(*);
    DECLARE (ITEM(80),I) BIN FIXED;
    DO I=1 TO N;
    ITEM(I)=A(I);
    END;
```

In this scheme the label XYZ starts in column 2. Location of declaration lines is not as simple as one might imagine at first glance. For example, our rule might be:

1. Locate a blank in column 2 and the string 'DCL' or 'DECLARE' in column 4 followed by a nonalphabetic character other than '=' and we have located a DECLARE.

The following lines of code prove that this rule does not work for all cases:

```
DECLARE DCL(10);
DCL(1)=1;
```

Using rule 1, both of these lines would qualify as DECLAREs and clearly the second line is an assignment statement.

We can make a second attempt at defining our rule:

2. Locate a blank in column 2 and the string 'DCL' or 'DECLARE' in column 5 and then make sure that the character '=' is not included to the end of the statement.

The following line of code proves that the second rule is also incomplete:

```
DCL A CHAR(4) INIT('XYZ=');
```

Rule 2 incorrectly identifies this line as an assignment statement and not a declaration.

By considering all pathological cases we can clearly develop a rule for identifying declarations, or for that matter, any other type of statement. Indeed, compilers do just this task as an early step in analyzing source code. The purpose of allowing the programmer freedom in spelling keywords or reserved words is to allow the introduction of some degree of style. But it is obvious that alternative forms complicate the task of compiler writers and writers of conversion software.

From the point of view of portability, the use of alternative forms of spelling accomplishes nothing. It does, however, have one negative effect: It complicates pattern recognition. The example above illustrates the increased complexity in locating declarations as the result of usage of alternatives forms. Standardization software should identify all keywords and reserved words that allow alternative forms and replace them by a unique form. The recommended policy is to *choose the shortest form*. By choosing the shortest form, we avoid added complications caused by increasing the size of some lines beyond the accepted maximum. If we would ultimately prefer to see the longer form of a particular keyword, we can perform appropriate replacements as a final step after the code has been passed through an automatic converter.

4.2.5 Punctuation

Punctuation is another area where some language rules permit alternatives. The classic example of punctuation freedom is the placement of commas in COBOL programs:

```
IF JANE = JOHN MOVE 1 TO C
          MOVE 2 TO D,
          ELSE MOVE 2 TO C
                 MOVE 1 TO D.
ADD D TO BILL.
```

We can see that usage of commas in this program segment has not been consistent. The suggested policy is to *always use punctuation marks in a consistent manner*. In the example above we could either remove all commas (e.g., after the statement MOVE 2 TO D,) or we could add commas where they have been omitted (e.g., after MOVE 1 TO C and after MOVE 2 TO C).

What is gained by consistent usage of punctuate marks? Once again, portability is enhanced by a consistent policy. If we can be sure, for example, that commas or periods are used to terminate all COBOL statements, this fact can be used to advantage in all pattern recognition schemes.

4.2.6 Command Syntax

Most language designers pride themselves on adding flexibility to the language syntax rules. A very rigid syntax is considered a sign of a low-level language. Programmers generally enjoy flexibility when it is available. The less one needs to remember, the easier the task of the programmer (but the more difficult the task of the compiler writer).

As examples of flexible syntax, consider the following alternatives:

COBOL:

```
IF A = B MOVE X TO Y.
IF A IS = B MOVE X TO Y.
IF A IS = B THEN MOVE X TO Y.
```

FORTRAN:

```
100  FORMAT(1H ,F10.3,3HYES)
100  FORMAT(' ',F10.3,'YES')
```

The three lines of COBOL are the same. The usage of the reserved words IS and THEN are optional (for some COBOL compilers). The two FORTRAN FORMATs are also identical. The usage of literals and Hollerith fields are interchangeable (for most FORTRAN compilers).
To enhance portability, standardize command syntax:

1. Eliminate usage of all optional words (or, alternatively, always include them). Elimination is a better policy because line lengths will be either shortened or left the same. Adding optional words increases line lengths and thus creates problems when the length exceeds the maximum allowable. (The optional words can always be added at a later stage in the conversion process.)
2. When two totally different forms of a language construction are available, choose one form as the standard. The shorter form is preferable if there is a length difference.

4.2.7 Continued Lines

Some languages include a fairly rigid policy regarding continued lines. For example, most FORTRANs use a nonblank character in column 6 to indicate a continued line. Another method of indicating continued lines is to include some character (e.g., an ampersand) at the end of a line to be continued. Other languages have no need to indicate continued lines because the language syntax requires an end-of-statement mark. For example, PL/1 uses a semicolon to indicate the end of a statement.

The portability of programs is enhanced by *selecting a standard policy for treating continued lines:*

1. Combine lines back to a single line where possible. For example, the following lines are valid PL/1 code:

```
A = B
+(C*D)
+E;
```

To simplify the task of writing conversion software, lines such as this should be combined:

```
A = B+(C*D)+E;
```

2. When continued lines are indicated by a nonblank character in a given column, use an increasing sequence of numbers (and/or letters) to indicate continuation level. For example, consider the following FORTRAN code:

```
COMMON A,    B,  CAT,
  *          DOG, E, FAT,
  *          XYZ
```

The preferred form is

```
COMMON A,    B,  CAT,
  1          DOG, E, FAT,
  2          XYZ
```

The continuation numbers can be used in subsequent conversion software to anticipate line lengths.

3. Ensure that a standard policy is maintained regarding where a line is broken. For example, do not break lines in the middle of a keyword or reserved word. Do not break lines in the middle of a literal (if possible). In arithmetic-type statements, break lines after operators. For example, consider the following COBOL code:

```
COMPUTE A = B + C + D
          + E.
```

The first line is a valid COBOL statement and only by looking at the following line would it be clear that the statement is continued. The code should be modified as follows:

```
COMPUTE A = B + C +
          D + E.
```

The first line is no longer a valid statement and this is apparent without the need for examining the following line.

4. If a continuation is indicated by a special character as the last non-blank character on the line, move the character to the final column. This policy simplifies subsequent conversion algorithms.

4.2.8 Subunit Identification

A conversion project is simplified if the original software is organized properly. For example, assume that we are given the task of converting a system consisting of 50 programs plus data and job control files. Our task is facilitated if each program is included on a separate file with *the file name corresponding to the program name.*

The problem becomes more complicated when each program includes several subroutines. An added degree of complexity is created when subroutines are used in more than one program in the same system. Some files may contain more than one program and/or subroutine. Often, source files are stored in libraries which are accessed differently than standard sequential files. When the libraries are incompatible with the target environment, additional problems are created.

Some thought should be given to the identification of subunits at the preconversion level. An analysis of file storage and naming techniques in both the source and target environments should reveal problems that require early action. A reasonable policy is to prepare each program and external subroutine (or function) as a separate sequential file. Unless a utility is available for moving entire libraries to the target environment, a simple procedure is to break down all libraries by creating separate files for each member.

The subunit identification policy can be extended to include subunits within a given program (e.g., internal PROCEDURES). A reasonable policy is to start and end all subunits on a separate line. Furthermore, several of the columns in the identification field can be used to identify the various subunits. As an example, the following PL/1 code is valid:

```
XYZ:   PROC OPTIONS(MAIN);
       GET LIST(N); BEGIN;
       DCL A(N),B(N); GET LIST(A);
DO I=1 TO N;
       B(I)=TRANS(A(I)); END;
TRANS: PROC(A);
       IF A<0 THEN DO;
                .
                .
                .
```

The modified form of this code might be:

```
XYZ:  PROC OPTIONS(MAIN);        XYZ00010
      GET LIST(N);               XYZ00020
BEGIN;                           XYZ00030
DCL A(N),B(N);                   XYZ00040
      GET LIST(A);               XYZ00050
      DO I=1 TO N;               XYZ00060
      B(I)=TRANS(A(I));          XYZ00070
      END;                       XYZ00080
TRANS: PROC(A);                  TRA00090
      IF A<0 THEN DO;            TRA00100
                 .
                 .
                 .
```

The change in the three-letter identification code within the identification field has no effect on the program; however, it could be exploited to facilitate the development of conversion algorithms.

A further level of sophistication can be obtained if a uniform policy is used regarding placement of subunits within a program. For example, PL/1 internal procedures could be moved to the bottom of BEGIN blocks. This task becomes much simpler if a method has been adopted for identifying subunits.

4.2.9 Placement of Comments

In some languages the placement of comments is very rigid. COBOL, for example, uses an asterisk in column 7 to indicate a comment. In most FORTRANs a C in column 1 indicates a comment. Some FORTRAN dialects allow several other characters (e.g., *) in column 1 to indicate a comment. Other languages allow a much more liberal policy regarding the placement of comments. PL/1 and Pascal permit placement of comments at any point in the program except within keywords and identifiers. A PL/1 comment is started by the character pair /* and terminated by */. The Pascal comment is similar: from (* to *).

For languages such as COBOL, the standard language syntax regarding comment identification is acceptable. In FORTRAN, if several different characters can be used to identify a comment, the standardization procedure should choose one of the alternatives. For languages with a liberal comment placement policy, the situation is complicated.

Clearly, placement of comments embedded within statements and immediately after statements can be used to generate well-documented code. For example, consider the following PL/1 program segment:

```
DCL I,                /* LOOP VARIABLE    */
    N,                /* NUM OF STUDENTS */
    COL CHAR(10);  /* COLLEGE          */

READ FILE(STU_REC) INTO (MAIN_AREA);  /* INPUT */
```

The comments following the declarations for I an N are embedded in the DCL statement. The other two comments are not embedded but are on the same line as their associated statement.

If the target environment for this code is a language that does not permit placement of comments as shown above, a policy must be developed for moving comments to an acceptable location. Even if the target environment permits liberal comment placement, their presence within and immediately after statements will clearly complicate the subsequent conversion process. If we choose a policy of moving the comments to a separate line, we enhance portability but adversely affect maintainability. It is an easy matter to move the comments; however, it is more complicated to automatically return them to their original location upon completion of the conversion.

If the problem appears to be too complex, it might be worthwhile to defer action to the conversion phase of the project. Embedded comments might be temporarily stored in a table and then replaced as a final conversion step. Comments at the ends of statements might be placed on a separate line for the duration of the conversion and then finally repositioned on the original line.

4.2.10 Flagging Special Problems

Potential problems can sometimes be identified during the standardization phase. Corrective action can then be taken as an early step in the conversion phase. Schematically, the processes would appear as shown in Figure 4.1. The treatment of special problems is considered as a conversion step and not a standardization step because the required changes will usually have an impact on the object code. The treatment of special problems is best handled automatically (i.e., using special software tools); however, some situations require manual intervention.

A COBOL example of a special problem is the usage of the reserved word ALTER. The following example of ALTER is from Brown [1]:

```
A20_SWITCH.
    GO TO A60_START.
A30_CONTINUE
```

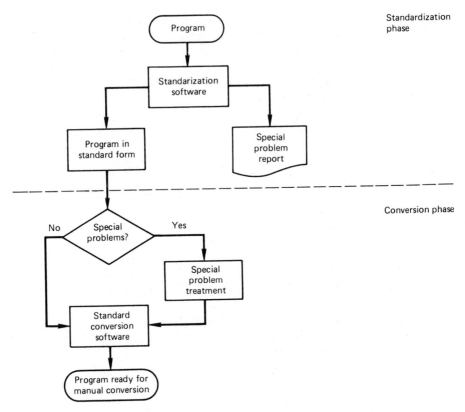

Figure 4.1 Treatment of special problems noted as a part of the program standardization process.

At some other point in the program the following line is included:

ALTER A20_SWITCH TO PROCEED TO B10_DONE.

Now the GO TO A60_START command acts as if it were GO TO B10_DONE. The effect on program readability (and convertability) is devestating and Brown's conclusion is clear: *Never use the ALTER statement.* In fact, most books on COBOL programming advise against the use of ALTER.

It is an easy matter to locate ALTER commands in the standardization phase. However, changes required to eliminate these commands will affect the program object code and are therefore part of the conversion phase. The recommended policy is to note their usage on an automatically generated special problem report. If the report indicates usage of ALTER, corrective medicine can be applied during conversion.

If no message appears in the report, the ALTER problem does not exist (for the particular program) and no special step need be taken.

An interesting example can be cited from the FORTRAN-to-PL/1 conversion problem. FORTRAN stores matrices by column, whereas PL/1 stores matrices by row. Consider the following FORTRAN code:

```
DIMENSION B(9),C(3,3)
EQUIVALENCE (B(1),C(1,1))
B(1)=1
B(2)=2
B(3)=3
```

The effect of this code on the C matrix is to set $C(1,1)$ to 1, $C(2,1)$ to 2, and $C(3,1)$ to 3; all other members of C are as yet uninitialized.

The PL/1 alternatives to EQUIVALENCE are DEFINED variables or BASED variables. However, when we use either of these devices to equivalence a vector and a matrix, the results are quite different from FORTRAN. For example, consider the following PL/1 code:

```
DCL B(9), C(3,3) DEF B;
B(1)=1;  B(2)=2;  B(3)=3;
```

The effect of this code is to set $C(1,1)$ to 1, $C(1,2)$ to 2, and $C(1,3)$ to 3. There are PL/1 techniques for solving this problem (e.g., use of iSUB in the DEFINE clause); however, the treatment of such cases is best handled as a special problem. In the standardization phase we would note all instances where arrays with differing numbers of subscripts or matrices of differing size are equivalenced. If instances of this problem are noted, the program would then require special treatment.

4.3 ENHANCING PERFORMANCE

When a conversion project is initiated, one usually has expectations regarding performance in the target environment. Indeed, the reason for moving to the new environment is often related to performance. The performance specifications might be stated in terms of CPU time, response time, through-put, or any other measure that satisfies the requirements of the specific application. The importance of meeting the targeted performance depends on the project mandate.

Performance requirements for the target environment are usually discussed at a very early stage in a conversion project. Often the feasibility of the move is influenced by the predicted performance, so performance specifications might be included in the initial project documentation (or contract if the conversion is being performed by an outside vendor). The specifications are often based on the manufacturer's claims regarding relative performance of the new and old systems. Benchmarking can also be used to yield some measures regarding expected performance. More recently, simulation techniques and analytical techniques have been used to predict performance [2].

Regardless of how one goes about predicting performance, an unfortunate fact of life is that actual performance can be measured only after the conversion has been completed. When measured performance fails to meet performance specifications, several lines of action are feasible:

1. Relax the specifications.
2. Modify the hardware configuration.
3. Enhance the software.

These three lines of action are not necessarily alternatives. The approach followed might include a combination.

In this section, only enhancement of software is considered. The approaches for enhancing software can be classified as either microscopic or macroscopic. The *microscopic* approach implies that we examine the code to locate small inefficiencies. If enough instances of inefficient programming are corrected, the cumulative effect might be enough to satisfy the performance specifications. The *macroscopic* approach implies that we discard the software modules responsible for degrading the performance and reprogram them for optimum performance in the target environment.

It is difficult to generalize which approach is preferable. However, some simple rules can be suggested. If the problem is one of timing (e.g., CPU time or response time), and if the measured performance is within a *factor of 2* of the required performance, the microscopic approach is often sufficient. In many cases it is possible to speed up programs by a factor of 2, especially programs that have been converted from one environment to another. Beyond a performance degradation factor of 2, the need for some reprogramming becomes increasingly probable.[2]

---

[2] Some interesting results for performance enhancement have been supplied by Rubin [3]. The results are related to conversions from a variety of mainframes (IBM, CDC, and DEC) to a CRAY vector processor. Direct conversion with no effort toward optimization for a variety of scientific applications resulted in reductions in CPU times by factors of 2 to 20. However, additional enhancements utilizing the unique architectural features of the CRAY resulted in additional reductions in CPU time of up to a factor of 6.

For cases where performance degradation can be traced to a shortage of main memory, a hardware solution is sometimes feasible. The price of add-on memory has dropped drastically in recent years and thus an upgrade of the available memory might be a reasonable solution. When a hardware solution is impossible or unacceptable, a software solution must be attempted. It is usually more difficult to reduce memory demands than to reduce CPU usage. Clearly program organization and attention to compiler core usage can result in reduced memory requirements; however, one should not expect to achieve much more than a 20% reduction. The only programs with a major potential for size reduction are those using large arrays, and these programs are usually run in environments exploiting virtual memory. (Memory is rarely a problem in virtual memory systems.) For most cases of severe memory shortages, solution becomes one of *segmenting* and *overlaying* sections of the largest programs in the system. Clearly, this process requires careful analysis to be most effective.

Analysis of the problems associated with performance can be vastly simplified if some useful measurement tools are available in the target environment. For example, a routine that allows one to call the CPU clock from within the programs under analysis is particularly valuable. In the following sections a variety of techniques for improving performance are discussed. Many of the techniques are well known and have been described in other references (e.g., Refs. 1, 4, and 5), but on a qualitative basis. In the following subsections most conclusions are supported by quantitative results. It is true that the numbers are applicable only to the specific test environment; however, they do give some indication of the impact on performance that one can expect in other environments.

4.3.1 Timing Measurements

In the following sections, results of timing measurements are included for a variety of statements using code generated from several compilers. Although the results are only strictly applicable to the specific environments under analysis, the measurement techniques can be generalized for most other environments.

The heart of any timing study is a routine that allows the programmer to access the CPU clock from within a test program. Most computer centers have available routines for performing this task. If not, it is usually a fairly simple matter to obtain such a routine or to program one in-house. The two routines used in the following studies are:

1. TIMER, a PL/1 function procedure that returns the incremental CPU usage in milliseconds from the previous access.

2. CCLOCK, a subroutine that can be accessed by FORTRAN programs. The second parameter is the incremental CPU usage in hundredths of a second from the previous CALL to the routine.

As an example, consider a test program designed to measure the time required to perform a mixed-mode assignment statement:

```
A = I;      (PL/1)
A = I       (FORTRAN)
```

In both cases A is a floating-point number [i.e., DEC FLOAT(6) in PL/1 and REAL*4 in FORTRAN) and I is an integer [i.e., BINARY FIXED(31) in PL/1 and INTEGER*4 in FORTRAN].

A PL/1 program for measuring the statement time is the following:

```
ASSIGN:  PROC OPTIONS (MAIN);
         /* MEASUREMENT OF MIXED MODE ASSIGNMENT TIME */
         DCL TIMER EXTERNAL ENTRY RETURNS(BIN FIXED(31));
         DCL(TO,T1,T2,N,I) BIN FIXED(31);
LO:      PUT SKIP LIST (' ENTER N');
         GET LIST(N);
         IF N=0 THEN EXIT;
         TO=TIMER;  /*INITIALIZES TIMER*/
         DO I=1 TO N;
         END;
         T1=TIMER;  /* T1 IS NULL LOOP TIME IN MILLISECS */
         DO I=1 TO N;
           A=I;
         END;
         T2=TIMER;  /* T2 IS GROSS TIME IN MILLISECS */
         TIME=1000.*(T2−T1)/N;
           /* TIME IS NET TIME PER ASSIGNMENT IN MICROSECS*/
         PUT SKIP DATA (N,TI,T2,TIME);
         GO TO LO;
         END ASSIGN;
```

The program has been written to run in an interactive mode. Note that if the results are not sufficiently accurate (i.e., T2-T1 is small), the value of N can be increased.

The program in FORTRAN is as follows:

```
C MEASUREMENT OF MIXED MODE ASSIGNMENT TIME
      INTEGER*4 TO,T1,T2
    5 WRITE(6,100)
  100 FORMAT(1H0,'ENTER N')
      IF(N.EQ.0) GO TO 90
```

```
C INITIALIZE CCLOCK
      CALL CCLOCK(L,TO)
      DO 10 I=1,N
   10 CONTINUE
C  TI IS TIME FOR NULL LOOP IN SECS/100
      CALL CCLOCK(L,T1)
      DO 20 I=1,N
   20 A=I
C  T2 IS GROSS TIME IN SECS/100
      CALL CCLOCK(L,T2)
      TIME=10000.*(T2-T1)/N
C TIME IS NET TIME PER ASSIGNMENT IN MICROSECS
      WRITE(6,110) N,T1,T2,TIME
  110 FORMAT(1HO,' N=',I6,' T1=',I6,' T2=',I6,' TIME=',F10.2)
      GO TO 5
   90 STOP
      END
```

Clearly, when routines such as TIMER and CCLOCK are available, they can be called from existing programs. One can thus gather information which helps identify high-activity areas within the programs. Enhancement efforts are then concentrated on these sections of the programs.

An alternative type of measurement tool generates a report that lists the number of times each source statement is executed. Tools of this type are available for many languages and are sometimes included as a compiler option (e.g., the COUNT parameter in the PL/1 Optimizing Compiler). Not only does the *COUNT Report* locate high-activity areas, *it can also be used to locate untested areas of code.* This information is invaluable in conversion testing.

While CPU time measurements and statement execution measurements are two of the most obvious performance evaluation tools, there are a variety of other techniques receiving increasing attention. Ferrari surveys both hardware and software tools in his book, *Computer System Performance Evaluation* [2]. He also discusses simulation techniques and analytical techniques for analyzing performance. Gilb suggests a variety of measures that can be used for the evaluation of software in his book, *Software Metrics* [6]. The entire subject of performance measurement and evaluation is in a state of rapid growth and useful tools are becoming more readily available.

4.3.2 Compiler and Run-Time Options

After bitter personal experience, I suggest that the first place to search for opportunities to improve performance is within the specification list of compiler and run-time options. Most compilers include a variety of options that can be specified at either compile-time or run-time. When a particular option is not specified (e.g., SOURCE or NOSOURCE), a default value is chosen. The computing center defines the defaults when the compiler is installed. The policy of the center usually dictates the choice of options. For example, the default for SOURCE or NOSOURCE might be chosen as NOSOURCE (i.e., do not print the source code listing with each compilation) in order to save paper. Alternatively, for student compilers in a university computing center, the SOURCE option would probably be chosen as the default.

My own two "horror stories" involve the PL/1 Optimizing Compiler. During the academic year 1975–1976 I spent a sabbatical leave developing some conversion software for a large time-sharing company. Version 1.0 of the package was completed and tested in August 1976 and I then returned to the Technion. A systems programmer from the company installed the package as a product the following month. I returned to the company the following summer to develop an improved version of the package. A number of bugs had been located during my nine-month absence and a number of ideas for new features had been proposed. In addition, a general complaint about excessive CPU demands was registered.

To analyze the CPU time problem, I ran a test case which I had timed just prior to my departure. To my amazement, the product version required six times as many CPU seconds as the development version! I reran the original test and confirmed that my original timing was correct. Something had happened to cause a 500% increase in CPU time in moving from the development to the product stage! The answer to this problem involved a run-time option that I had never heard about —ISASIZE. The ISASIZE parameter specifies the size of the ISA (initial storage area). Execution of PL/1 programs is faster if all PL/1 storage is contained in the ISA. If additional storage is required, PL/1 uses two macro instructions called GETMAIN and FREEMAIN, which can add considerable overhead to the execution time. The systems programmer who installed the package decided to reduce core storage requirements by 100K. To accomplish this she reduced the ISASIZE to a small value. She was not aware of the massive degradation that this change caused on performance.

The second horror story involves the same package. It was installed sometime in 1977 on an in-house computer (an IBM 370/168) of a large Fortune 500 company. Within a few months, the load module from this in-house version was moved to the computing center of another large company (to an IBM 370/148). The program required a suspiciously large running time on the 370/148 and a complaint was registered.

Once again I returned in time to handle the problem. This time, however, I was armed with my knowledge of ISASIZE and I was sure that I would be able to solve the problem in a few minutes. Much to my chagrin, setting ISASIZE to the maximum possible value had absolutely no effect on the performance!

Fortunately, I located the compiler output from the 370/168 installation. From the compiler options list I noticed one suspicious parameter—FLOW. The FLOW parameter, when specified as a compiler option, allows the programmer to trace the logical flow through the program. By specifying NOFLOW at run-time, the option can be "turned off." I ran a series of tests and once again discovered a massive degradation in performance! For a small test program the use of FLOW caused about a 10% increase in program size but a 470% increase in CPU time! When NOFLOW was specified as a run-time option (after specifying FLOW during compilation), the increase in CPU was reduced to 240%, still a massive degradation. The incredible fact about this story is that the 370/168 installation was routinely using the FLOW option as the compiler default without being aware of the tremendous waste of resources that this parameter was causing in their production PL/1 programs!

The following analysis utilizes another small PL/1 program to measure the effect of several PL/1 options. The program merely zeros several matrices and consists of a series of nested DO loops. The program includes calls to a timing routing before and after execution of the loops (i.e., similar to the program shown in Section 4.3.1). The results are included in Table 4.1 for several combinations of options. The results were obtained on an IBM 370/168 under the MVS operating system using the PL/1 Optimizing Compiler (V1 R3.0 PTF 69). Usage

TABLE 4.1   Measured CPU Times for PL/1 Test Programs[a]

| Case | Compiler Options | | | Run-Time Options[b] | | CPU Time (msec) |
	OPT	COUNT	FLOW	COUNT	FLOW	
1	TIME	NOCOUNT	NOFLOW	N.A.	N.A.	199
2	TIME	COUNT	NOFLOW	COUNT	N.A.	6559
3	TIME	COUNT	NOFLOW	NOCOUNT	N.A.	2529
4	TIME	NOCOUNT	FLOW	N.A.	FLOW	4399
5	TIME	NOCOUNT	FLOW	N.A.	NOFLOW	2497
6	0	NOCOUNT	NOFLOW	N.A.	N.A.	288

[a]Programs run on an IBM 370/168 under MVS using the PL/1 Optimizer (V1 R3.0 PTF 69).

[b]N.A., not applicable.

of the COUNT option yielded some additional information: a total of 260,800 statement executions were recorded (i.e., one count is noted each time the program passes a single source statement).

The results in Table 4.1 are, of course, valid only for the test program run in the specific environment described above. Nevertheless, they dramatically illustrate the extreme effects that compiler and run-time options can have on program performance. The OPT option sets the degree of optimization that the compiler will attempt on the source code. If OPT is set to TIME, the generated object code is optimized to minimize CPU time, and if OPT is set to zero, no optimization is attempted. A comparison of cases 1 and 6 shows that for the test program, a 31% savings resulted from specifying TIME. (The price one pays for using the TIME option is an increase in compilation time.)

The COUNT option allows the programmer to get an exact count on the number of executions of each source statement. This information can be invaluable when one is attempting to identify the high-activity and zero-activity statements in a program. However, we see that the overhead caused by this option is considerable. A comparison of cases 1 and 2 show that the COUNT option required 33 times more CPU time for the test program. Case 3 shows that even if NOCOUNT is specified at run-time, if COUNT was specified at compile-time, we still must pay for a considerable amount of overhead. [We can compute the overhead per statement by dividing the increase in CPU time by the total number of executed statements. For case 2 we obtain $(6559 - 199)/260,800 = 0.024$ msec per statement and for case 3 we obtain $(2529 - 199)/260,800 = 0.009$ msec per statement.]

The FLOW option allows the programmer to track the flow of logic throughout a program by yielding a trace of executed statements in the order that they are executed. Once again the results indicate a massive degradation in performance. (Note cases 1 and 4.) Even when NOFLOW is specified at run-time, case 5 shows that the degradation is considerable.

The results included in Table 4.1 should not be considered as a complete analysis of the dangerous PL/1 Optimizer options. Indeed, there are many other options and the programmer involved in running PL/1 Optimizer production programs should read the appropriate sections in the PL/1 Optimizer *Programmers Guide* [7]. However, the results yield several conclusions which are valid for *all compilers in all languages:*

1. Compiler and run-time options can have considerable effects on program performance.

2. Options useful for debugging usually cause considerable overhead and should therefore be removed from production programs.

3. Some options can be specified at compile-time and turned off at run-time. However, even when the option is turned off at run-time it still might cause considerable overhead.

4. Before attempting to improve performance by altering code, *make sure that all compiler and run-time options have been specified properly.*

4.3.3 Mixed-Mode Numeric Operations

All compilers in all languages generate more efficient object code if numeric operations use only items of the same mode (i.e., data type). For example, consider the following simple assignment statements:

```
MOVE I TO A.        (COBOL)
A = I;              (PL/1)
A = I               (FORTRAN)
```

If I and A are variables of the same mode, the assignments are efficient. If, however, I and A are different (e.g., in FORTRAN if A is REAL and I is INTEGER), the assignment must include some overhead for mode conversion.

This problem is particularly acute in COBOL programs because numeric data can be stored in such a variety of different modes. A well-known technique for improving COBOL programs is to eliminate usage of mixed-mode COMPUTE, ADD, SUBTRACT, DIVIDE, MULTIPLY, MOVE, and IF statements [8]. The following example illustrates this point:

```
WORKING_STORAGE SECTION.
77 X PICTURE S999V99.
77 Y PICTURE S99V9.
77 Z PICTURE S99V99.
    .
    .
    .
PROCEDURE DIVISION.
    COMPUTE Z = X + Y.
```

The statement will execute considerably faster if both Y and Z are defined as S999V99. (The change will also save storage because the extra object code required to convert the data types to the same mode is eliminated.)

A series of FORTRAN and PL/1 mixed-mode assignment measurements are summarized in Table 4.2. The measurements were made using programs similar to those shown in Section 4.3.1. The results indicate that a large penalty is paid for mixed-mode assignments. For all cases the ratios of mixed-mode to regular assignment times are greater than 4!

TABLE 4.2   Comparison of Mixed-Mode and Regular Assignment Times[a]

| | | CPU Time (μsec) | | |
| | | PL/1 Optimizer (VI R3.0 PTF 69) | | |
Statement[b]	Mixed Mode	Time Optimization	No Optimization	FORTRAN IV-G Level 21
A = B	No	0.32	0.40	0.38
A = L	Yes	1.87	1.93	1.82
K = L	No	0.32	0.40	0.38
K = B	Yes	1.70	1.85	2.04

[a]The measurements were made on an IBM 370/168 under MVS.
[b]A and B are DEC FLOAT (6) (PL/1) or REAL∗4 (FORTRAN); L and K are BIN FIXED (31) (PL/1) or INTEGER∗4 (FORTRAN).

How can one exploit this knowledge to enhance programs? The obvious answer is to avoid mixed-mode numeric usage wherever possible. For example, consider the following FORTRAN loop:

```
        DO 100 I = 1,N
        A(I) = A(I)+C*I
        B(I) = A(I)-I
100  CONTINUE
```

An improved version of this loop is

```
        DO 100 I = 1,N
        AI = I
        A(I) = A(I)+C*AI
        B(I) = A(I)-AI
100  CONTINUE
```

We can use the results in Table 4.2 to estimate the savings that this change should cause. The time required to convert I to AI is approximately 1.8 microseconds (μsec). Usage of AI allows us to avoid two conversions in the following two statements. Thus the net saving should be about $1.8N$ μsec for the entire loop. If N is large or if this loop is repeated many times, the saving might be significant.

Timing results for some simple additions are shown in Table 4.3. Once again we see that mixed-mode usage (i.e., cases 3 and 4) requires much more time than do statements in which all numeric items are of the same mode. A comparison of cases 1 and 2 is interesting. Early FORTRAN "lore" warned programmers *not* to use statements such as case 1 because this form required a data conversion. The suggested policy was to use statements such as case 2. The results show that case 1 is actually faster. Both compilers tested are clever enough to avoid data conversion for both of these statements.

In summary, the obvious conclusion is to avoid mixed-mode numeric operations when possible. The main reason why programmers use different modes for storing numeric data is to facilitate printing. However, it is a relatively simple matter to do all time-consuming calculations in an efficient manner and, only on completion, move the final results to suitable print fields. When one is attempting to speed up programs in a given target environment, it is extremely useful to have a quantitative idea as to how various programming techniques affect program execution time.

TABLE 4.3   CPU Time for Some Simple Additions[a]

Case	Statement[b]	PL/1 Optimizer (VI R3.0 PTF 69) Time Optimization	PL/1 Optimizer (VI R3.0 PTF 69) No Optimization	FORTRAN IV-G Level 21
1	A = B+1	0.38	0.55	0.52
2	A = B+1.0	0.57	0.87	0.79
3	A = B+K	2.58	2.43	2.18
4	A = K+B	2.41	2.49	2.18
5	A = B+C	0.36	0.48	0.60

[a]The measurements were made on an IBM 360/168 under MVS.

[b]A, B, and C are DEC FLOAT(6) (PL/1) or REAL*4 (FORTRAN), and K is BIN FIXED (31) (PL/1) or INTEGER*4 (FORTRAN).

4.3.4 Looping Techniques

Many programs utilize loops to perform repetitive operations. Most higher-level languages have specific commands for defining loops. For example:

COBOL:

```
PERFORM XYZ 100 TIMES.
```

PL/1:

```
DO I = I TO 100;
        .
        .
        .
    END;
```

FORTRAN:

```
    DO 200 I = 1,100
        .

200  CONTINUE
```

BASIC:

```
FOR I = 1 TO 100 STEP 1
    .
    .
    .
NEXT I
```

Loops can be nested within other loops. For example:
FORTRAN:

```
    DO 105 L1 = 1,N
    DO 100 L2 = 1,M
        .
        .
        .
100  CONTINUE
        .
105  CONTINUE
```

For this example, each statement in the innermost loops is performed $N \times M$ times (unless an exit command (e.g., GO TO) is encountered).

Timing studies can be used to locate loops that consume significant portions of the program running time. Effort can then be directed toward optimizing these loops. Usually, the most time-consuming loops are the innermost loops within a group of nested loops.

To speed up loops, the following advice is valid in most languages:

1. Remove portions of computations from loops when the intermediate results remain constant. For example:

    PL/1:

```
L1:  DO I = 1 TO N;
     DO J = 1 TO 100;
       A(I,J) = EXP(I*ALPHA)*B(J)*C*D;
     END L1;
```

The more efficient form for this loop is

```
     CD = C*D;
L1:  DO I = 1 TO N;
       EIA = EXP(I*ALPHA);
     DO J = 1 TO 100;
       A(I,J) = EIA*B(J)*CD,
     END L1;
```

The multiplication C*D is performed only once and the calculation EXP(I*ALPHA) is performed only N times. In the preceding version, both calculations are performed $100N$ times.

One might expect that this form of loop optimization is a task that is routinely performed by an *optimizing compiler*. If an optimizing compiler is being used in the target environment, it is a simple matter to write a little test program to check whether or not such optimization is performed. [Experiments with the PL/1 Optimizer (Version V1 R3.0) show that optimization does very little removal of repetitive calculations from inside loops.]

2. Minimize loop openings and closings. For example:

    FORTRAN:

```
     DO 100 I = 1,1000
     DO 100 J = 1,2
       V(I,J) = B(I)*C(J)
100  CONTINUE
```

The more efficient version of this loop is

```
           DO 100 J = 1,2
           DO 100 I = 1,1000
           V(I,J) = B(I)*C(J)
       100 CONTINUE
```

The improved version reduces the number of loop openings and closings from 1001 to 3. Loops in any language require some overhead for openings and closings. Results from timing measurements for PL/1 and FORTRAN compilers are shown in Table 4.4.

TABLE 4.4   Loop Opening and Closing Overhead[a]

Language	Compiler	Optimization	Loop Opening and Closing Overhead (μsec)
PL/1	Optimizer V1 R3.0	None	2.3
		Time	6.7
FORTRAN	IV-G Level 21	None	4.5

[a]Measurements performed on an IBM 370/168 running under MVS.

It is interesting to note that the overhead for opening and closing loops is greater when the PL/1 Optimizing Compiler uses time optimization. The loop indexing generated by the optimization process is much faster than without optimization (see Table 4.5); however, additional overhead is required to open and close these fast loops.

3. Use the most efficient method for indexing a loop. For example, in PL/1, use BINARY FIXED indices for loops:

```
           DCL (I,N) BIN FIXED(31):
           DO I = 1 TO N;
                     •
                     •
                     •
```

In some languages (e.g., COBOL and PL/1), the programmer is free to use any type of variable for the loop index. However, the time required to increment an index (or counter) is increased considerably if the preferred variable type is not used. Results for several types of PL/1 loops are summarized in Table 4.5. Note that the time to increment BINARY FIXED indices is considerably less than the time required to increment other index types.

TABLE 4.5   Time to Increment the Index of a Loop for Four Different
Types of PL/1 Index Variables[a]

	Time (μsec) to Increment Index[b]			
Optimization	BIN FIXED(31)	DEC FLOAT(6)	DEC FIXED(6)	BIN FLOAT(53)
Time	0.32	1.29	2.82	2.43
None	1.45	2.01	2.84	2.44

[a]The results were obtained using the PL/1 Optimizing Compiler (V1 R3.0 PTF 69) running on an IBM 370/168 under MVS.
[b]BINARY FIXED indices are the preferred type of index.

In COBOL programs, the incrementing of loops is more subtle. Application of the concepts suggested above are valid; however, inefficiencies are not so obvious. For example, the following statement is inefficient:

ADD 1 TO LOOP_COUNT.

The number 1 is stored as a numeric literal and this statement requires a conversion to the same data type as LOOP_COUNT. The most efficient data type for counters is *signed syncronized binary* (i.e., S9 COMP SYNC). The recommended change for the statement above is [8]

77 LOOP_COUNT PIC S9(9) COMP SYNC.
77 ONE PIC S9(9) COMP SYNC VALUE 1.
.
.
.
ADD ONE TO LOOP_COUNT.

It should be emphasized that the internal form of numeric data and the precision of intermediate results are not specified in the ANS COBOL standard, but vary from computer to computer [1]. Therefore, when the target environment includes a particular COBOL compiler, it is worthwhile to become familiar with the method of treating various numeric data types and the most efficient methods for counting loops.

In some languages, selection of an inefficient type of loop index is impossible. For example, FORTRAN requires that all loop indices must be INTEGER variables. The line

DO 100 I = 1,N

is a valid FORTRAN statement as long as I is an integer variable. This limitation reduces the programmers "freedom of choice"; however, inadvertant usage of inefficient data types for looping is avoided.

4. For compilers that generate very inefficient code for looping, some improvement can be made by *unrolling* the loop [4]:
FORTRAN:

```
        DO 100 K = 1,1000
          A(K) = 0
100     CONTINUE
```

The unrolled version of this loop reduces the number of increments by half:

```
        DO 100 K = 2,1000,2
          A(K-1) = 0
          A(K)   = 0
100     CONTINUE
```

There is a loss of clarity in the second version, so such a "desperation" technique would only be used in extreme circumstances.

5. Loops can sometimes be combined without a loss of clarity:
PL/1:

```
        DO I = 1 TO N;
          A(I) = AC;
        END;
        DO I = 1 TO N;
          B(I) = BC;
        END:
```

The combined version of these loops is

```
        DO I = 1 TO N;
          A(I) = AC;
          B(I) = BC;
        END;
```

Van Tassel calls this technique *loop jamming* [4]. The combined version reduces storage as well as execution time.

4.3.5 Locality of Data and Subroutines

Many computers use a form of architecture called *virtual memory*. A program is segmented into *pages*, and pages are brought into memory as they are needed. Thus at any given moment the real memory contains only a small fraction of a program under execution. Whenever execution requires a jump to a statement not currently in memory, the appropriate page must be brought into the memory. Similarly, usage of data and subroutines not in memory require *paging*.

Van Tassel defines *locality* as the degree to which a program favors some subset of the program [4]. The amount of paging can be reduced if locality is increased. For example, if a few subroutines are used within a high-activity loop, they should be loaded concurrently. Similarly, data that are used repeatedly should be grouped as close as possible.

Van Tassel describes a classic example of an inefficient FORTRAN loop for zeroing an array:

```
DIMENSION X (512,20)
DO 15 K = 1,512
DO 15 L = 1,20
15   X(K,L) = 0.0
```

The reason for this inefficiency is due to the fact that FORTRAN arrays are stored by columns. Thus X(K,L) and X(K,L+1) are not stored concurrently. The array member X(K,L+1) is stored 512 numbers beyond X(K,L). If each member requires 4 bytes of storage, and each page is 2048 bytes, *we see that every value of X addressed in this manner must be on a new page.* The number of times we must move to a new page is thus $512 \times 20 = 10,240$. By reversing the order of the DO statements, we reduce the number of new page references to 20:

```
DO 15 L = 1,20
DO 15 K = 1,512
15   X(K,L) = 0.0
```

From the point of view of loop openings and closings, the second variation is clearly preferable (see Section 4.3.4). The remaining question concerns the importance of data locality. An experiment was performed on an IBM 370/168 running under MVS (a virtual memory operating system) to test the effect of locality using both FORTRAN and PL/1. Two loops were timed in both languages:

PL/1:

```
DCL V1(1000,2),V2(2,1000);
                .
                .
                .

LOOP1:  DO J = 1 TO 1000;
        DO K = 1 TO 2;
        V1(J,K) = 0;
        END LOOP1;
                .
                .
                .

LOOP2:  DO K = 1 TO 1000;
        DO J = 1 TO 2;
        V2(J,K) = 0;
        END LOOP2;
```

FORTRAN

```
        DIMENSION V1(1000,2),V2(2,1000)
                .
                .
                .

   C  LOOP1
        DO 1  J  =  1,1000
        DO 1  K  =  1,2
   1        V1(J,K)  =  0.0
                .
                .
                .

   C  LOOP2
        DO 2  K  =  1,1000
        DO 2  J  =  1,2
   2        V2(J,K)  =  0.0
```

The results are summarized in Table 4.6. In PL/1, arrays are stored by rows and therefore Loop1 should be more efficient from the point of view of locality. In FORTRAN, since arrays are stored by columns we would expect exactly the opposite to happen. The results indicate that *no measurable difference was detected.* This rather surprising conclusion is explained by the "cleverness" of the operating system. More than one page can be stored in memory simultaneously, and jumps from page to page do not increase user CPU time as long as the appropriate pages are in memory. However, as the load on the system increases, there is an increasing probability that pages will be swapped out of the memory

TABLE 4.6   CPU Time per Loop for Two Loops Run with Two
Different Compilers[a]

| | CPU Time/Loop (msec) | | |
| | PL/1 Optimization (V1 R3.0 PTF 69) | | FORTRAN IV-G |
Loop	Time Optimization	No Optimization	Level 21
1	5.2	10.0	5.6
2	5.2	10.0	5.6

[a]The experiments were performed on IBM 370/168 under MVS.

during execution. Thus lack of locality can result in a measurable degradation of performance under certain circumstances. Clearly, the locality problem can be important in other environments. The user is therefore warned against dismissing locality as a factor influencing performance without suitable testing in his or her own environment.

4.3.6 Arithmetic Operations

Processing arithmetic statements constitutes a significant fraction of the total running time for some CPU intensive programs. Typically, scientific and engineering programs fall within this catagory. When running time is a problem, often revision of the algorithms upon which the calculations are based can lead to impressive improvements in speed. However, if the conversion is being performed by personnel with no understanding of the basic algorithms, they can hardly be expected to suggest refinements in the algorithms. Nevertheless, using the techniques described in Sections 4.3.3 and 4.3.4, arithmetic operations can be improved.

In this section, some additional observations are made regarding arithmetic operations. Timing measurements for a variety of arithmetic statements are included in Table 4.7 for FORTRAN and PL/1 programs run on an IBM 370/168 under MVS. One can expect similar results (on a relative basis) for other computers, compilers, and languages. An analysis of the results leads to some conclusions:

1. Adding and subtracting is several times faster than multiplying and dividing.

2. Raising a number to an integer power is considerably faster (more than 20 times faster) than raising to a decimal power (even if there are only zeros after the decimal point).

TABLE 4.7   CPU Time for Some Arithmetic Statements[a]

| | CPU Time (μsec) | | |
| | PL/1 Optimizer (V1 R3.0 PTF 69) | | FORTRAN IV-G Level 21 |
Statement	Optimization	No Optimization	
A = B+C	0.32	0.43	0.60
A = B–C	0.32	0.72	0.60
A = B*C	1.28	1.44	1.60
A = B/C	1.38	1.87	1.80
A = B**3	2.60	2.79	2.70
A = B**3.0	51.72	51.77	39.00
A = B**6	3.88	4.08	3.60
A = EXP(B)	23.87	23.70	21.50
A = SQRT(B)	20.85	20.60	14.50
A = SIN(B)	23.10	23.30	18.50
A = MOD(B,2)	4.51	3.50	2.50

[a]The measurements were run on an IBM 370/168 under MVS. The variables are DEC FLOAT(6) for PL/1 and REAL*4 for FORTRAN.

3. Usage of mathematical functions such as EXP, SQRT, and SIN require about a factor of 20 more CPU time than the simple operations.

An awareness of the run-times for basic operations can help estimate the improvement that one might expect from revision of arithmetic operations. For example, consider the following segment of a FORTRAN program run in the same environment as the test programs used to obtain Table 4.7:

```
      DO 100 I = 1,200
      DO 100 J = 1,200
      A(I,J) = EXP(–I*ALPHA)*EXP(–J*BETA)
  100 CONTINUE
```

A revised form of this program segment is as follows:

```
      DIMENSION EALPHA(200),EBETA(200)
```
          .
          .

```
      DO 90 I = 1,200
        EALPHA(I) = EXP(-I*ALPHA)
        EBETA(I) = EXP(-I*BETA)
   90 CONTINUE
      DO 100 I = 1,200
      DO 100 J = 1,200
        A(I,J) = EALPHA(I)*EBETA(J)
  100 CONTINUE
```

This change results in the reduction of calls to the EXP function from 80,000 to 400, for savings of 79,600 $\times$ 21.5 = 1,711,400 μsec = 1.71 sec. If this loop is within a larger loop the savings might be considerable. We have also reduced the number of mixed-mode arithmetic statements (i.e., I*ALPHA and J*BETA) from 80,000 to 400, but from the results in Section 4.3.4 we see that this savings is small compared to the elimination of calls to EXP. We can reduce the running time even further by using the following:

```
      EALPHA(1) = EXP(-ALPHA)
      EBETA(1) = EXP(-BETA)
      DO 90 I = 2,200
        EALPHA(I) = EALPHA(I-1)*EALPHA(1)
        EBETA(1) = EBETA(I-1)*EBETA(1)
   90 CONTINUE
```

In this manner we reduce the number of calls to EXP from 400 to 2; however, we have now lost a great deal of clarity. In addition, the values of EALPHA and EBETA are less and less accurate as I increases (due to propagated round-off errors). This accuracy degradation might or might not be a problem. The very small improvement in run-time would probably not warrant the loss in clarity and precision unless the loop was repeated many times.

4.3.7 Input/Output Techniques

Many programs tend toward high input/output activity rather than high CPU activity. Typically, data processing programs using large files fall within this category. The methods used to organize the data files, read the files, and post results must be converted from the original environment to the target environment. Often, in conversions, the emphasis is on getting the system to run in the new environment and very little emphasis is placed on efficiency. When performance becomes a pressing issue for I/0-bound systems, the conversion team must address the problem of input/output efficiency. Several concepts are applicable to many different languages, compilers, and hardware configurations:

1. Proper blocking of sequencial files can result in major reductions in input/output overhead. Blocking is a process that organizes a series of records into a single block. Besides saving disk (or tape) space by reducing the number of interblock gaps, the CPU time required to read (or write) a block is *not* proportional to the block length. Thus for large blocks, the read and write overhead per record is small.

2. For most systems, there is a maximum block size beyond which performance tends to be degraded. For disk files, the maximum block size is usually limited to the largest block that will fit on a single track. For smaller systems where memory is at a premium, specification of a large block size for files might degrade performance because buffers are required to hold the block that is read into memory.

3. Many computer languages allow alternative methods for input and output of data. The choice of methods can have a profound impact on performance. In general, *unformatted* I/0 is faster than *formatted* I/0. A comparison of different I/0 statements for FORTRAN and PL/1 is shown in Table 4.8. All I/0 results are based on reading and writing records of 80 characters. The coding was as follows:

PL/1:
```
DCL LINE CHAR(80);
DCL INPUT1 FILE INPUT;
DCL INPUT2 FILE INPUT RECORD;
DCL OUTPUT1 FILE OUTPUT;
DCL OUTPUT2 FILE OUTPUT RECORD;

/* FORMATTED I/0 */
    GET FILE(INPUT1) EDIT(LINE)(COL(1),A(80));
    PUT FILE(OUTPUT1) EDIT(LINE)(SKIP,A);
/* UNFORMATTED I/0 */
    READ FILE(INPUT2) INTO(LINE);
    WRITE FILE(OUTPUT2) FROM (LINE);
```

FORTRAN:
```
REAL*4 LINE1(20)
REAL*8 LINE2(10)
        .
        .
        .
```

TABLE 4.8   CPU-Time (microseconds) for Input/Output Operations[a].

| I/0 Type | Organization | PL/1 Optimizer (V1 R3.0 PTF 69) | | FORTRAN IV-G Level 21[b] | |
		Time Optimization	No Optimization	LINE1	LINE2
Read	Formatted	82	114	660	360
Write	Formatted	74	214	730	640
Read	Unformatted	34	34	N.A.	N.A.
Write	Unformatted	26	98	N.A.	N.A.

[a] All results were measured on an IBM 370/168 under MVS.
[b] N.A., not applicable.

```
        READ(7,100) (LINE1(L),L = 1,20)
        WRITE(8,100) (LINE1(L),L = 1,20)
100 FORMAT (20A4)
                        .
                        .
                        .
        READ(7,200) (LINE2(L),L = 1,10)
        WRITE(8,200) (LINE2(L),L = 1,10)
200 FORMAT(10A8)
```

Examining the PL/1 results, we see a clear advantage for un-formatted I/0. The FORTRAN IV-G compiler does not allow unformatted I/0 and the results show that reading character data is a notoriously slow process. (Other FORTRAN compilers allow unformatted I/0.)

4. For jobs requiring several files that are used together in high-activity areas of a program, place the files on different disks when possible. For some cases, the operating system will allow some overlapping of file processing. In addition, disk head motion is reduced if jumps from one file to another are eliminated.

5. Use of multiple buffers can sometimes reduce I/0 overhead. For jobs that require a large amount of I/0, it is useful to measure the effect of the number of buffers on execution time. Conversely, for programs where space is a problem, reduction in the number of I/0 buffers can be used to free memory. For some I/0-bound jobs, if memory space is a problem, one solution might be to reduce block size and increase the number of buffers.

6. When an indexed sequential file is used, degradation of perfor-mance can occur if a significant number of records have been added to the file. For most environments using this type of file,

extra records are stored in an *overflow area*. As the number of records in the overflow areas increases, the efficiency of a search for a record decreases. The normal procedure for improving performance is to reorganize the files periodically.

7. Explore alternative access methods for file I/0. If a system has been well designed, the methods for organizing files in the original environment were selected for valid reasons. However, these reasons might not be valid in the new environment.

8. Some languages allow the programmer to specify details concerning files from within the program or at the job control level (e.g., COBOL and PL/1). The recommended policy is to specify as little about the file as possible within the converted programs. This policy simplifies experimentation aimed at improving I/0 performance.

9. Some languages include OPEN and CLOSE commands for files (e.g., COBOL and PL/1). By opening files only when they are needed and closing them when they are no longer needed, storage requirements for buffers, internal I/0 tables, and so on, can be minimized. For some systems the savings might have a positive effect on performance.

4.3.8 Calls to Procedures

Use of procedures (i.e., functions and subroutines) is common to many programming languages. The main advantage of procedures is that code can be reused for several combinations of variables. In addition, their use can vastly improve the readability and maintainability of programs. However, there are some inherent inefficiencies associated with procedures. An awareness of the sources of these inefficiencies can sometimes be used to enhance performance.

1. There is a basic overhead for using a procedure. Measurements using the PL/1 Optimizer and the FORTRAN IV-G Compiler or an IBM 370/168 under MVS indicate that this overhead is about 14 μsec. (Clearly, this overhead varies from machine to machine and from manufacturer to manufacturer.) Comparing this value to measured times for basic operations (e.g., Tables 4.2 and 4.3), we see that procedure usage is relatively expensive. For some systems the relative overhead can be much greater. Depending on the circumstances, one might consider combining or eliminating some very small subroutines that are being called from within very high activity loops.

2. The overhead associated with procedure usage increases as a function of the length of the parameter list. For example, we would expect that

                              CALL PROC1(A,B,C)

would require more overhead than

                              CALL PROC2(A)

There are several methods of reducing the length of the parameter
list. For example, FORTRAN allows parameter sharing using
COMMON lists. Usage of internal procedures (e.g., in PL/1) allow
parameters to have a global scope (i.e., the parameter is known
throughout the program, including the internal procedures). The
declaration of parameters as *external* (e.g., in PL/1) permits their
usage in external procedures without the need to pass them
through the parameter list.

3. Some languages permit the saving of parameters within a procedure. Usage of such devices can sometimes result in significant
   performance enhancement. As an example, consider the following
   PL/1 procedure:

                      XYZ: PROC(T);
                      DCL VEC(3) INIT(10,20,30);

   Every time the XYZ procedure is called the VEC array must be
   initialized. Assuming that the values of VEC remain constant, this
   initialization process can be eliminated by using the STATIC
   attribute:

                      XYZ: PROC(T);
                      DCL VEC(3) INIT(10,20,30) STATIC;

   Other languages employ similar devices to accomplish the same
   purpose. The FORTRAN equivalent is to store VEC in a COMMON
   list and initialize VEC prior to the first usage of XYZ.

4. Some compilers require additional overhead to use parameters
   from the parameter list as compared to internal parameters. For
   example:

       FORTRAN:

                      SUBROUTINE SKL(T,U,V)
                              .
                              .
                              .
                      B = T
                      C = A

In this subroutine, A is an internal parameter and T is a passed parameter (from the parameter list). If the statement B = T is within a loop and is less efficient than C = A, the performance can be enhanced by the following change:

```
SUBROUTINE SKL(T,U,V)
TT = T
      .
      .
      .
B = TT
C = A
```

Clearly, a change of this type reduces clarity, so it is recommended only if the passed parameters (i.e., T, U, and V in this example) are used many times in the subroutine and the subroutine is called many times.

5. Usage of procedures can reduce storage by avoiding the need for repetitive code. Sometimes the opportunities for shared usage of a procedure are not obvious. However, if procedures are written in a general manner, the probability that they can be used in several places in a program increases.

4.3.9 Sorting and Searching

A reality of computer usage is that more than 25% of the total running time on many computers is spent sorting data [9]. The data might be numeric or character. The purpose of the sort might be to order a list in a manner suitable for generation of a report. (For example, we might want to sort a group of student records alphabetically.) Alternatively, the purpose of the sort might be to order a list to facilitate a subsequent searching operation. (For example, sort the students by grade average and then use the sorted list to analyze the grades.) Regardless of the specific application of sorting and searching software, if the time spent in performing these operations is relatively large, this software might offer an important potential for enhancing performance.

In Knuth's well-known book, *Sorting and Searching* [9], about 25 sorting algorithms are described. Many other algorithms have been developed and are not discussed in the book. This profusion of different methods for accomplishing the same purpose leads us to some obvious questions: Why are there so many different methods? Isn't there one theoretically best method? And if there is a best method, why don't we use it and forget about its competitors? Knuth's answer is quite clear: "Unfortunately there is no known *best* way to sort: there are *many* best methods, depending on what is to be sorted on what machine for what purpose." Knuth goes on to quote Rudyard Kipling: "There are nine and sixty ways of constructing tribal lays, and every single one of them is right."

For applications that include a significant sorting and searching component, there are several possible situations regarding the original software:

1. Sorting and/or searching is accomplished using available library or utility routines.
2. Sorting and/or searching is accomplished using routines developed in-house.
3. Sorting and/or searching is embedded within the applications software.

The methods used for sorting and searching might or might not have been "optimized" for use in the original environment. Even if they were optimized there is no guarantee that they are best for the new environment. Even if high-quality library or utility routines were used in the orginal environment, there is no reason to assume that duplication of the routines is best for the new environment. Clearly, a process of analysis and experimentation related to the sorting and searching algorithms for the new environment is desirable if one is attempting to enhance performance.

In general, sorting can be subdivided into two groups: *internal sorting* and *external sorting*. Internal sorting implies that the records are stored in the computer memory. External sorting implies that only a fraction of the records are stored in the memory at a given time. The other records are usually stored in an external file on some direct access device (e.g., a disk). Internal sorting is clearly the more efficient process because transferal of data from memory to external storage and back again is avoided. When the conversion is to a new system with much greater available memory (or virtual memory), *one should not overlook the possibility of converting external sorts to internal sorts.* The impact on performance might be dramatic if the external sort accounts for an important fraction of the running cost of the system.

When sorts are being converted, it is worthwhile to consider acquisition of a commercial sort or sort-merge package. A number of companies advertise such packages (e.g., CA-SORT by Computer Associates and SyncSort by Whitlow Computer Systems), which outperform manufacturer-supplied sort-merge utilities. Clearly, the research required to develop a high-performance package is considerable, so if a good-quality package is available, it is often worth acquiring. When the conversion is to a new environment with no available sort-merge software, one must either develop a package in-house or subcontract the effort to a software house (preferably with expertise in this area).

In many applications, sorting is a prelude to *searching*. Knuth comments that: "Searching is the most time-consuming part of many programs, and the substitution of a good search method for a bad one often leads to a substantial increase in speed. In fact it is often possible to arrange the data or the data structure so that searching is eliminated entirely, i.e., so that we always know just where to find the information we need [9]." The searching problem is sometimes referred to as the *table-lookup* problem. The purpose of a search is to find a particular data record which has been stored with a given identification. The search might be *successful* or *unsuccessful*. As with sorting, searching can be subdivided into two groups: *internal searching* and *external searching*. There are a variety of available searching algorithms, and different algorithms are best for different situations. Some are good for small internal tables, others perform well on external files, and still others are good for huge data bases. Clearly, some effort should be spent in converting searching routines to the new environment. An algorithm that was good for the original environment might not be so good for the new environment.

It is beyond the scope of this book to go into details regarding specific search and sort algorithms. However, the magnitude of the differences in various algorithms is impressively illustrated in a table comparing performance in Knuth's book, *Sorting and Searching*. The comparison considered 14 different algorithms and was based on two internal sorting test problems, one with only 16 records and the second with 1000 records. The fastest method for the short sort was the *list insertion method* requiring 433 time units. (This method required 1,248,615 time units for the 1000 record search.) The slowest method for the short sort (the *distributed counting method*) required 10,352 time units, which was 24 times slower than list insertion! For the 1000-record sort, distributed counting was fastest and required only 32,000 time units, which is 39 times faster than list insertion. The slowest method for the larger sort was the *comparison counting method*, which required 3,992,427 time units and was 125 times slower than distribution counting. The table also compares storage requirements for the various methods; however, the differences are much less impressive.

The conclusion that should be made from this discussion is that sorting and searching provide excellent opportunities for enhancing performance. Many applications require heavy use of sorting and searching algorithms, so improving the algorithms (or replacing them by better algorithms) can reduce the time required to run the system. When storage is a problem, different algorithms requiring less storage can be selected. It is not a simple matter to choose the "best" algorithm for a given situation. The correct choice of algorithm requires an in-depth knowledge of the subject. If this knowledge is not available in-house, it might be worthwhile to seek the advice of an expert.

4.4 ENHANCING MAINTAINABILITY

An awareness of the importance of program maintainability has been growing in recent years. Frank noted that 60% of ongoing software efforts are committed to maintenance [10]. Because maintenance accounts for such a large fraction of the average software budget, reduction in maintenance costs can have a substantial impact on the profitability of a data processing operation.

Recognizing the importance of maintainability, a serious effort has been made to introduce a methodology for developing maintainable software. Perhaps the one phrase that summarizes this activity is *structured programming*. An exact definition of SP (structured programming) is rather elusive. McClure defines SP as a software methodology that provides consistency and form to the program; however, she admits that "one can find almost as many definitions of SP as there are articles on the subject" [11]. Regardless of how one defines SP, it is clear that the methodology begins early in the design stage and is relevant to implementation (i.e., programming) and maintenance.

Credit for SP is generally given to Dijkstra. He wrote a number of papers on the subject starting in the late 1960s. A summary of his work (up to 1976) is included in [12]. Since then, the number of articles published on the subject and conferences devoted to the subject has grown in geometric proportions. Many books devoted to SP and/or its application to a specific language have been published in recent years (e.g., Refs. 1, 11, 13-17). The advocates of SP all agree that best results are achieved by initiating SP concepts in the early design phases of pro-programming development projects.

From the point of view of portability, it is clearly easier to move well-designed, programmed, and documented systems from one environment to another. Thus systems developed using SP concepts are usually easier to convert than systems that were developed in the "old way." However, when a conversion project is initiated, the conversion team has absolutely no control over the original programs. The original programs are inputs to the project. The conversion team can only influence the form of the converted programs.

Unfortunately, poorly designed and implemented programs can be corrected only by redesign and reprogramming. If we wish to do a straight conversion and keep reprogramming to a minimum, we will have to carry some of the poor features of the original system over to the new environment. This policy might be asthetically repugnant; however, from the point of view of the project economics, it might be the best solution (i.e., see Section 2.4). The question that should be asked is: Within the framework of a conversion project can we enhance maintainability without redesigning and reprogramming the major modules of the system?

In the following subsections a number of concepts are discussed which can be used to enhance maintainability in a system that has undergone conversion:

1. Program readability
2. Uniform labeling
3. Order of statements
4. Documentation preamble and comments
5. Control reorganization

In reading the following subsections one should remember that these concepts are relevant to programs that have been (or are undergoing) conversion. Clearly, if one is attempting to build maintainability into new programs, a much more drastic approach should be taken.

4.4.1 Program Readability

The U.S. Marine Corps conducted a survey among 18 maintenance programmers to determine the relative merits of various software documentation tools [18]. The results of the survey confirmed the importance of source listings. There was general agreement that the source listing is by far the most important document for maintenance programmers. The conclusion of the study was that a well-commented, readable, and structured source listing is a highly desirable tool for facilitating ongoing program maintenance.

The subject of program readability is often discussed in terms of *program style*. Many books on programming discuss *elements of style* which are considered good programming practice (e.g., Refs. 1 and 19). Van Tassel considers a number of topics that are normally included in programming standards and form the basis for developing readable programs (see Section 1.4.3) [4].

Many of the topics included in Section 1.4.4 were discussed from the point of view of portability (see Section 4.2). There are, however, major differences between the demands of portability and the demands of readability. For example, consider the following lines of PL/1 code:

```
DO I=1 TO N;
IF A(I)=B(I) THEN
A(I)=C(I)+B(I);
ELSE
A(I)=C(I)-B(I);
END;
```

From the point of view of portability, automatic pattern recognition is simplified by aligning the statements in this manner. However, this code is painful to the eye! The following realignment improves the code considerably:

```
DO I=1 TO N;
   IF   A(I)=B(I)
        THEN A(I)=C(I)+B(I);
        ELSE A(I)=C(I)-B(I);
   END;
```

The advice given in Section 4.2 regarding comments, sequence numbering, standard abbreviations, and punctuation is generally applicable to readability. A consistent treatment of these topics improves the appearance of a program. The advice regarding blank spaces is not necessarily applicable. In Section 4.2 it was suggested that all unnecessary blank spaces be removed. While this policy improves portability, it leads to horrible-looking code, especially in a language like FORTRAN. To improve readability we might want to add blanks before and after keywords, around operators, and so on. The specific policy regarding blanks is, of course, language dependent and a matter of style. However, it is important to standardize on a particular style and use this style consistently.

The inclusion of blank lines can be used to separate various sections of a program. For example, in COBOL programs, a reasonable policy is to place a blank line before each paragraph name in the procedure division. Some COBOL compilers include an EJECT statement which causes page breaks in the source listing. The EJECT statement can be used to list various sections of a program on separate pages. In PL/1 programs, blank lines (or page breaks) can be used before internal procedures and BEGIN blocks. Use of blank lines and page breaks can enhance readability in almost any programming language.

The use of descriptive names for variables, files, paragraphs, and procedures is recommended in all texts dealing with programming style. From the point of view of maintainance, it is much easier to understand the statement

COST_TOTAL=COST_BASE + COST_VARIABLE

than

C=B + V

However, in conversion projects, there are some problems associated with the introduction of descriptive names:

1. If the conversion team is unfamiliar with the application, the task of choosing "better" names is quite difficult.
2. If the language allows *implicit declaration* of variables, a name change can inadvertantly change a variable type and thus introduce a bug into the program. For example, consider the following FORTRAN or PL/1 example:

A=B/I

where none of the variables are explicitly declared. If we change this line of code to

AREA=MASS/INDEX

The variable B has been changed from REAL [or DEC FLOAT (6)] to INTEGER (or BINARY FIXED). The computed value of AREA might be quite different than the value of A. We could correct this bug by either choosing a variable name starting with B (for example) or by explicitly declaring MASS as REAL [or DEC FLOAT (6)].

3. Name changes must be made uniformly throughout a program and throughout an entire system of programs for those names that are passed on to other modules (e.g., through FORTRAN common blocks or as PL/1 external variables). The safest way to accomplish such a change is through the use of a table-driven conversion tool. Tools of this type are relatively easy to write using the type of language discussed in Chapter 7.

Use of alphabetized lists is an excellent method for improving program readability. For example, consider the following FORTRAN COMMON block:

```
COMMON X,Y,A,B,D
+C,JOHN,JOE,ETA,VEL,
+BINARY
```

The following is much easier to use:

```
COMMON A,    B,    BINARY, C,    D,
1            ETA,  JOE,  JOHN,   VEL,  X,
2            Y
```

Examples of other lists that can be alphabetized are parameter lists for procedures and subroutines, declaration lists, and elements in structures. However, *alphabetizing lists in converted programs can introduce extremely subtle bugs.*

The following incident illustrates the problems associated with changing the order of lists. I was once asked to help locate a bug that occurred in a large FORTRAN program that was being moved from one mainframe to another. The bug was occurring under very strange circumstances and the programmer working on the conversion had wasted about a week trying to locate the error. (This incident took place back in the old batch processing days.) The manager responsible for the conversion also tried to find the bug and could not. When I looked at the code, I was suspicious about a common block that had been changed. However, they assured me that the block had been modified uniformly throughout all subroutines. On further examination I located the following statements in one subroutine:

```
COMMON/C2/A,B,C,D,ETA,GOOD
DIMENSION P(6)
EQUIVALENCE (P(1),A)
```

The effect of these statements is to force P(1) and A to share the same location in memory, P(2) and B to share the same location, and so on. Clearly, any change in COMMON will affect the relationships between the Ps and the variables in COMMON. The reason why the bug was so difficult to locate is because the effect of the change did not become apparent until the program had proceeded far beyond the offending subroutine.

In summary, the readability of converted programs can be improved by following some basic policies. Furthermore, the institution of the policies in the form of a programming standard can be partially executed using software tools. However, several topics that would normally be included in a standard for new program development might cause problems when applied to converted programs. For example, name changes and changes in the order of lists can result in difficult-to-find logical errors. The changes made to improve readability should be balanced against the associated risk of introducing additional program bugs.

4.4.2 Uniform Labeling

Most programming languages include some form of statement label. Usually, the label is optional. Labels can be numeric (e.g., BASIC and FORTRAN) or alphanumeric (e.g., ALGOL, COBOL, Pascal, and PL/1). All discussions of programming style include suggestions for treatment of labels.

For some languages (e.g., BASIC), the line number is the statement label, and therefore the BASIC programmer has no control over the choice of labels. In FORTRAN, only numeric labels can be used. Many FORTRAN compilers reserve columns 1 to 5 for the statement label. Thus FORTRAN labels can be any number from 1 to 99999. However, the programmer is free to label any statement in the program with any number in this range. For example, the following is valid FORTRAN code:

```
   23   IF(A-B)3004,7,19856
19856   X=Y
        A=B+C
        GO TO 982
    7   A=B-C
        GO TO 981
 3004   A=B+2*C
        X=Y+1
  982   WRITE (6,17) A
   17   FORMAT(1H ,' A=',F10.3)
        GO TO 14
  981   WRITE(6,492) X
  492   FORMAT(1H  ,' X=',F10.3)
   14   CONTINUE
```

The labels in this segment could be changing to improve the clarity of the code:

```
 10   IF(A-B)40,30,20
 20   X=Y
      A=B+C
      GO TO 50
 30   A=B-C
      GO TO 60
 40   A=B+2*C
      X=Y+1
 50   WRITE(6,10000) A
```

```
10000    FORMAT(1H ,' A=',F10.3)
         GO TO 70
   60    WRITE(6,10010) X
10010    FORMAT(1H  ,' X=',F10.3)
   70    CONTINUE
```

Following the logical flow in the revised segment is obviously easier. (We could further improve the segment by moving the FORMAT statements out of the main line.)

Programming standards have been written for FORTRAN programs. The Coopers and Lybrand labeling standard[3] helps identify the various sections of a program [20]:

1. 10000-19999 for initialization logic,
2. 20000-59999 for processing logic,
3. 60000-69999 for normal termination logic,
4. 70000-79999 for abnormal termination logic,
5. 80000-89999 for input or input/output FORMATS,
6. 90000-99999 for output FORMATS.

Institution of such a standard in converted programs is a difficult task because it would be almost impossible to accomplish this scheme without some manual intervention. Nevertheless, programs conforming to this standard would clearly have a maintainability advantage.

Labels in ALGOL, Pascal, and PL/1 programs and paragraph names in COBOL programs are alphanumeric, so they can be much more descriptive than the numeric labels in FORTRAN. For programs with many labels, it is often difficult to locate a particular label. Van Tassel offers a simple solution to this problem [4]: Use descriptive names for labels and add a sequence number to each label to identify its relative position in the program. For example, consider the following COBOL paragraph names:

```
TEST_LOOP
RUN_ERROR
REPORT_OUT
```

The suggested change is as follows [4]:

```
TEST_LOOP_600
RUN_ERROR_610
REPORT_OUT_620
```

[3] Courtesy of Coopers & Lybrand.

In procedure-oriented languages such as ALGOL, Pascal, and PL/1, procedures may be nested within other procedures. The recommended labeling convention is to prefix the internal procedure names by the name of the outer procedure [4]. For example:

```
SCAN: PROCEDURE
        .
        .
        .
    SCAN_CHECK : PROCEDURE
        .
        .
        .
```

This advice can also be applied to statement labels within procedures. For example:

```
SCAN: PROCEDURE
        .
        .
        .
    SCAN_10 :  IF A>B  THEN GO TO SCAN_20;
        .
        .
        .
    SCAN_20 :  CALL SCAN_CHECK;
```

Clearly, intelligent labeling can be used to simplify the task of following the logical flow within a program. Most of the concepts discussed in this subsection can be instituted in an automatic manner and can thus be included within the framework of the conversion software. By improving the statement labeling, the maintainability of the converted programs is enhanced.

4.4.3 Order of Statements

Some programming languages allow the programmer considerable freedom regarding the order of statements. For example, PL/1 permits placement of DECLARE statements anywhere within a block. Other languages tend to force the programmer into a consistent style. For example, a COBOL program consists of four divisions ordered as follows: Identification, Environment, Data, and Procedure Divisions. Current thinking regarding the structure of computer programs tends to support a *rigid set of rules regarding statement order.* For example,

Pascal (a relatively modern language) requires all declarations to appear immediately after the PROGRAM statement and in the following order: LABEL, CONST, TYPE, and VAR.

Regardless of how much freedom a given language permits, maintainability can be enhanced by enforcing a well-defined order for program statements. This order can be accomplished automatically within the framework of the conversion software. As an example, consider the order that Coopers and Lybrand specifies in their FORTRAN programming standard [20]:

1. FUNCTION, SUBROUTINE, or BLOCK DATA statements
2. Documentation preamble
3. Specification statements
4. DATA statements
5. Executable statements
6. END statement

A rigid order for specification statements is specified in the standard:

1. CHARACTER
2. DOUBLE PRECISION
3. INTEGER
4. LOGICAL
5. REAL
6. PARAMETER
7. COMMON
8. DIMENSION
9. EQUIVALENCE

This sequence is followed for each *logical grouping* (e.g., first declaration of arguments, then variables and arrays appearing in each common block, then local variables and arrays appearing in input/output lists for each data file, and finally all other local variables and arrays). Array dimensions are only permitted in COMMON and DIMENSION statements. The standard includes the following example, which illustrates this structure:

```
      SUBROUTING NAME (ARG1, ARG2, ARG3)
C DOCUMENTATION PREAMBLE
C ARGUMENT DECLARATIONS
      DOUBLE PRECISION ARG1, ARG2, ARG3
```

```
C
C COMMON BLOCK1 DECLARATIONS
      INTEGER VAR1, VAR4
      COMMON/BLOCK1/VAR1,VAR2,VAR3,VAR4(10)
      EQUIVALENCE (VAR2,VAR5)
C
C DATA FILE1 DECLARATIONS
      DOUBLE PRECISION OUT1, OUT5
C
C WORKING STORAGE DECLARATIONS
      INTEGER TEMP1, TEMP2, TEMP3
C
                    .
                    .
                    .
```

For procedure-oriented languages (e.g., ALGOL, Pascal, and PL/1) the problem is more complicated because each internal procedure may contain the various statement types. The recommended policy is to reorder each procedure according to a standard and then move the internal procedures to a well-defined position within the main procedure (e.g., in alphabetic order at the end of the block or procedure in which they are defined).

4.4.4 Documentation Preamble and Comments

All books on programming style emphasize the concept that programs should be self-documenting. Nicholls suggests that "a programming language should be successful in communicating to other users as well as to machines [21]." In Section 4.4.1 we discussed a survey of maintenance programmers which confirmed that the program listing is by far the most important documentation tool [18]. A well-written documentation preamble vastly enhances the readability of the code and thus the maintainability of the program. Furthermore, use of comments throughout the body of the program simplifies the maintenance task.

The *documentation preamble* is a set of comment lines that are prefixed to all program units (i.e., main program and all subprograms). The Coopers and Lybrand standard for FORTRAN programs [20] is applicable to most other languages. The standard specifies the following content and order for the preamble:

1. PROGRAM UNIT NAME/LEVEL
   (The level is zero for the initial version and is increased by one each time the production version is changed.)

2. CREATION DATE/AUTHOR
3. CHANGE DATE/NAME
   (Coopers and Lybrand suggests saving the last three changes.)
4. PURPOSE OR FUNCTION
5. INTERFACES
   a. ARGUMENT LIST
   (Including description and usage, where USAGE = I, O or I/O for input, output, and input/output.)
   b. COMMON AREA(S)
   (List only those variables actually referenced in the program and indicate their usage.)
   c. EXTERNAL DATA
   (This list refers to data files and includes usage.)
6. SUBPROGRAMS
   [List of subprograms invoked, their type (i.e., FUNCTION or SUB-ROUTINE), and a description of their use or purpose.]
7. NOTE
   (Include any other critical information about the use of this programming unit, *including potential conversion problems.*)
8. LEGAL NOTICE

An optional extra section of the preamble is a list of principal local variables with some descriptive material.

From the point of view of a conversion team, the documentation preamble presents several problems:

1. Name changes of variables, files, subprograms, and so on (due to language or dialect differences) can be made automatically throughout the program *with the exception of usage within comments.* Thus if the original program includes a preamble, there might be discrepancies between names in the converted program and in the preamble.

2. There is no guarantee that the original preamble was maintained in an up-to-date status.

3. If no preamble was included in the original program, the task of writing the descriptive portions of the preamble requires an understanding of the program purpose and details. Usually, conversions can be performed without this level of understanding.

One method of partially solving all these problems is to *generate some sections of the preamble automatically.* In particular, the *interface* and *subprogram* lists (but without descriptive material) can be generated.

From the point of view of a maintenance programmer, the usage information can be the most valuable information included in the preamble. It is a relatively simple matter to build tables that include all names used in the program plus their type and usage. Once the tables have been completed, they can be used to generate appropriate comments at the beginning of the program.

The appearance of comments throughout the program also presents problems. The usual procedure in conversion work is to leave comments unchanged. However, name changes can make comments misleading. For example, consider a CDC-to-IBM FORTRAN Conversion in which seven-character names must be changed to six-character names:

CDC FORTRAN:

```
C CALCULATION OF CALCULA
      CALCULA=CALCUL+ CALCUL1
```

The conversion of the second line of code might be:

IBM FORTRAN:

```
CALC$1=CALCUL+CALC$2
```

The conversion of this line can be done automatically, but note what might happen if we try to automatically convert the comment:

```
C CALC$1TION OF CALC$1
```

To avoid problems such as this, automatic conversion of comments should not be attempted. Several alternative policies can be followed:

1. Convert all comments manually.
2. Generate a table of all name changes and include the table in the documentation preamble.
3. Avoid the issue and just do nothing (clearly the most painless option).

4.4.5 Control Reorganization

Programs that are correct from the point of view of function and output might be disastrous from the point of view of maintainability. Van Tassel illustrates this concept with the following lovely PL/1 example [4]:

```
GOTO: PROCEDURE OPTIONS (MAIN);
      /* A PROGRAM THAT USES TOO MANY GO'S.*/
      /* WHAT DOES THE PROGRAM PRINT?        */
      K=O;
      GO TO L4;
  L2: PUT LIST('D'); GO TO L3;
  L7: PUT LIST('E'); GO TO L5;
  L4: PUT LIST('H'); GO TO L7;
  L3: PUT LIST('O'); GO TO L1;
  L5: PUT LIST('L'); K=K+1;
      IF K<2 THEN GO TO L5;
      GO TO L3;
  L1:
      /* DOES YOUR PROGRAM USE GO TO'S LIKE THIS? */
  END GOTO;
```

Programs rarely start out in such an incredible form; however, after a series of bug fixes and modifications, we often end up with code that starts to resemble this example.

Many books and articles on structured programming point to the GO TO statement as the main cause of indecipherable code. When the logical flow jumps all over the program, it becomes harder and harder to follow what is actually happening. To simplify the logical flow, several concepts are usually suggested:

1. *Top-down programming* (i.e., subdivide the program into smaller and smaller functionally related parts).
2. *Modular design* (i.e., break the code down into reasonably sized subprograms).
3. *GO TO-less programming* (i.e., avoid GO TOs by using other control-type statements, such as IF–THEN–ELSE, DO loops, and CASE statements. Brown adds a sobering note to the great GO TO debate [1]: "Structured programming has given the GO TO some bad press, much of it deserved. However, the GO TO is not all bad, and one need not be fanatical about it. It may be used but do not transfer backward or intertwine the code with GO TOs as this makes the logical flow hard to follow.")

Applying these (and other) structured programming concepts is fairly straightforward when we are developing new programs. It is more difficult to apply these concepts to converted programs that were originally written in an unstructured manner. Some "patterns" can be recognized and changed automatically; however, some revisions intended to "structurize" a program will require manual intervention.

As an example, consider a FORTRAN-to-PL/1 conversion. The GO TO cannot be avoided in FORTRAN because there is no IF–THEN–ELSE in this language. Let us take the following lines of FORTRAN code:

```
      IF(A.EQ.B) GO TO 20
      X=Y
      GO TO 30
   20 X=-Y
   30 C=A+X
```

A direct conversion of this code to PL/1 yields

```
        IF(A=B) GO TO L20;
        X=Y;
        GO TO L30;
   L20: X=-Y;
   L30: C=A+X;
```

If we reorganize the control statements, we get an equivalent GO TO-less form:

```
   IF(A=B) THEN X=-Y; ELSE X=Y;
   C=A+X;
```

Clearly, this revised version is more readable. However, simple changes like this can often lead to errors. If, for example, there is a GO TO 20 statement somewhere else in the program, we are in trouble. Algorithms for affecting changes of this sort must take such possibilities into consideration.

4.5 SUMMARY

In this chapter we have discussed methods for enhancing portability, performance, and maintainability in programs undergoing conversion. The portability-motivated changes are suggested as a preconversion step that should be executed completely automatically (i.e., using software tools). These changes should be limited to the original source code and should not cause changes in the original object code.

Performance enhancement might or might not be necessary, depending on test results from the converted system. However, in all circumstances it is worthwhile to examine the effect of compiler and run-time options on performance. When additional performance enhancement is necessary, automatic methods can sometimes be used to improve the source code. There are also available software tools for improving performance by modifying the object code (e.g., Capex Corp.'s OPTIMIZER II [22] for IBM COBOL object code). Some performance enhancement techniques require manual modification of the source code.

Maintainability can also be enhanced, and this is usually accomplished as a final step in the code conversion phase of a project. Although the best time to build maintainability into a program is in the initial design stages of the program development cycle, some improvements can be introduced at a much later stage. There are many changes that can be introduced using software tools.

In general, enhancement techniques are associated with some degree of risk. However, the risk can be minimized if high-quality software tools are used to introduce the necessary program modifications. If suitable tools are unavailable, they can either be developed or the changes can be made manually. Clearly, the choice between these options is an economic decision. As the number of programs to be converted increases, the available budget for acquisition or development of software tools should be increased. Some modifications can only be made manually, and such changes introduce a higher risk than software-driven changes. Before introducing manual changes, the associated risk should be weighed against the potential benefits.

REFERENCES

1. Brown, G. D., *Advanced ANS COBOL with Structured Programming*, Wiley-Interscience, New York, 1977.

2. Ferrari, D., *Computer System Performance Evaluation*, Prentice-Hall, Englewood Cliffs, N.J., 1978.

3. Rubin, D., Midgdar Ltd., Tel Aviv, private communication, May 1980.

4. Van Tassel, D., *Program Style, Design, Efficiency, Debugging and Testing*, Prentice-Hall, Englewood Cliffs, N.J., 1974.

5. Wolberg, J. R., *Application of Computers to Engineering Analysis*, McGraw-Hill, New York, 1971.

6. Gilb, T., *Software Metrics*, Winthrop Publishers, Cambridge, Mass., 1977.

7. *OS PL/I Optimizing Compiler: Programmers Guide*, IBM SC33-0006-4, July 1979.

8. McGuire, N., "COBOL Efficiency Techniques Affect Computer Run Costs," *Journal of Systems Management*, April 1977.

9. Knuth, D. E., *Sorting and Searching*, Vol. 3 of *The Art of Computer Programming*, Addison-Wesley, Reading, Mass., 1973.

10. Frank, W., "The Ten Great Software Myths," *Computerworld*, March 6 and 13, 1978.

11. McClure, C., *Reducing COBOL Complexity through Structured Programming*, Van Nostrand Reinhold, New York, 1978.

12. Dijkstra, E., "Structured Programming," in *Software Engineering Techniques*, Petrocelli/Charter, Princeton, N.J., 1976.

13. Tremblay, J. P., R. Bunt, and J. Richardson, *Structured PL/1 (PL/C) Programming*, McGraw-Hill, New York, 1979.

14. Trembley, J. P., and R. Bunt, *Structured FORTRAN (WATFIV-S) Programming*, McGraw-Hill, New York, 1979.

15. Trembley, J. P., R. Bunt, and L. Opseth, *Structured Pascal*, McGraw-Hill, New York, 1980.

16. Yourden, E., *Structured Walkthroughs*, Prentice-Hall, Englewood Cliffs, N.J., 1979.

17. Welsh, J., and R. M. McKeag, *Structured Systems Programming*, Prentice-Hall, Englewood Cliffs, N.J., 1980.

18. Anderson, G. E., and K. C. Shumate, "Documentation Study Proves Utility of Program Listings," *Computerworld*, May 21, 1979.

19. Weinberg, G. M., *PL/I Programming: A Manual of Style*, McGraw-Hill, New York, 1970.

20. *NEDP Standards Program FORTRAN Programming Standards*, Coopers and Lybrand, New York, 1979.

21. Nicholls, J. E., *The Structure and Design of Programming Languages*, Addison-Wesley, Reading, Mass., 1975.

22. OPTIMIZER II, Capex Corp., Phoenix, AZ 85002.

5

Conversion Software

5.1 INTRODUCTION

Like many people in the computer industry, my introduction to the subject of conversion software resulted from the need to perform a specific conversion. In the late 1960s, the Rambam Hospital in Haifa received a program from a hospital in Denmark for planning radiotherapy treatments. I agreed to help the Oncology Department establish a similar planning capability using the Technion computer (at that time an Elliott 503). We received the program on a punched paper tape in a language called *Gear* ALGOL. This ALGOL differed from *Elliott* ALGOL in several respects: The character codes for several characters were different, and there were several minor syntactical differences.

Our first surprise came when we tried to read the paper tape. For both systems, the middle column on the tape was used as a *parity* check. However, each system used a different parity (one odd, the other even). The first character on the tape caused a parity error and input was terminated. Furthermore, there was no option in the operating system for overriding the parity check. Our solution to this problem was truly elegant. We opened up the back panel of the computer, located the wire from the parity circuit to the reader, and cut it! After we successfully read the tape, the wire was repaired and the program was outputted as a new tape (but with proper parity).

Once we had a readable paper tape, we addressed the problem of correcting the characters and syntax. I wrote three little programs, each completing a different task in the conversion. The first task was to read the original program (but with the parity reversed) and scan (in core) for the incorrect characters. Each time one of the characters was located, it was replaced by the Elliott equivalent. Upon completion of the task a corrected tape was produced. The following tasks made the appropriate syntactical changes and the output of each task was an updated tape. The final tape generated was the converted radiotherapy planning program, and to our surprise it worked perfectly for all the test cases.

For this simple conversion project, we could have avoided the need to develop an automated conversion process and conversion software. The alternative of retyping the program from the program listings was our *fallback position*. However, the need for conversion software becomes increasingly apparent as the size of the task grows. If we are faced with the conversion of a few program modules and let us say less than 5000 lines of code, a manual conversion is still possible. As the size increases beyond this rather arbitrary limit, the use of conversion software becomes easier to justify on the basis of cost effectiveness. Qualitative arguments related to the impact of conversion software on the cost of conversion were presented in Chapter 2.

In this chapter a variety of conversion tools and aids are discussed. Software can be used to facilitate many different phases of the conversion process, including the following:

1. *Program conversions*
2. *Data conversion*
3. *Testing*
4. *Project management*

We shall consider features of the various tools and aids that one often encounters to perform these tasks. No attempt is made to catalog all existing software for a number of reasons:

1. Any list of available software would rapidly become *out of date* because new tools and aids are constantly reaching the marketplace.
2. Software developed by companies specializing in conversion work is often unavailable because the companies consider the software as *proprietary*.
3. Many conversion tools and aids are developed within the framework of *special in-house projects*. Typically, no attempt is made to market the resulting software.

4. Current lists of available conversion software can easily be obtained (see below).

The emphasis is therefore on features rather than specific products. An awareness of useful features is helpful in either designing new software or evaluating commercially available products. To illustrate some of the features, some commercial products are mentioned, but it should be clear that other products are available from a wide variety of sources.

When confronted with a need to obtain conversion software, the reader should search the current literature to locate suppliers of suitable tools. There are a number of useful sources of information. For example, Datapro includes extensive lists of translators and conversion aids in the Programming Aids section of their reports [1]. The *ICP* listings of available software include information on conversion support systems [2]. Advertisements related to conversion tools and services are regularly included in journals such as *Datamation* and *Computer Decisions*. *Computerworld* also includes conversion-related advertisements. Probably the most extensive list of conversion software is distributed by the U.S. Federal Conversion Support Center [3]. The August 1980 listing is 138 pages long, and each entry includes detailed information regarding function, applicable hardware and operating systems, and source and target details, plus references to additional information.

5.2 PROGRAM STANDARDIZERS

In Section 4.2 we discussed *program standardization* as a method for enhancing portability. Software to affect standardization can be extremely helpful in simplifying the entire conversion process. Standardizers can also be used on the converted code to improve the subsequent maintainability of the programs. Elements often found in standardizers are discussed in Section 4.2 and include *statement alignment, blank spaces, sequence numbering, spelling, punctuation, command syntax, continued lines,* and *comment placement*. Commercial standardizers are available for the most popular languages and do many if not most of the tasks described in Section 4.2.

As examples of program standardizers, consider the following three products:

Language	Product	Company	Figure
COBOL	MetaCOBOL	Applied Data Research	5.1
FORTRAN	FORDOC	J. Toellner & Associates	5.2
PL/1	PLISTAN	O.L.I. Systems	5.3

```
Before

CHECK_BATCH_CODE.

    IF BATCH_CODE = 'B' PERFORM BATCH_HEADER

    ELSE IF BATCH_CODE = 'A' OR 'C' OR 'D'

    PERFORM BATCH_DETAIL ELSE

    PERFORM BATCH_ERROR.

BATCH_HEADER.


After

0050_CHECK_BATCH_CODE.

    IF BATCH_CODE = 'B'

        PERFORM 0060_BATCH_HEADER

    ELSE

        IF BATCH_CODE = 'A' OR 'C' OR 'D'

            PERFORM 0070_BATCH_DETAIL

        ELSE

            PERFORM 0080_BATCH_ERROR.

0060_BATCH_HEADER.
```

Figure 5.1 *Before* and *after* example using the QDM (Quality Assurance, Documentation, and Maintenance) product of MetaCOBOL. This example illustrates sequence numbering of paragraphs and the introduction of structure into the program. (From MetaCOBOL Product Group, *Applied Data Research*, Product Description, ADR, Princeton, N.J.)

As a group, these products include most of the features that one would like to see in a standardizer.

MetaCOBOL is representative of the many commercial products available for upgrading COBOL source code. MetaCOBOL is actually a group of products for converting COBOL programs from one level to another, auditing for conformance to local programming standards, interfacing COBOL with data communications and data base management systems, structuring the COBOL language, and performing other important tasks [4]. As an example of the standardization aspects of MetaCOBOL, consider Figure 5.1. This figure illustrates two typical features of program standardizers:

1. Sequence numbering
2. Indentation to highlight the program structure

Prefacing paragraph names by sequence numbers is an extremely useful method for improving readability of COBOL programs. Indentation also improves readability, but as mentioned in Section 4.2.1, it should only be introduced just prior to the manual phase of a conversion.

An example of FORDOC is shown in Figure 5.2. (FORDOC is available on National CSS time sharing.) The example illustrates several interesting features:

1. Automatic generation of a cross-reference list and inclusion of the list in the program documentation preamble

```
C*                                                               EXA00010
CTEXAMPLE                                                        EXA00020
C*                                                               EXA00030
      SUBROUTINE EXAMPLE                                         EXA00040
      COMMON L, A, SUM,     ADD, TOTAL                           EXA00050
      DIMENSION SUM(10),   ADD(100), TOTAL(1000), A(80)          EXA00060
      INTEGER    A                                               EXA00070
C                          TEST                                  EXA00080
C                          ROUTINE                               EXA00090
C                          TO PUT THE FORDOC                     EXA00100
C                          SYSTEM THROUGH ITS PACES              EXA00110
C                          IT USES NONSENSE STATEMENTS           EXA00120
  900 IF(L.EQ.1)  GO TO 220                                      EXA00130
CX        READ AND WRITE RECORDS 2 TO 9                          EXA00140
      READ(4'L,121)A                                             EXA00150
      CALL GET(A,&900,&220)                                      EXA00160
      READ(5,121,END = 95,ERR=95) A                             EXA00170
  121 FORMAT(I1,T1,I2,T1,I3,T4,I4,T5                             EXA00180
     1,I7,T10,I1,I2,I3,I4,I5,                                    EXA00190
     3I3,I3,I3)                                                  EXA00200
      WRITE(6,1011)                                              EXA00210
     1        A                                                  EXA00220
 1011 FORMAT(1X,80A1)                                            EXA00230
CX    START LOOPS                                                EXA00240
  220 DO 100 I = 1,10                                            EXA00250
C INITIALIZE THE SUM TO ONE                                      EXA00260
      SUM(I) = 1.0                                               EXA00270
      DO   200 J= 1, 10                                          EXA00280
C             INITIALIZE THE ARRAY TO 1.0                        EXA00290
      ADD(I,J)=1.0                                               EXA00300
      DO 300 K=1,10                                              EXA00310
C INITIALIZE THE MATRIX TO 1.0                                   EXA00320
      TOTAL(I,J,K)=1.0                                           EXA00330
  300 CONTINUE                                                   EXA00340
  200 CONTINUE                                                   EXA00350
  100 CONTINUE                                                   EXA003C0
      L = L + 1                                                  EXA00370
      IF(L-10) 220,                                              EXA00380
     1        900,                                               EXA00390
     2        900                                                EXA00400
C*                                                               EXA00410
   95     REWIND 6                                               EXA00420
      STOP                                                       EXA00430
      END                                                        EXA00440
```

Figure 5.2 FORDOC example. (a) Before: example program purposely prepared with very sloppy coding.

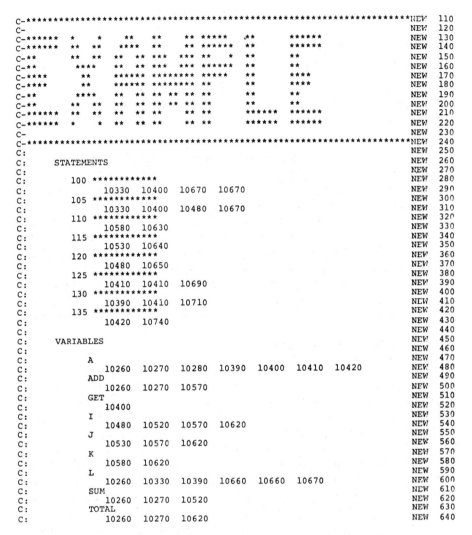

Figure 5.2 (b) After: program deck produced using FORDOC program header and cross-reference list.

2. Renumbering of numeric FORTRAN statement labels

3. Indentation to highlight the program structure

4. Blank removal

5. Movement of code (e.g., FORMATs to the bottom of the program)

6. Combining unnecessarily continued lines [e.g., IF(L-10)···]

7. Highlighting comments by adding blank comment lines before and after each comment

```
C:                                                                            NEW  650
         SUBROUTINE EXAMPLE                                                   NEW10250
         COMMON L,A,SUM,ADD,TOTAL                                            NEW10260
         DIMENSION SUM(10),ADD(100),TOTAL(1000),A(80)                        NEW10270
         INTEGER A                                                           NEW10280
C                                                                            NEW10290
C        TEST  ROUTINE  TO PUT THE FORDOC  SYSTEM THROUGH ITS PACES  IT      NEW10300
C        USES NONSENSE STATEMENTS                                            NEW10310
C                                                                            NEW10320
     100 IF(L.EQ.1)GO TO 105                                                 NEW10330
C-****************************************************************************NEW10340
C-*                                                                          *NEW10350
C-*          READ AND WRITE RECORDS 2 TO 9                                   *NEW10360
C-*                                                                          *NEW10370
C-****************************************************************************NEW10380
         READ(4'L,130)A                                                       NEW10390
         CALL GET(A,&100,&105)                                                NEW10400
         READ(5,130,END=125,ERR=125)A                                         NEW10410
         WRITE(6,135)A                                                         NEW10420
C-****************************************************************************NEW10430
C-*                                                                          *NEW10440
C-*   START LOOPS                                                            *NEW10450
C-*                                                                          *NEW10460
C-****************************************************************************NEW10470
     105 DO 120 I=1,10                                                        NEW10480
C                                                                            NEW10490
C           INITIALIZE THE SUM TO ONE                                         NEW10500
C                                                                            NEW10510
            SUM(I)=1.0                                                        NEW10520
            DO 115 J=1,10                                                     NEW10530
C                                                                            NEW10540
C              INITIALIZE THE ARRAY TO 1.0                                    NEW10550
C                                                                            NEW10560
               ADD(I,J)=1.0                                                   NEW10570
               DO 110 K=1,10                                                  NEW10580
C                                                                            NEW10590
C                 INITIALIZE THE MATRIX TO 1.0                                NEW10600
C                                                                            NEW10610
                  TOTAL(I,J,K)=1.0                                           NEW10620
     110          CONTINUE                                                    NEW10630
     115       CONTINUE                                                       NEW10640
     120 CONTINUE                                                             NEW10650
         L=L+1                                                                NEW10660
         IF(L-10)105,100,100                                                  NEW10670
C-****************************************************************************NEW10680
     125 REWIND 6                                                             NEW10690
         STOP                                                                 NEW10700
     130 FORMAT(I1,T1,I2,T1,I3,T4,I4,T5                                       NEW10710
        $,I7,T10,I1,I2,I3,I4,I5,                                             NEW10720
        $I3,I3,I3)                                                           NEW10730
     135 FORMAT(1X,80A1)                                                      NEW10740
         END                                                                 NEW10750
```

Figure 5.2 (c) After: program deck produced using FORDOC. (From *FORDOC Users Manual*, National CSS Form 305-1, NCSS, Norwalk, Conn., March 1975.)

An example of PL/1 standardization is shown in Figure 5.3. PLISTAN is a member in the National CSS CONVERT library of conversion products [5]. Documentation for members in the library is obtained by first attaching the library (i.e., *attach convert*) and then issuing the command *help member name*. The features illustrated in Figure 5.3 include the following:

1. Proper layout of data structures
2. Indention to highlight program structure

```
TEST_CASE: PROC OPTIONS (MAIN);
/*  THIS IS AN EXAMPLE OF THE O.L.I. PL/I STANDARDIZER: PLISTAN */
   DCL 1 STRUCTURE, 2 MEMBER1 CHAR (10), 2 MEMBER2, 3 SUB_MEM 2_1
   CHAR (5), 3 SUB_MEM 2_2 CHAR (15), 2 MEMBER3 BIN FIXED (31);
   GET LIST (N); B1: BEGIN; DCL A(N, N);
   L1: /* START CALCULATION */ A=0;
   L2:  DO I=1 TO N; DO J=1 TO N; A(I, J) = I*J;  END L2;  IF N > 10
   THEN GET LIST (MEMBER1, SUB_MEM 2_1, SUB_MEM 2_2); ELSE DO;
   MEMBER3=N+1; MEMBER1=' N >10 ';  END; L3: DO I=1 TO N;  PUT SKIP;
   DO J=1 TO N;  PUT DATA (A (I, J); END; END;  END TEST_CASE;
```

```
TEST_CASE:
PROC OPTIONS (MAIN);
/*  THIS IS AN EXAMPLE OF THE O.L.I PL/I STANDARDIZER: PLISTAN */
DECLARE
           1 STRUCTURE,
             2 MEMBER1 CHAR (10),
             2 MEMBER2,
                3 SUB_MEM 2_1 CHAR (5),
                3 SUB_MEM 2_2 CHAR (15),
             2 MEMBER3 BIN FIXED (31);
     GET LIST (N);
B1:
BEGIN;
DECLARE A(N,N);
   L1:                                          /* START CALCULATION */
        A = 0;
   L2:
        DO I = 1 TO N;
          DO J = 1 TO N;
            A (I, J) = I * J;
        END L2;
        IF N > 10 THEN GET LIST (MEMBER1,   SUB_MEM 2_1,   SUB_MEM 2_2);
        ELSE DO;
          MEMBER3 = N + 1;
          MEMBER1 = 'N > 10   ';
        END;
   L3:
        DO I = 1 TO N;
          PUT SKIP;
          DO J = 1 TO N;
             PUT DATA (A (I, J));
          END;
        END;
     END TEST_CASE;
```

Figure 5.3 *Before* and *after* example using the CONVERT library member PLISTAN for PL/1 standardization. (From PLISTAN Documentation, CONVERT library, NCSS, Norwalk, Conn.)

3. Blanks around operators

4. Labels and statements on separate lines

The three products discussed in this section illustrate basic features often included in standardization software. Usage of this type of tool can be applied at the early stages of a conversion project and/or upon completion of the automatic phase of the conversion. By improving the readability of the source and the target code, the entire process is simplified.

The products discussed above represent typical solutions to the standardization problem. A number of novel solutions have been proposed. A provocative article by Bates discusses standardization of Pascal programs [6]. He suggests that the code

```
A := 1;
if B = 2
then C := 3
else D := 4
```

might be reformatted as follows:

```
;  A := 1
;  if B = 2
   then C := 3
   else D := 4
```

The rationale behind this scheme is that the leading semicolons clearly show where each statement begins. However, I am not sure that the world is quite ready for this degree of innovation!

5.3 DOCUMENTATION TOOLS

There is general agreement that source listings of programs are extremely useful tools for purposes of program maintenance [7]. Listings are also invaluable for program conversions. The original listings are the primary documents upon which program conversions are based.

In addition to the program listings, several additional computer generated documents are extremely useful for facilitating conversions:

1. Cross-reference lists
2. Data attribute lists
3. Block, level, and nesting indicators

Many compilers (and interpreters) will yield some or all of this information if the proper options are specified at the Job Control level. For situations where the information cannot be obtained directly from the compiler, tools can be developed to provide the needed documents [8].

Other documents are often needed in conversion projects; however, they are not usually obtained directly from a computer analysis of the source code. The major documents in this category include:

1. System instruction manuals
2. Installation documents
3. Charts (e.g., HIPO charts) which indicate how the various program modules interact
4. Charts to indicate the flow of data between the various program modules

With the exception of the program listing, the cross-reference list and data attributes list are probably the two most important documents for purposes of maintenance and conversion. Usually, these two documents can be combined. An example from the PL/1 Optimizing Compiler is shown in Figure 5.4. This list includes a large amount of useful information related to the associated program. For example, we see that the variable NID is explicitly declared in statement 122 as a BINARY FIXED (15) array. The notation (*) just prior to word AUTOMATIC indicates that NID is a one-dimensional array. A two-dimensional array would be noted as (*,*). The numbers under that ATTRIBUTES specification (i.e., 136, 137, 148, etc.) indicate the statements in which NID is referenced. The following two parameters in the list are both N2. (PL/1 permits a variable name to be used more than once in a single program as long as each usage is in a different block or procedure.) The first occurrence of N2 is not declared explicitly and it is used twice in statement 194 [e.g., IF (N2 > NS | N2 > NUMSTR) THEN GO TO MESSAGE;]. The final three parameters (i.e., ONSOURCE, O1, and PCHK) are a BUILTIN PL/1 parameter, a statement label, and an internal procedure, respectively.

DCL NO.	IDENTIFIER	ATTRIBUTES AND REFERENCES
122	N1D	(*) AUTOMATIC ALIGNED BINARY FIXED (15, 0) 136, 137, 148, 236, 243, 248
******	N2	AUTOMATIC ALIGNED BINARY FIXED (15, 0) 194, 194, 196, 228, 230
1247	N2	AUTOMATIC ALIGNED BINARY FIXED (31, 0) 1284, 1311, 1321, 1330, 1336
15	ONSOURCE	BUILTIN 30, 148, 918, 1204
446	O1	/* STATEMENT LABEL CONSTANT */ 453, 459
405	PCHK	ENTRY RETURNS (DECIMAL /* SINGLE */ FLOAT (6)) 382, 387, 497

Figure 5.4 Sample output from the PL/1 Optimizing Compiler Attributes and Cross-Reference List.

Several important questions are not answered directly in this list and one must refer back to the appropriate lines in the program for answers:

1. What is the nature of each reference (e.g., *assignment, IF statement, read, write, arithmetic statement*, etc.)?
2. What is the scope of each variable (i.e., is the variable a *global* variable or limited to a particular *internal procedure* or *block*)?
3. Which of the variables are parameters of internal procedures?
4. From which internal procedure is each of the various references made?

Some of these questions are relevant only to PL/1 (and other ALGOL-like languages that permit internal procedures). The first question (i.e., the nature of each reference) is relevant to all cross-reference lists. Rand Information Systems (RIS) uses a program called QUIKREF, which provides a simple solution to this problem for COBOL programs. In addition to the statement reference, the actual statement is also included in the list. An example of some QUIKREF output is shown in Figure 5.5.

```
NPS4

        057040              10 NPS4                  PICTURE 9999

        126000              IF NPS4 = 0

        126200              IF NPS4 = 2

        129200              MOVE 1 TO NPS4.

        132400              MOVE 0 TO NPS4.

        136900              MOVE 2 TO NPS4.
NPS5

        057050              10 NPS5                  PICTURE 9999

        110710              IF NPS5 = 1

        110740              MOVE ZERO TO NPS5.

        112210              IF NPS5 = 1

        141100              MOVE ZERO TO NPS5.

        141710              MOVE 1 TO NPS5.
```

Figure 5.5 Sample output from QUIKREF, an RIS cross-reference generator for COBOL programs. (From *Rand Conversion Software*, Rand Information Systems, San Francisco, Calif.)

PARAMETER	TYPE	USE	
A	REAL *8 (4, 4)	CALL	12
		READ	6
		WRITE	9
		IF	13
		ARITHMETIC	11
		EQUIV	5
		DECLARE	1, 2, 3, 4
		ASSIGN	13
AA	REAL *8 (400)	CALL	12
		EQUIV	5, 5
		DECLARE	3, 4, 4
B	REAL *8	CALL	12
		ARITHMETIC	11
		EQUIV	5
		DECLARE	1, 3, 4
B10	DIMENSION (100)	IF	13
		ARITHMETIC	13
		DECLARE	2
		ASSIGN	8
C	REAL *8	WRITE	9
		ARITHMETIC	11
		EQUIV	5
		DECLARE	1, 3
D	DEFAULT	READ	6
		WRITE	9
		EQUIV	5
FLOAT	FUNCTION	ARITHMETIC	8
I	DEFAULT	CALL	12
		READ	6, 6
		DO	7
		ARITHMETIC	8, 8
J	DEFAULT	READ	6, 6
N	DEFAULT	READ	6
		DO	7
		ARITHMETIC	11
SIN	FUNCTION	ARITHMETIC	11
SUBR	SUBROUTINE	CALL	12
VAR 12	DEFAULT	ASSIGN	11

Figure 5.6 Cross-reference list which includes data attributes and usage information. This list was developed to provide supplementary information to the IBM FORTRAN IV-G compiler listings. (From J. R. Wolberg and M. Rafal, "Using CONVERT to Transform Source Code," *Software —Practice and Experience*, Vol. 9, pp. 881–890, 1979.)

I was personally involved in the development of a data attributes and cross-reference list generator for use with an IBM FORTRAN IV-G compiler [8]. The IBM compiler did not generate the required lists and the information was needed in a CDC-to-IBM conversion. (The information was available from the original CDC listings; however, it was deemed necessary to obtain similar information after conversion). Sample output is shown in Figure 5.6. The interesting feature of this list is that all references are qualified by *usage* (e.g., CALL, READ, WRITE, IF, ARITHMETIC, EQUIVALENCE, DECLARE, ASSIGN, and DO). A glance at the list helps the analyst determine, for example, in which statements a particular variable might have its value changed.

5.4 AUTOMATIC CONVERTERS

The real workhorses of the conversion business are the automatic converters. For any serious conversion effort (let us say above 5000 lines of source code), most changes should be performed automatically. Not only is it cost-effective to allow the computer to do the work, unnecessary clerical errors are avoided by reducing human intervention.

In Section 1.4 we discussed *intralanguage* converters (i.e., from one dialect to another dialect of the same language) and *interlanguage* converters (i.e., from one language to another). A list of some commercially available interlanguage converters is shown in Table 1.7. For up-to-date information regarding intra and interlanguage converters, the reader should consult the current literature (e.g., Refs. 1–3).

The most popular areas for commercial converters are shown in Figure 5.7. Other converters are available (e.g., the DASD NEAT-3-to-COBOL converter); however, for the sake of brevity, only the most

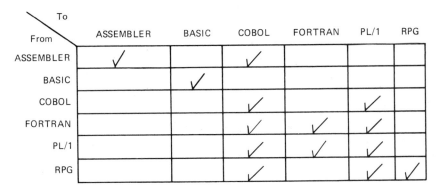

To From	ASSEMBLER	BASIC	COBOL	FORTRAN	PL/1	RPG
ASSEMBLER	✓		✓			
BASIC		✓				
COBOL			✓		✓	
FORTRAN			✓	✓	✓	
PL/1			✓	✓	✓	
RPG			✓		✓	✓

Figure 5.7 Availability of commercial converters for the most widely used programming languages. (Compiler transformations from higher-level languages to Assembler are not included in this chart.)

widely used languages are included in the chart. If a check is noted in the box of interest, all that can be said is that the probability of locating a specific converter is higher. If, for example, you are interested in Assembler-to-Assembler converters, the check in this box is encouraging. If your specific need is to convert Burroughs Basic Assembler to IBM DOS ALC, you are in luck: IBM supplies a suitable converter. However, there are many other desirable Assembler-to-Assembler converters which are not currently covered by suitable products. There are other available conversion aids which concentrate on the operating systems rather than the actual code. For example, University Computing Company provides a product called UCC TWO, which allows IBM DOS object programs to be run within an OS region or partition [9].

The lack of a check in a particular box in Figure 5.7 does not mean that a particular converter is undesirable. It merely means that I am unaware of the existence of a suitable commercial converter. For example, a market exists for BASIC-to-COBOL and/or BASIC-to-PL/1 converters, but I have not seen any mention of the availability of such software. Similarly, other languages could have been added to the chart (e.g., ALGOL, APL, Pascal); however, I am unaware of any widely distributed converters related to these languages. We should, however, be seeing some converters to Pascal in the near future. Another language that should eventually encourage converter development is the new U.S. Department of Defense Language Ada. If Ada really catches on, there will be a major incentive to move programs to this language.

To appreciate the task of developing a high-quality converter, consider the following example, which was presented to me by the late Jack Merkin of Rand Information Systems. Jack postulated the following simple Assembler-like program:

```
LD R1,A
LD R2,B
AD R2,R1
ST R2,C
```

The LD command means that the current value of A is *loaded* into register 1. The AD command means that the current value of register 1 is *added* to register 2. The ST command means that the current value of register 2 is *stored* in C. He then noted that it is an easy matter to write a converter to a higher-level language if all we plan to do is a line-by-line translation:

```
R1 = A
R2 = B
R2 = R2 + R1
C = R2
```

However, it is a much more difficult matter to recognize that the original four lines of "Assembler" is merely:

$$C = A + B$$

If we include the added complexity of branches into and out of the original code, the complexity of the conversion problem becomes considerable.

Nevertheless, a wide variety of highly sophisticated automatic converters are either commercially available or can be used through companies providing conversion services. As an example of a high-quality converter, let us consider the O.L.I. FORTRAN-to-PL/1 Converter FORPLI [10]. I have chosen this particular converter for several reasons:

1. Most readers are familiar with either FORTRAN or PL/1.
2. The converter solves some very complex conversion problems.
3. The converter goes far beyond a line-by-line treatment of the code.
4. I am thoroughly familiar with this converter: I managed its development.

A flowchart of the conversion process is shown in Figure 5.8 and the relevant files are shown in Figure 5.9. The converter *input* is the file *EXAMPLE FORTRAN* and the output is *EXAMPLE PLI*. The small file *EXAMPLE FLAG* is a message file that helps the analyst complete any required manual changes to the resulting PL/1 program. The converter is written in the CONVERT language (see Chapter 7), and thus the CONVERT interpreter is required to drive the conversion.

Before considering specific features of this converter, it is useful to consider the general concept suggested by Figure 5.8. Use of a problem-oriented language simplifies the task of writing converters but reduces the converter portability. This converter cannot be used on a system that does not support the CONVERT interpreter. It can be argued that it hardly matters on which machine a program is converted because this process takes place only once per program. Nevertheless, portability is a problem when one is interested in acquisition of a converter rather than use of a conversion service. Dataware has solved the portability problem by writing their large line of converters in ANS COBOL [11]. RIS has taken a different approach for conversion from Assembly languages to higher-level languages (i.e., COBOL, FORTRAN, and PL/1) [12]. They have a line of converters that transform Assembly language programs from a variety of manufacturers to a single *meta-language*. They then use other converters which translate meta-language code to the desired target language.

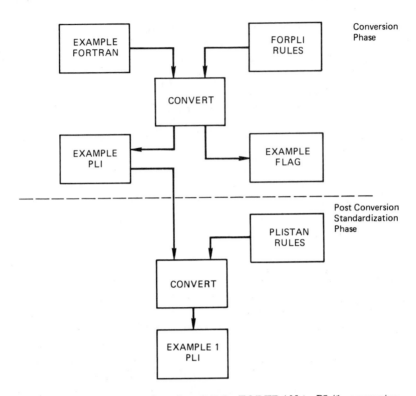

Figure 5.8 Flowchart for the O.L.I. FORTRAN-to-PL/1 converter FORPLI and post-conversion standardizer PLISTAN. The EXAMPLE FORTRAN file is the FORTRAN program to be converted and EXAMPLE PLI is the resulting PL/1 program. EXAMPLE FLAG is a message file. EXAMPLE PLI is then reformatted in a standard form (EXAMPLE 1 PLI) using PLISTAN RULES. Both FORPLI and PLISTAN are written in the CONVERT language. (From O.L.I. Systems, New York, NY)

Returning our attention to the FORPLI converter, consider the declarative statements included in Figure 5.9(a): COMMON, DIMENSION, REAL*8, EQUIVALENCE, and DATA. The FORTRAN language permits declarative information regarding a particular variable to be spread over several statements. For example, we see that VAR1 is placed in blank COMMON, and that it is DIMENSIONed as (10,10) in the next statement. VAR2 is dimensioned in COMMON and it is EQUIVALENCEd to VAR4 in a separate statement. VAR3 is placed in a named COMMON, it is declared as REAL*8, and it is dimensioned in the REAL*8 statement. VAR5 is also dimensioned in the REAL*8 statement and it is initialized in a separate DATA statement. VAR6 is DIMENSIONed as (4) and initialized in a DATA statement with character data. The PL/1 language uses a single declaration (i.e., DCL or

```
EXAMPLE  FORTRAN  P ID=DVOLI      13.17.21  TUESDAY 1 FEBRUARY 1981        PAGE 1
NATIONAL CSS, INC. (STAMFORD DATA CENTER)              HSYS


C*********** THE O.L.I. FORTRAN IV TU PL/I CONVERTER **************    EXA00010
C   FORTRAN USES NAMED & UNNAMED COMMONS.  THE PL/I                    EXA00020
C   EQUIVALENT IS EXTERNAL STRUCTURES.  VAR2 IS DIMENSIONED            EXA00030
C   IN COMMON BUT VAR1 & VAR3 ARE DIMENSIONED SEPARATELY,             EXA00040
C   PL/I COMBINES ALL INFORMATION IN A SINGLE DECLARATION,            EXA00050
C*******************************************************************   EXA00060
      COMMON/LIMITS/VAR3                                              EXA00070
      COMMON VAR1,VAR2(100)                                          EXA00080
      DIMENSION VAR1(10,10),VAR4(10),VAR6(4)                        EXA00090
      REAL*8 VAR3(20),VAR5(3)                                        EXA00100
C*******************************************************************   EXA00110
C   THE FOLLOWING LINES INCLUDE EQUIVALENCE AND DATA STATEMENTS.     EXA00120
C   PL/I USES BASED VARIABLES INSTEAD OF EQUIVALENCE.  IF ONE OF THE  EXA00130
C   VARIABLES IS IN COMMON THE POINTER MUST ADDRESS THIS VARIABLE.   EXA00140
C   NOTE VAR6 IS INITIALIZED WITH CHARACTER DATA,                    EXA00150
C*******************************************************************   EXA00160
      EQUIVALENCE (VAR4(1),VAR2(91)),(VAR1(1,1),VAR7)               EXA00170
      DATA VAR5/1.0, 7.5, -92.0/                                    EXA00180
      DATA VAR6/'PROG','RAM ','HEAD','ING '/                       EXA00190
C*******************************************************************   EXA00200
C   DO LOOPS, LOGICAL IF'S, AND READS & WRITES HAVE SIMPLE PL/I      EXA00210
C   EQUIVALENTS BUT THERE IS NO SIMPLE FORM FOR THE ARITHMETIC IF.   EXA00220
C*******************************************************************   EXA00230
      READ(5,100) (VAR3(I),I=1,20),N,M                             EXA00240
  100 FORMAT(8F10.0)                                                EXA00250
      WRITE(6,110) (VAR6(I),I=1,4)                                  EXA00260
  110 FORMAT(1H1,4A4)                                               EXA00270
      DO 20 I=1,9                                                   EXA00280
      DO 20 J=2,10,2                                                EXA00290
      IF (VAR3(I)) 10,15,15                                        EXA00300
   10 IF(VAR1(I,J).GT.0.AND.VAR1(I,J).LT.VAR5(2)) GO TO 20         EXA00310
   15 VAR1(I+1,J)=VAR1(I,J) + VAR3(I)                             EXA00320
   20 CONTINUE                                                      EXA00330
C*******************************************************************   EXA00340
C   COMPUTED GO TO'S REQUIRE A PL/I ARRAY OF LABELS.  LITERALS       EXA00350
C   IN FORMATS MUST BE MOVED TO WRITE LISTS IN PL/I.  FOR OTHER     EXA00360
C   CONVERTER FEATURES CONTACT O.L.I. FOR A DETAILED DEMONSTRATION.  EXA00370
C*******************************************************************   EXA00380
      GO TO (60,70,60),M                                           EXA00390
   60 VAR1(1,1)=0                                                  EXA00400
   70 VAR1(1,2)=1                                                  EXA00410
      WRITE(6,120) N,M                                             EXA00420
  120 FORMAT(1H1, 'N=', I4, '   M=', I4)                          EXA00430
      STOP                                                          EXA00440
      END                                                           EXA00450
```

(a)

Figure 5.9 (a) Sample input for the FORTRAN-to-PL/1 converter FORPLI.

DECLARE) for each variable. The converter had to be programmed to gather all the relevant information for each variable in a series of passes through the code and then replace the FORTRAN declarations by the equivalent PL/1 code. A further complication is noted in the EQUIVALENCE statements. One (but not both) of the variables in an *equivalence pair* can also be in COMMON. The PL/1 version of EQUIVALENCE is BASED variables; however, the address (i.e., ADDR) must be to the variable in COMMON regardless of how the pair is ordered in FORTRAN. Although not shown in the example, if neither member of an equivalence pair is in COMMON but one is a scalar

```
EXAMPLE  PLI      P ID=DVOLI     13.17.31  TUESDAY % FEBRUARY 1981      PAGE 1
NATIONAL CSS, INC. (STAMFORD DATA CENTER)                    HSYS


GO: PROC OPTIONS(MAIN);                                               EXA00010
    DEFAULT RANGE(I:N) FIXED MIN VALUE(FIXED BIN(31));               EXA00020
/************** THE O.L.I. FORTRAN IV TO PL/I CONVERTER **************/EXA00030
/*    FORTRAN USES NAMED & UNNAMED COMMONS.  THE PL/I                */EXA00040
/*    EQUIVALENT IS EXTERNAL STRUCTURES.  VAR2 IS DIMENSIONED        */EXA00050
/*    IN COMMON BUT VAR1 & VAR3 ARE DIMENSIONED SEPARATELY.          */EXA00060
/*    PL/I COMBINES ALL INFORMATION IN A SINGLE DECLARATION.         */EXA00070
/*******************************************************************/EXA00080
    DCL 1 LIMITS_C EXT,2 VAR3(20) BIN FLOAT(53);                    EXA00090
    DCL 1 HCOMM_C EXT,2 VAR1(10,10) ,2 VAR2(100) ;                  EXA00100
/*******************************************************************/EXA00110
/*    THE FOLLOWING LINES INCLUDE EQUIVALENCE AND DATA STATEMENTS.   */EXA00120
/*    PL/I USES BASED VARIABLES INSTEAD OF EQUIVALENCE. IF ONE OF THE*/EXA00130
/*    VARIABLES IS IN COMMON THE POINTER MUST ADDRESS THIS VARIABLE. */EXA00140
/*    NOTE VAR6 IS INITIALIZED WITH CHARACTER DATA.                  */EXA00150
/*******************************************************************/EXA00160
    DCL VAR4(10)  BASED($$PT1); $$PT1=ADDR(VAR2(91));               EXA00170
    DCL VAR7   BASED($$PT2); $$PT2=ADDR(VAR1(1,1));                 EXA00180
    DCL VAR5(3) INIT(1,0,7.5,=92.0)BIN FLOAT(53);                  EXA00190
    DCL VAR6(4) INIT('PROG','RAM ','HEAD','ING ')CHAR(4);          EXA00200
/*******************************************************************/EXA00210
/*    DO LOOPS, LOGICAL IF'S, AND READS & WRITES HAVE SIMPLE PL/I    */EXA00220
/*    EQUIVALENTS BUT THERE IS NO SIMPLE FORM FOR THE ARITHMETIC IF. */EXA00230
/*******************************************************************/EXA00240
    DCL $$5 FILE INPUT;                                             EXA00250
    GET FILE($$5) EDIT((VAR3(I) DO I=1 TO 20),N,M1(R($100));        EXA00260
$100: FORMAT((8)F(10,0));                                           EXA00270
    DCL $$6 FILE OUTPUT;                                            EXA00280
    PUT FILE($$6) EDIT((VAR6(I) DO I=1 TO 4))(R($110));            EXA00290
$110: FORMAT(PAGE,(4)A(4));                                         EXA00300
    DO I=1 TO 9;                                                    EXA00310
    DO J=2 TO 10 BY 2;                                              EXA00320
    IF(VAR3(I))<0 THEN GO TO $10; ELSE IF (VAR3(I))=0 THEN GO TO $15; EXA00330
      ELSE GO TO $15;                                               EXA00340
$10: IF (VAR1(I,J)>0 & VAR1(I,J)<VAR5(2)) THEN                     EXA00350
      GO TO $20;                                                    EXA00360
$15: VAR1(I+1,J)=VAR1(I,J)+VAR3(I);                                EXA00370
$20: END; END;                                                     EXA00380
/*******************************************************************/EXA00390
/*    COMPUTED GO TO'S REQUIRE A PL/I ARRAY OF LABELS.  LITERALS     */EXA00400
/*    IN FORMATS MUST BE MOVED TO WRITE LISTS IN PL/I.  FOR OTHER    */EXA00410
/*    CONVERTER FEATURES CONTACT O.L.I. FOR A DETAILED DEMONSTRATION.*/EXA00420
/*******************************************************************/EXA00430
    DCL LABARRAY1(3) LABEL INIT($60,$70,$60);                      EXA00440
    GO TO LABARRAY1(M);                                            EXA00450
$60: VAR1(1,1)=0;                                                  EXA00460
$70: VAR1(1,2)=1;                                                  EXA00470
    PUT FILE($$6) EDIT('N=',N,'  M=',M)(R($120));                 EXA00480
$120: FORMAT(PAGE,A,F(4),A,F(4));                                  EXA00490
    STOP;                                                          EXA00500
    END;                                                           EXA00510
                              (b)
```

Figure 5.9   (b) Sample output from the FORTRAN-to-PL/1 converter
FORPLI.

and the other a vector, the vector member should be addressed. An examination of Figure 5.9(b) shows that all problems related to the FORTRAN declarations are properly resolved in the resulting PL/1 version of the program.

The lines of code located in the middle of Figure 5.9(a) (i.e., EXA00240 to EXA00330) illustrate some relatively simple tasks performed by the converter: simple READ and WRITE statements, DO loops, and IF statements. The arithmetic IF is slightly more complicated

```
EXAMPLE  FLAG      P ID=DVOLI      13,17,39  TUESDAY 5 FEBRUARY 1961      PAGE 1
    NATIONAL CSS, INC, (STAMFORD DATA CENTER)                    HSYS


NEITHER ITEM IS SCALAR LINE  17 RULE 204          DCL VAR4(10) BASED(SSPT1)J
SSPT1=ADDR(VAR2(91))J
```

(c)

Figure 5.9 (c) An auxiliary output file from FORPLI. This message
file helps the analyst complete any required manual changes.

than the logical IF but both can be performed on a line-by-line basis.
The only moderately challenging feature illustrated in this section is the
placement of two END statements at $20 in the PL/1 version.

The final section illustrates a clever solution to the FORTRAN
computed GO TO: usage of an array of labels. The last feature illustrated in this section is the solution to one of the most challenging
problems in FORTRAN-to-PL/1 conversions: literals in FORMAT statements. In FORTRAN, literals to be printed in the program output may
be included in FORMAT statements. In PL/1 the literals must be moved
to the list of items following PUT EDIT. Proper placement of the literals
is a very difficult problem indeed.

It should be glaringly obvious from this example that this conversion could not be executed on a line-by-line basis. The only way a
manual conversion could be performed is to examine and mark up the
FORTRAN listings thoroughly. The amount of changes per line is large,
so the danger of clerical errors is considerable. Even for very small conversions (i.e., a few hundred lines of code), use of an automatic converter for FORTRAN-to-PL/1 conversions is cost-effective.

The conversion illustrated in Figure 5.9 yields PL/1 code which
passes through the PL/1 checkout compiler with only warning and in-
formative messages. Nevertheless, the converter detected one potential
problem that might materialize during program execution. A warning
message is printed on the EXAMPLE FLAG file shown in Figure 5.9(c).
The problem is related in the conversion of EQUIVALENCE statements
and is described in Section 4.2.10. This problem arises from the different manner in which FORTRAN and PL/1 store arrays and can lead to
problems that are extremely difficult (if not impossible) to correct algorithmically (and therefore automatically). The best the converter can
do for problems such as this is to call the analyst's attention to the
potential danger.

This conversion can be carried one step further on an automatic
basis. By passing the generated PL/1 code through the PLISTAN standardizer described in Section 5.2 (see Figure 5.3), the program can be
put into a more readable form which simplifies the manual phases of
the conversion. The resulting code is easier to maintain. O.L.I. uses this
combination of software on a routine basis for FORTRAN-to-PL/1

conversions. The output from this post conversion standardization phase is shown in Figure 5.9(d).

A few words about the history of this converter are of interest. The need for the converter arose as the result of an attempt by a large corporation to use a FORTRAN IV-to-PL/1 converter supplied by IBM. The IBM converter left many problems unsolved and a large manual effort was required to complete the conversion. O.L.I. was approached to develop a better converter. At the time, I was on a sabbatical leave

```
EXAMPLE1 PLI      P ID=DVOLI      13.17.48  TUESDAY 3 FEBRUARY 1981        PAGE 1
       NATIONAL CSS, INC. (STAMFORD DATA CENTER)             HSYS


       GO;
       PROC OPTIONS(MAIN);
          DEFAULT RANGE(I;N) FIXED BIN VALUE(FIXED BIN(31));
       /************** THE O.L.I. FORTRAN IV TO PL/I CONVERTER **************/
       /*   FORTRAN USES NAMED & UNNAMED COMMONS.  THE PL/I                */
       /*   EQUIVALENT IS EXTERNAL STRUCTURES.  VAR2 IS DIMENSIONED        */
       /*   IN COMMON BUT VAR1 & VAR3 ARE DIMENSIONED SEPARATELY.          */
       /*   PL/I COMBINES ALL INFORMATION IN A SINGLE DECLARATION.         */
       /*****************************************************************/
       DECLARE
              1 LIMITS_C EXT,
                2 VAR3(20) BIN FLOAT(53);
       DECLARE
              1 BCOMM_C EXT,
                2 VAR1(10,10) ,
                2 VAR2(100);
       /*****************************************************************/
       /*   THE FOLLOWING LINES INCLUDE EQUIVALENCE AND DATA STATEMENTS.  */
       /*   PL/I USES BASED VARIABLES INSTEAD OF EQUIVALENCE. IF ONE OF THE */
       /*   VARIABLES IS IN COMMON THE POINTER MUST ADDRESS THIS VARIABLE. */
       /*   NOTE VAR6 IS INITIALIZED WITH CHARACTER DATA.                 */
       /*****************************************************************/
       DECLARE VAR4(10) BASED(SSPT1);
          SSPT1 = ADDR(VAR2(91));
       DECLARE VAR7 BASED(SSPT2);
          SSPT2 = ADDR(VAR1(1,1));
       DECLARE VAR5(3) INIT(1,0,7.5, - 92.0)BIN FLOAT(53);
       DECLARE VAR6(4) INIT('PROG','RAM ','HEAD','ING ')CHAR(4);
       /*****************************************************************/
       /*   DO LOOPS, LOGICAL IF'S, AND READS & WRITES HAVE SIMPLE PL/I   */
       /*   EQUIVALENTS BUT THERE IS NO SIMPLE FORM FOR THE ARITHMETIC IF. */
       /*****************************************************************/
       DECLARE SS5 FILE INPUT;
          GET FILE(SS5) EDIT((VAR3(I) DO I = 1 TO 20),N,M)(R(S100));
       S100;
          FORMAT((8)F(10,0));
       DECLARE SS6 FILE OUTPUT;
          PUT FILE(SS6) EDIT((VAR6(I) DO I = 1 TO 4))(R(S110));
       S110;
          FORMAT(PAGE,(4)A(4));
          DO I = 1 TO 9;
             DO J = 2 TO 10 BY 2;
             IF(VAR3(I)) < 0
             THEN GO TO S10;
             ELSE IF (VAR3(I)) = 0
             THEN GO TO S15;
             ELSE GO TO S15;
       S10;
             IF (VAR1(I,J) > 0 & VAR1(I,J) < VAR5(2))
             THEN
             GO TO S20;
       S15;
             VAR1(I + 1,J) = VAR1(I,J) + VAR3(I);
       S20;
             END;
```

```
EXAMPLE1 PLI        P ID=OVOLI      13,17,48  TUESDAY 3 FEBRUARY 1981      PAGE 2

   END;
/*********************************************************************/
/*   COMPUTED GO TO'S REQUIRE A PL/I ARRAY OF LABELS,  LITERALS     */
/*   IN FORMATS MUST BE MOVED TO WHITE LISTS IN PL/I,  FOR OTHER    */
/*   CONVERTER FEATURES CONTACT O.L.I. FOR A DETAILED DEMONSTRATION, */
/*********************************************************************/
   DECLARE LABARRAY1(3) LABEL INIT($60,$70,$60);
     GO TO LABARRAY1(M);
   $60:
     VAR1(1,1) = 0;
   $70:
     VAR1(1,2) = 1;
     PUT FILE($%6) EDIT('N=',N,'  M=',M)(R($120));
   $120:
     FORMAT(PAGE,A,F(4),A,F(4));
     STOP;
   END;
```

(d)

Figure 5.9 (d) Sample output from the post-conversion standardizer PLISTAN. (From O.L.I. Systems, New York, NY)

from the Technion and was managing O.L.I.'s conversion efforts. While searching for solutions for some of the problems associated with this conversion, I was very lucky to come across Gary Brown's book, *Fortran to PL/1, PL/1 to Fortran Dictionary* [13]. In one reference we located well-researched solutions to most of the problems associated with this conversion. Unfortunately, very few documents such as this are available for the many conversions that one might want to perform. Thus most high-quality converters represent not only a large software development effort, but also an important research effort to determine how one goes about mapping from the source to the target language.

5.5 DATA GENERATORS

Van Tassel lists three general categories of test data [14]:

1. *Constructed data*
2. *Actual data with modifications*
3. *Actual data in volume*

Each of these types of data is needed to test converted programs and systems. Software for generation of these different types of data is used in most serious conversion projects.

 Constructed test data are the data created by the programmer to see if the program works. Constructed data can be either *controlled* (i.e., generated directly by the programmer) or *random* (i.e., generated by a data generator but based on the file descriptions in the programs to be tested). Some data generators are included in the manufacturer's utility library (e.g., IBM's utility program IEBDG); others can be obtained commercially or developed in-house. Use of constructed data for initial testing of programs is clearly preferable to initial testing with large real files. At the early stages, using too many test data is actually counterproductive. Computer resources are wasted and the analyst is confronted with massive amounts of output. Better to work with small but carefully prepared files of test data!

There are advantages and disadvantages to using *controlled* and *random* test data. Controlled data allow the analyst to prepare tests that maximize the number of options and paths tested. However, the drawback with using controlled data is that only those problems recognized by the analyst as problems are tested. Use of randomly generated data can sometimes create situations that were not previously recognized as potential problem areas. Probably, a combination of controlled and random test data should be used for early unit testing of programs. The files of test data should be saved for reuse each time the program is changed. Experience has shown that enhancements and corrections to programs often introduce new bugs.

Use of actual data but with modifications is the next level of data that one should use in serious testing. The types of modifications that one might consider are elimination of essentially repetitive records and changes in some data fields to activate various minor options is in the programs or system being tested. The advantage of using actual records from real files is that the analyst can verify that his or her interpretation of how the data are organized is actually correct. Misunderstandings related to the data are often identified at this level of testing. *Software can be used to extract records from actual data files to create a test data file.*

Volume testing using entire real files is the final stage of testing. Normally, volume tests are run in parallel using the same data on the original system. Often, failures in communication between the users of the original system and the analysts performing the conversion are discovered at this stage of testing. Occasionally, errors are located in the original system which were somehow corrected during conversion. *The need for software is sometimes required for conversion of the real data files.* For example, the codes for character data might be different in the two systems. For some conversions there might have been a need to change the format of the data. Clearly, changes in large data files should be made automatically. It would be foolish to reenter all the original data into the new system manually.

As an example of a test data generator, RIS uses a program called FILESCAN to copy, extract, or display selected records from data files [15]. It provides a means of creating limited test files containing specific types of records. Records can be selected on the basis of one or more test fields and/or on a random basis. The program can also be used to generate unit test files according to the specifications provided for each file. The merge option of FILESCAN enables transaction file keys to be matched to main file keys for the selection of the appropriate matching records. The merge selection may be further controlled by field selection parameters. Thus a comprehensive test file can be generated from several separate but related large-volume files.

5.6 DATA CONVERTERS

An important aspect of many conversion projects is the *migration of data from the source to the target environment*. Often, this migration can be accomplished quite simply: data tapes are created in the source environment and then physically transported to the target system. The tapes are then read into the target computer and stored on the chosen medium (e.g., the target system disks). The data might have to undergo some conversion process. For example, character data might require a conversion from one character set to another (e.g., EBCDIC to ASCII; see Section 6.7).

Most computer systems include a variety of utility programs for execution of the most obvious *data conversion tasks*. Many installations have developed their own data conversion software to accomplish tasks that are not covered by the normal utility routines. RIS uses several data conversion tools whose features are typical of what one most often requires [15]. Their GENER program copies source machine data files to the target machine format. The program can drop file header records or copy them into data records if necessary. The program can also be used to truncate characters from the beginning or end of a record, provide input and output totals, change the logical record length or record format, add or insert records into existing files, translate character strings to different character strings, and calculate and indentify file size and format statistics.

More complex data conversion tasks are accomplished using another program called FILECONV [15]. It can restructure or rearrange fields within records according to external record descriptions which are prepared for each record type. The following features are supported by FILECONV:

1. Changing bits to characters, characters to bits, and characters to different characters
2. Replacing zones

3. Dropping checkpoint records
4. Handling carriage control characters
5. Dropping or including header records
6. Separating variable-lengths records which have been compressed into one block
7. Modifying fields in a record
8. Printing the output and/or input in alphabetic, octal, hexidecimal, or a combination of characters
9. Producing a map of data formats
10. Providing a shorthand parameter specification to handle the identification and conversion of all records
11. Reconverting a portion of a file using altered parameters.
12. Examining and altering records and dynamically supplying parameters for conversion.

The most difficult data conversion tasks are associated with large data bases. When a conversion includes movement from one DBMS to another, the data stored in the original data base might require a thorough reorganization. This can often be a complex problem and one should make a serious attempt to locate suitable software for accomplishing the task. The supplier of the target DBMS is usually the best source of information regarding data base conversions.

5.7 TEST VALIDATION SOFTWARE

In Section 5.5 the generation of test data was discussed. It was mentioned that a serious testing program proceeds from small constructed data files for unit testing to volume testing of the entire system using real complete files. The *final testing* of a converted system is usually a series of *parallel tests* in which the same data are processed in the source and target environments. It is a nontrivial matter to prove that the results of the parallel tests are the same or are different but in an acceptable manner.

Parallel testing can be simplified if software is available for comparison of the resulting output from the two systems. A typical tool is the RIS program COMPARE [15]. This program identifies those records that do not match and then pinpoints only those bytes that mismatch. A number of useful options are included:

1. Masking unnecessary fields such as carriage control positions on print fields or known fields that mismatch

2. Selecting the maximum number of mismatched records to be printed
3. Merging compared files upon specified key fields (so that missing or extra records do not generate subsequent mismatches)
4. Selectively comparing portions of a large file
5. Comparing only portions of records in a file

Another useful RIS program for test validation is PCTEXEC (i.e., Percentage Execution) [15]. An important question during program testing is the percentage of the program statements that are executed as a result of the test data. Van Tassel [14] correctly states that we *hope* that 100% of the code is tested. The figure of 100% might be a reasonable goal for *new system development* but it is not practical for conversion work (due to dead code and code required for all instances of abnormal termination). RIS suggests that 70% is an adequate level for testing and uses PCTEXEL to measure the actual level obtained as a result of the test data [16]. The PL/1 checkout and optimizing compilers include an option called COUNT, which can be used to obtain similar information from executing PL/1 programs (see Section 4.3.2).

Much of the literature on the testing, verification, and validation of new software is applicable to conversion projects. Several recent books consider these subjects in detail and include references to recent work in these areas. For example, the fifth chapter of *Software Engineering* by Deutsch is devoted to the subject of *verification and validation* [17]. Gunther includes a chapter on *managing software product tests* in his book, *Management Methodology for Software Product Engineering* [18]. The methodology and software described in these references is particularly relevant to testing of large systems.

5.8 PROJECT MANAGEMENT TOOLS

A well-recognized trend is to computerize a number of planning and reporting tasks associated with the management of large projects. This trend is applicable to software development in general and to conversion projects in particular. For large conversion projects the number of programs might be in the hundreds or thousands. Similarly, the data to be converted might consist of many megabytes of information spread over hundreds or thousands of files. In addition, job control files and utilities must be considered as parts of the project.

For large projects it therefore becomes necessary to use software tools to keep track of the status of the various phases of the conversion. Inventory systems that provide details concerning the files to be converted, schedule dates, current status, and so on, are extremely useful. Similarly, common management tools used for planning and scheduling can be applied to conversion projects. The reader is referred to Section 3.7 for a more detailed discussion related to a *management tool* that has been used by Philips to control large conversion projects.

5.9 SUMMARY

A variety of different types of conversion software have been discussed in this chapter. No attempt has been made to include complete lists of available software. The emphasis is on features that one would like to see in the various types of tools under discussion. Some examples have been included to illustrate some of the most important features and concepts.

One point has *not* been mentioned specifically but should be emphasized: The normal tools included in most systems are extremely useful in conversion work. For example, many compilers and interpreters utilize a variety of debugging aids which are most helpful in finding errors in the converted systems. Cross-reference lists, editors, utility programs, and so on, are the basic tools we have come to expect from any decent system. It is much easier to convert to an environment that includes powerful general-purpose software tools than to a system in which all the basic tools must be either developed or acquired.

REFERENCES

1. *Datapro Directory of Software*, Datapro Research Corp., Delran, NJ 08075.

2. "ICP INTERFACE," *Data Processing Management Quarterly Journal*, International Computer Programs, 9000 Keystone Crossing, Indianapolis, IN 46240.

3. *Conversion Products/Aids Survey*, Federal Conversion Support Center, 5203 Leesburg Pike, Falls Church, VA 22041, August 1980.

4. MetaCOBOL Product Group, *Applied Data Research*, Product Description, ADR, Route 206 Center, CN-8, Princeton, NJ 08540.

5. PLISTAN Documentation, CONVERT library, NCSS, 187 Danbury Rd., Wilton, CT 06897.

6. Bates, R. M., "A Pascal Prettyprinter with a Different Purpose," *SIGPLAN Notices*, March 1981.

7. Anderson, G., and K. Shumate, "Documentation Study Proves Utility of Program Listings," *Computer World*, May 21, 1979.

8. Wolberg, J. R., and M. Rafal, "Using CONVERT to Transform Source Code," *Software—Practice and Experience*, Vol. 9, pp. 881–890, 1979.

9. *UCC TWO Product Information*, University Computing Company, 8303 Elmbrook, Dallas, TX 75247.

10. FORPLI Documentation, CONVERT library, NCSS, 187 Danbury Rd., Wilton, CT 06897.

11. Dinkel, R., Private communication, Dataware, 2565 Elmwood Avenue, Buffalo, NY 14217.

12. *The Solution to Your Computer Conversion Problems*, Rand Information Systems, 98 Battery St., San Francisco, CA 94111.

13. Brown, G. D., *Fortran to PL/I, PL/I to Fortran Dictionary*, Wiley-Interscience, New York, 1975.

14. Van Tassel, D., *Program Style, Design, Efficiency, Debugging and Testing*, Prentice-Hall, Englewood Cliffs, NJ 1974.

15. *Rand Conversion Software*, Rand Information Systems, 98 Battery St., San Francisco, CA 94111.

16. *Conversion Special Report: Changing to New Technology*, Rand Information System, 98 Battery St., San Francisco, CA 94111.

17. Deutsch, M., in *Software Engineering*, R. Jensen and C. Tonies, Prentice-Hall, Englewood Cliffs, NJ 1979, pp. 329–408.

18. Gunther, R. C., *Management Methodology for Software Product Engineering*, Wiley-Interscience, New York, 1978.

Conversion Algorithms

6.1 INTRODUCTION

An *algorithm* can be defined as an unambiguous ordered sequence of steps that leads to the solution of a given problem [1]. One of the early tasks in a conversion project is to list the various technical problems confronting the conversion team. *Conversion algorithms* are the methods of solutions for these problems.

    An algorithmic approach to problem solving is not a new concept. Knuth described ancient Babylonian algorithms in a 1972 ACM Communication [2]. Computer analysts are confronted with the need to express algorithms at two levels: *design* and *implementation*. There has been a considerable effort to develop programming languages that facilitate implementation of algorithms. The ALGOL language (for ALGOrithmic Language) was developed in the 1950s and has had a major impact on the general direction of programming languages. Gries summarized the contribution of ALGOL: "Of prime importance was its sense of simplicity, structure and conciseness—its mathematical elegance if you will" [3]. The influence of ALGOL on more recent languages (e.g., PL/1 and Pascal) is acknowledged by the term *ALGOL-like* which is used to describe various languages.

    The development of methods for expressing algorithms at the design level has received much less attention than the development of programming languages. ALGOL, PL/1, and more recently Pascal are often used to express mathematical algorithms. For tasks of a more general nature, a "pidgin-ALGOL-like" scheme of notation is sometimes used [4]. The difference between the description of algorithms at the design and implementation level can best be understood when we consider the purpose of the algorithm. Implementation (i.e., programming) is directed to a computer and must be expressed precisely according to a set of formal rules. Expression of algorithms at the design level is directed toward human beings and the notation can therefore be less precise. However, the purpose of each step must be *clear and unambiguous, the order of the steps must be well defined,* and the solution must be *obtainable in a finite number of steps.*

In this chapter a number of conversion algorithms are discussed. The purpose of the chapter is threefold:

1. To illustrate how one goes about expressing conversion algorithms.
2. To provide examples of common techniques used in a variety of conversion algorithms.
3. To discuss topics of general applicability in conversion work but from an algorithmic point of view.

Conversion algorithms are building blocks used to specify the technical methodology associated with a conversion project. *The algorithms can be used as design specifications for automatic converters or conversion aids. Alternatively, the algorithms may be included in handbooks used by programmers for manual conversions.*

It is useful to be able to classify conversion algorithms according to some basic properties. The following two properties are relevant for classification:

1. *The number of passes through the source file* required to execute the algorithms (e.g., zero-pass, single-pass, and multipass algorithms)
2. *The type (or types) of operations* required by the algorithm (e.g., replacement, insertion, and translation algorithms)

In Section 6.3, for example, we discuss two algorithms: *Algorithm 6.3.1* is an example of a *single-pass replacement algorithm* and *Algorithm 6.3.2* is an example of a *zero-pass insertion algorithm.*

One of the basic tasks that we will specify in most algorithms is to search a program (or program unit) for a particular pattern of characters (e.g., the word GOTO followed by an integer number followed by a blank). We can simplify the task of describing algorithms if we adopt a simple method for defining patterns. In Section 6.2 a method is presented and is then used throughout the remainder of the chapter [5]. This method is also used to define patterns in the conversion language discussed in Chapter 7.

6.2 DEFINING PATTERNS

A *pattern* consists of one or more characters. In the notation scheme described in this section, a pattern is defined as a series of *elements* in a specified order [5]. The element types are usually noted by a letter followed by a number (e.g., N3 and A7). The only exception to this scheme is a string that is delimited by apostrophes (e.g., '*' and 'A STRING'). Patterns consisting of more than one element are noted by dots used to connect the elements (e.g., N3. '*' and A6.'A STRING' .N2). An element can be noted as *optional* by placing it within parentheses [e.g., A1.(P10) and N3.(B20).'*'] . The negative of an element can be specified by preceeding it with a *not* (i.e., ¬) character (e.g., B10.¬ B1 and ¬ A1.A1.P5).

TABLE 6.1   Element Types for Pattern Definition[a]

Element Type	Fixed or Variable Length	Length	Description
A	Fixed	I	Alphabetic characters
B	Variable	1 to I	Blanks
C	Fixed	I	Any characters
D	Variable	4 to I	Double-precision number
E	Variable	4 to I	Floating-point number
F	Variable	2 to I	Fixed-point number
H	Variable	See Sec. 6.2.4	H-table member
L	Variable	1 to I	Numeric characters
N	Fixed	I	Numeric characters
P	Variable	2 to I	Parentheses group
Q	Variable	1 to I	V or V.P
S	Fixed	See Sec. 6.2.6	Defined string I
T	See below	See Sec. 6.2.7	Any member of table I
U	Variable	0 to I	Unspecified
V	Variable	1 to I	First character A, then zero to (I-1) Z characters
X	Variable	1 to I	User-defined variable group
Y	Fixed	I	User-defined fixed group
Z	Fixed	I	Alphanumeric characters
String	Fixed	See Sec. 6.2.6	Literal

[a] All fixed-length elements and T type can be preceded by a NOT (i.e., ¬) character. All types except C and U can be specified as optional by enclosing the element in parentheses. The parameter I is the numeric suffix attached to the *type* (e.g., A3, X7).

Source: CONVERT Instruction Manual, Version 2.0, National CSS, Inc., Form 401-2, September 1978.

A list of all element types is included in Table 6.1. Some types are of fixed length and others are of variable length. Only fixed-length elements can be preceded by a *not* character because a *not* prior to a variable-length element is ambiguous. All element types except C and U can be specified as optional.

6.2.1 A, C, N, Y, and Z Type Elements

All elements in this family are of fixed length and furthermore, the numeric suffix is the element length. For example, A5 denotes five alphabetic characters, C2 denotes any two characters, and Z17 denotes 17 alphanumeric characters. Examples of A5 patterns include the following:

$$\text{EDBCA} \quad \text{RRRRR} \quad \text{HOUSE}$$

Examples of C3 patterns include the following:

$$\text{ABC} \quad \text{A*C} \quad \text{bb2}$$

(where b denotes a blank). Examples of N4 patterns (i.e., four numeric characters) include

$$1234 \quad 0000 \quad 9812$$

Elements of type Y first require a user-supplied definition of the Y group of characters. For example, if Y is defined as follows:

$$Y = (AB*123)$$

then Y5 would include

$$\text{AAAAA} \quad 12312 \quad \text{A11*2}$$

Examples of Z4 patterns include

$$1237 \quad \text{AABB} \quad \text{F101}$$

More complex patterns can be developed by combining several elements together. For example, A1.N4 refers to patterns consisting of a single alphabetic character followed by four numeric characters:

$$\text{Q0000} \quad \text{D1793} \quad \text{X1008}$$

The use of these element types can be enhanced if we allow redefinition of the groups of characters for each type. For example, in some versions of FORTRAN IV, the dollar sign (i.e., $) is considered as an alphabetic character. By redefining the A character set:

$$A = (\$ABCDEFGHIJKLMNOPQRSTUVWXYZ)$$

we can then use A elements to locate patterns that include all characters in the expanded alphabet set in FORTRAN programs.

6.2.2 B, L, V, and X Type Elements

All elements in this family are of variable length. The numeric suffix is the maximum length of the element and the minimum length is a single character. For example, B5 denotes one to five blank characters and L3 denotes one to three numeric characters. Examples of L3 patterns include the following:

$$1 \quad 73 \quad 881$$

The V type elements are very useful for patterns encountered in conversion algorithms because many languages define variable names starting with an A (i.e., alphabetic) character and then followed by from zero to a specified number of Z (i.e., alphanumeric) characters. For example, V6 patterns include the following:

$$J \quad MIG21 \quad SOLVER$$

For some languages the definition of a variable is superficially radically different but can easily be forced into the framework of V type elements by redefining either the A or Z or both character sets. For example, some dialects of BASIC define variables as a single alphabetic character or a single alphabetic character followed by a numeric digit. The pattern V2 covers all BASIC variables if we redefine Z:

$$Z = (0123456789)$$

Examples of V2 patterns would then include

$$X \quad X7 \quad A0$$

but patterns such as GO would (correctly) not be recognized as BASIC variables.

The X element type is a user-defined variable-length element. For example, if X is defined as follows:

$$X = (+-/*1234567890)$$

then X5 would include

$$+ \quad -2 \quad 3*4/6$$

More complex patterns can be developed by combining elements. For example, L2.A3.V4 is a pattern that can vary from five to nine characters in length, starting with one or two numeric characters, followed by three alphabetic characters, followed by an alphabetic plus zero to three alphanumeric characters.

6.2.2 B, L, V, and X Type Elements

Many languages use noninteger numeric constants and it is useful to have elements that can identify the most important of these types. The D type is a double-precision floating-point number, the E type is a regular floating-point number and the F type is a fixed-point number. The numeric suffix is the maximum length of the element. Examples of D9 type elements include

$$1.235D-2 \quad -.12DO3 \quad +113.D+12$$

Example of E20 type elements include

$$1.235E-2 \quad -.12EO3 \quad +113.E+12$$

Example of F80 type elements include

$$+.123 \quad 178. \quad -1.09$$

A problem arises because we have included the leading sign as part of the pattern. If, for example, we are searching for the pattern E20 in the following statement:

$$Q = A+.123E-12$$

the pattern +.123E-12 would be located. However, if we search for the pattern Y1.E20, where Y=(+-*/), we would locate the same pattern but the second element would not include the plus sign.

Another problem arises if the specified length is just a little too short. For example, if we search for E8 in the statement above, we would locate the pattern +.123E-1! We should always specify the length to be as large or larger than the longest pattern that might appear in the code.

6.2.4 H Type elements

It is useful to be able to store character type information for every line in the source code. To accomplish this, tables that maintain a one-to-one correspondence with the source lines are required. Let us define these tables as H1, H2, ... For every line of source code there is a corresponding string in each of the H tables. The H-table string can then be used in subsequent pattern searches.

As an example, consider the following lines of code and the associated H tables (in this case only H1 and H2):

Line Number	Line	H1	H2
1	A = B+C	B	+
2	D = XYZ–D/E	D	/
3	XYZ = B+REN*E/A	REN	+

Searches for the patterns H1.H2.C1 would locate B+C on the first line and D/E on the second line. The search would be *unsuccessful* on the third line.

6.2.5 P and Q Type Elements

Most computer languages use parenthetical groups. The P type elements refer to groups starting from a left parenthesis. The numeric suffix is the maximum length of the group. Examples of P10 patterns include

$$( )   (A+B)   (X(1,1)+B)$$

The pattern (X(1,1)+BC) would not be located because it includes more than 10 characters.

The Q type elements are V type elements or V type elements followed by P type elements. This element type is extremely useful when we are trying to analyze patterns in an arithmetic type statement. If some of the variables are arrays, pattern definition is considerably simplified using Q type elements. Examples of Q10 patterns include

$$X \quad Y1(2) \quad AB(I+J(K))$$

To understand the value of Q type elements, consider the following pattern:

$$Q10.'='.Q10.'+'.Q10$$

(i.e., a Q10 element followed by the character = followed by a Q10 element followed by the character + followed by a Q10 element). All of the following lines satisfy this pattern:

$$A(I)=B+C(J)$$
$$DET=X(I,I)+YY(J*K)$$
$$XYZ=E+F$$

without Q type elements it would be very difficult to define a single pattern that is satisfied for each of these lines.

6.2.6 S and String Type Elements

These elements are strings either defined separately (e.g., S3='JOE SMITH') or within the pattern itself (e.g., Q20.'='). If we wish to include the apostrophe in the string, we can use another character (e.g., ") to delimit the string:

$$S7 = "JOE'S BOOK"$$

A reasonable question is why bother with two types of strings? Isn't it simpler to include the string directly in the pattern? For example, two alternative forms for expressing the same pattern are:

1. S1 = 'GO TO '
   Pattern = S1.L5
2. Pattern = 'GO TO '.L5

For this example there is no difference. However, many algorithms require first locating a pattern, then saving the pattern as a string (e.g., S5 = *located pattern*) and finally searching for a new pattern which

includes the defined string (e.g., S5.N3). The ability to define and refer
to a pattern symbolically is very useful in pattern searching problems.

6.2.7 T Type Elements

It is extremely useful to be able to reference an entire table in a
pattern. For example, if Table 7 includes three members (e.g., '10',
'48', and '103'), then the pattern

'GO TO '.T7

would locate the following patterns:

GO TO 10
GO TO 48
GO TO 103

but not the following:

GOTO 10
GO TO 11
GO TO   48

When developing conversion software it is important to be able to
easily build, manipulate, and search tables. Many algorithms consist of a
table generation step (or steps) and then a pattern search based on the
table. For example, Algorithm 6.5.1 (NAME_CHANGE) utilizes tables.
The algorithm first specifies generation of a table of names that will be
illegal in the new environment. The next step is to generate a suitable
replacement table and the final step is to replace all illegal names.

6.2.8 U Type Elements

The U type element is similar to the C type element in that it can
include any character. However, it is variable in length. For example,
U10 specifies any zero to 10 characters. This element type is useful
only in conjunction with other elements. For example, the pattern
A3.U2.L2 can be from four to seven characters in length and would
include the following:

MIG23   MIG 23   MIG**23

This element is extremely useful when we wish to save or use whatever appears between two other elements. For example, consider the following pattern:

'='.U80.';'

The U80 element includes everything between the equal sign and the semicolon. For this pattern the separation between the equal and semicolon signs may be from zero to 80 characters.

6.2.9 Optional Elements

We define an element as being optional by including it within parentheses. All elements except C and U types can be specified as optional. As an example, consider the pattern 'GO'.(B20).'TO' (i.e., the word GO followed by 0 to 20 blanks followed by the word TO). Examples of strings satisfying this pattern include

GOTO   GO TO   GO   TO

The string GO*TO does not satisfy the pattern. The usage of optional elements can often simplify definition of a complex pattern.

6.3 SOME SIMPLE EXAMPLES

In this section two conversion algorithms are discussed. They have been chosen because they are conceptually quite simple. We can therefore easily introduce the *algorithmic notation scheme* used throughout the chapter. The scheme is similar to the method used by Tremblay and Bunt [1]. It is an "ALGOL-like" method for describing algorithms and requires very little explanation for anyone with some prior programming experience. Algorithms expressed in this manner can be used as part of the design specifications for conversion software, or directly in a handbook for manual conversions.

The first algorithm specifies conversion of CDC FORTRAN *two-branch logical IF* statements to a FORTRAN IV–acceptable form. This algorithm is a *single-pass replacement algorithm*. Each offending line of code is replaced by two new lines, so the code "grows" as a result of the replacements.

Algorithm 6.3.1 TWO-BRANCH. This algorithm converts CDC FORTRAN two-branch logical IF statements to an acceptable FORTRAN IV form. The original form [i.e., IF (*logical expression*) *Label 1*, *Label 2*] means that if the logical expression is true, then go to label 1; else, go to label 2.

1. [Initiate loop]
   Repeat through step 3 for every line in program unit.
2. [Search for offending statement]
   If line is not comment
   Then if pattern C6.'IF'.P100.L5.','.L5.B1 is located in column 1
   Then replace line with two lines:
   Elements 1 through 3. ' GOTO '. Element 4
   '   GOTO '. Element 6
3. [Terminate loop]
   Continue
4. [Terminate algorithm]
   Exit

[Assumptions]
   The code has been stripped of all unnecessary blanks and all continued IF lines have been combined prior to execution of this algorithm. Furthermore, the largest possible parenthetical group (i.e., element 2) is 100 characters.

[Example (before conversion)]

```
          IF (A.EQ.B)20,207
       20 IF (X.GT.Y.AND.T.LE.S)100,90
```

[Example (after conversion)]

```
          IF (A.EQ.B) GOTO 20
          GOTO 207
       20 IF (X.GT.Y.AND.T.LE.S) GOTO 100
          GOTO 90
```

This algorithm illustrates several points:

1. In Section 4.2.2 it was mentioned that blank removal enhances portability. Here we note that if blanks are removed prior to execution of the algorithm, we can use the fairly simple pattern defined in step 2.

2. By combining all continued IF lines prior to execution of the algorithm, we eliminate the problem of searching for patterns that might span more than one line. One might ask: What happens when a combined line exceeds the legal FORTRAN IV limit (i.e., 72 characters)? Clearly, a subsequent algorithm is needed to break all long lines back down to legal length (e.g., step 12, Algorithm 6.4.1).

3. Use of the pattern notation scheme described in Section 6.2 reduces the verbiage that would be required to describe the algorithm. For example, in step 2 the same pattern stated in words is: any six characters followed by the string 'IF' followed by a parenthetical group of up to 100 characters followed by a numeric label of one to five characters followed by a comma followed by a second numeric label of one to five characters and terminated by a blank.

4. The elements included in the replacement lines (step 2) clearly refer to the elements located in the pattern defined in the same step.

5. The final B1 in the pattern is required to distinguish between a *two-branch logical* if and the *arithmetic IF* which can be used in both CDC FORTRAN and in standard FORTRAN IV.

6. This algorithm is programmed in the CONVERT language in Section 7.6.

Algorithm 6.3.2 DEFAULT. This algorithm modifies program units converted from FORTRAN IV to PL/1 so that the default precision of undeclared integer variables in PL/1 is BINARY FIXED(31) (i.e., 4 bytes). These variables then have the same precision in PL/1 as in the original FORTRAN IV program units.

1. [Examine for IMPLICIT statements]
   If program unit is main program
   then examine statement 1
   else examine statement 2

2. [Build table]
   If no IMPLICIT statement
   then members of table are I,J,K,L,M,N
   else members of table are only those letters
   in range I-N not specified in IMPLICIT.

3. [Create DEFAULT statement]
   Insert the following statement immediately

after the first statement in the PL/1
program (i.e., the PROCEDURE statement):

DEFAULT RANGE (member 1, member 2, . . .) BIN FIXED(31);

4. [Terminate algorithm]
   Exit

[Assumptions]
   The default precision for undeclared integers in the FOR-
TRAN IV program units is INTEGER*4 (i.e., 4 bytes). A
subsequent algorithm is required to specify conversion of the
IMPLICIT statement (if included) for each program unit.

[Example with IMPLICIT statement in FORTRAN]

IMPLICIT (G-K) INTEGER*2

[Example of inserted DEFAULT statement in PL/1]

DEFAULT RANGE (L,M,N) BIN FIXED (31);

   This algorithm (6.3.2) solves a problem related to the default precision for integer variables in FORTRAN IV-to-PL/1 conversions. The
algorithm is a *zero-pass insertion algorithm*. We do not require a search
through each program unit. We must only examine the first statement
(for main programs) or the second statement (for subprograms) of the
FORTRAN IV program units to see if an IMPLICIT statement is included. A new statement is inserted in the PL/1 versions (but perhaps
modified as a result of the IMPLICIT statement).
   This algorithm (6.3.2) solves a problem related to the default precision for integer variables in FORTRAN IV-to-PL/1 conversions. The
consider algorithms that are based on generation and then use of tables
to accomplish a particular task. The conversion language discussed in
Chapter 7 includes a variety of table-oriented tools which simplify the
development of converters and conversion aids.

6.4 BLANK REMOVAL

In Section 4.2.2 blank removal is considered as a means of enhancing
portability. Algorithm 6.3.1, for example, exploits the fact that unnecessary blanks have already been removed from the program unit and

thus utilizes a simpler pattern for the two branch logical IF statements. In Section 4.4 treatment of blanks is again considered but from the point of view of program readability.

In this section two algorithms for removal of blanks are discussed:

Algorithm	Task
6.4.1	Removal of unnecessary blanks in FORTRAN IV program units
6.4.2	Removal of multiple blanks in COBOL Procedure Division

Blank removal is a task that can easily be performed automatically. Both algorithms can easily be implemented to develop suitable blank removal tools.

Algorithm 6.4.1 REMOVE_1.   This algorithm removes all unnecessary blanks from a FORTRAN IV program unit. The necessary blanks are those used in comments, literals, and Hollerith fields, and those in columns 1 through 6. Two character variables are used in the algorithm: APO is the apostrophe character and NFC is a non-FORTRAN character.

1. [Initiate main loop]
   Repeat through step 13 for every line in program unit.
2. [Skip over comment lines]
   If 'C' in column 1 then go to (13).
3. [Combine continued lines]
   If ¬'C'.C4.¬B1 in column 1 of next line
      then combine from column 7 to current line,
         go to (3).
4. [Initiate line preparation loop]
   Do through step 6 for i = 7 to line_length
5. [Convert all necessary blanks to NFC]
   If Char (i) = APO
      then do i = i+1 by 1 while (Char(i)¬=APO)
         if Char(i) = blank
            then Char(i) = NFC
      else if pattern = ¬Z1.L3.'H' starts at i
         then n = value of element 2
            k = position of element 3 + 1
            do i = k to k+n-1
               if Char (i) = blank
                  then Char (i) = NFC

6. [Terminate line preparation loop]
   Continue

7. [Initiate blank stripping loop]
   Do through step 9 for i = 7 to line_length

8. [Remove all blanks]
   If pattern B10.⌐B1 starts at i
      then replace element 1 by null string,
         i = i – 2.

9. [Terminate blank stripping loop]
   Continue

10. [Initiate translate loop]
    Do step 11 for i = 7 to line length

11. [Translate NFC back to blank]
    If Char (i) = NFC
       then Char (i) = blank)

12. [Break long lines back to 72 characters]
    n = position of last nonblank character on line.
    If n > 72
       then break line at 72,
          put ∗ in column 6 of next line,
          go to (13).

13. [Terminate main loop]
    Continue

14. [Terminate algorithm]
    Exit

[Example before conversion]

```
C REMOVE ALL BLANKS
234 DO 100 I = 1, N
        WRITE(6,1000) X
        A = B+
    *  C  +  D
100   CONTINUE
C BUT NOT IN LITERAL OR HOLLERITH FIELD
1000 FORMAT(1H  ,' X=', F10,3)
```

[Example after conversion]

```
C REMOVE ALL BLANKS
234 DO100I=1,N
        WRITE(6,1000)X
        A=B+C+D
```

```
100  CONTINUE
C BUT NOT IN LITERAL OR HOLLERITH FIELD
1000 FORMAT(1H  ,' X=',F10.3)
```

This algorithm includes a number of interesting aspects:

1. Step 3 examines the following line to see if it is *not* a comment but *is* a continuation line. Our notation scheme allows us to very simply define this pattern using two negative elements (i.e., not 'C' in column 1 and a not blank in column 6). The purpose of element 2 (any four characters) is to ensure correct positioning for element 3.

2. The most difficult step in the algorithm is step 5. In this step the necessary blanks are temporarily converted to NFC (a non-FORTRAN character) but are translated back to blanks in step 11.

3. The pattern search in step 8 is for 1 to 10 blanks followed by a nonblank character. We might wonder what happens if more than 10 blanks are followed by a nonblank character. By reducing i by 2, we ensure that even those blanks beyond 10 will be stripped. (Ten is an arbitrary value.)

4. Step 12 shows how we can return the line lengths to the legal maximum of 72 characters. However, if this algorithm is being implemented with other algorithms in the framework of a conversion tool, we might prefer to leave the lines combined until supplementary tasks have also been completed.

5. The notation *Char(i)* is used to indicate the character located in column i of the current line. We will have many occasions to use this function.

Algorithm 6.4.2 REMOVE_2.   This algorithm removes all multiple blanks from COBOL Procedure Divisions except those in comments and literals. The QUO character refers to either a single quote (i.e., ') or a double quote (i.e., "), depending on which character is used for enclosing literals in the particular COBOL of interest. The algorithm also aligns all lines to column 8 or 12.

1. [Locate Procedure Division]
    Examine line for 'PROCEDURE DIVISION'.
2. [Initiate main loop]
    Repeat through step 7 for all remaining lines in program
3. [Skip over comment lines]
    If '' in column 7 then go to (7)*

4. [Realign line to standard positions (column 8 or 12)]
   istart = 12
   n = position of first nonblank character after column 6
   If n = 7 (continued literal)
       then locate next nonblank and
                realign to column 12
       else if n < 12 (paragraph or section name)
           then realign to column 8,
                istart = 8.
       else realign to column 12

5. [Initiate loop on current line]
   Repeat through step 6 for i = istart to 72
       if char(i) = QUO
           then do i = i+1 to 72,
                   If char(i) = QUO then go to (6).
           go to (6).
       if pattern = B80.⌐B1 starting at i
           then replace element 1 by a single blank

6. [Terminate loop on current line]
   Continue

7. [Terminate loop on all lines]
   Continue

8. [Terminate algorithm]
   Exit

[Example before conversion]

```
        COUNT_TROUBLES_C10 SECTION.
    *        LIFE IS TOUGH. . .
        IF  THRILL  =  ULTIMATE
            THEN MOVE  '*JOY* '  TO WORLD
            ELSE ADD          1 TO DISAPPOINTMENT.
```

[Example after conversion]

```
        COUNT_TROUBLES_C10 SECTION.
    *        LIFE  IS  TOUGH. . .
        IF  THRILL  =  ULTIMATE
            THEN MOVE  '   *JOY*   '  TO  WORLD
            ELSE ADD 1 TO DISAPPOINTMENT.
```

This algorithm has been arranged in a more efficient manner than *Algorithm 6.4.1.* We have eliminated the need to convert blanks in literals to some non-COBOL character and then translate them back to blanks. We have also managed to destroy the *structure* of the program! However, as explained in Section 4.2.1, we can enhance portability by aligning all statements in this manner. Ultimately, we will reindent the program but in strict adherence to a set of rules.

This algorithm differs from *Algorithm 6.4.1* in another important aspect. No attempt has been made to combine continued lines. This is a simple task for FORTRAN programs and was incorporated in Algorithm 6.4.1. However, for COBOL programs the logic is more complex, and is best handled in a separate algorithm. One would also include logic for starting all new statements on separate lines.

6.5 IDENTIFIER NAMES

A common conversion problem is modification of identifier names due to differences in the definitions of valid names. Table 6.2 includes definitions of identifier names for a variety of languages and dialects. We note differences in maximum lengths, character sets, and in the rules for constructing a valid name. These differences often result in the need to change the names of some identifiers in a variety of conversion situations.

Most COBOL compilers adhere to the ANS standard for identifier names and therefore name changes are rarely required in COBOL-to-COBOL conversions. There are differences in the various PL/1 definitions; however, these differences are not particularly important. (Very few PL/1 programmers elect to use names longer than 31 characters!) The FORTRAN differences, however, are quite significant. Unless limited by an enforced standard, CDC and GE FORTRAN programmers will often use seven- and eight-character identifiers. Usage of these long names will cause problems if a subsequent attempt is made to convert the programs to standard FORTRAN IV.

Interlanguage conversions will involve naming problems if the move is from a language with a liberal set of rules for constructing identifiers to a restricted set of rules. For example, conversions from COBOL to RPG or FORTRAN to BASIC will require some effort to modify identifier names. Conversions in the opposite direction should be relatively simple (from the point of view of identifier name changes).

The most difficult problem associated with identifiers is the need to reduce the maximum length of a valid name. We are confronted with this problem in a variety of conversion situations (e.g., CDC FORTRAN

TABLE 6.2 Identifier Names for a Variety of Languages and Dialects

Language	Dialect	Maximum Length	Character Set	Rules of Construction
ALGOL		Unlimited	A–Z, 0–9	First character must be A–Z; some compilers treat only six or eight characters as significant
BASIC	VS	2	A–Z, 0–9, $	First character must be A–Z, second character must be 0–9 or $.
COBOL	ANS	30	A–Z, 0–9, _	The break character (i.e., _) cannot be first or last; must include at least one A–Z; cannot be reserved word
FORTRAN	IV	6	A–Z, 0–9, $	First character not 0–9
FORTRAN	CDC	7	A–Z, 0–9	First character must be A–Z
FORTRAN	GE	8	A–Z, 0–9	First character must be A–Z
Pascal		Unlimited	A–Z, 0–9, _	First character must be A–Z; cannot be reserved word; some compilers consider only first eight characters, others first 31
PL/1	IBM	31	A–Z, 0–9, $, #, @, _	First character not 0–9 or _; some keywords are reserved
PL/1	PL/C	31	A–Z, 0–9, $, #, @, _	First character not 0–9 or; some keywords are reserved
PL/1	CDC	40	A–Z, 0–9, $, #, @, _	First character not 0–9 or _; may be keyword
PL/1	Burroughs	63	A–Z, 0–9, $, #, @, _	First character not 0–9 or _; may be keyword
RPG II	System 3	8 (file names) 6 (field names)	A–Z, 0–9, $, #, @	First character not 0–9

to FORTRAN IV, ANS COBOL to VS BASIC, FORTRAN IV to VS BASIC). The typical approach to solution of this problem is:

1. List all identifier names that will not be valid in the target environment.
2. Generate a replacement table for all these names.
3. Replace all the illegal names.

This process can either be performed manually or automatically. However, the risk associated with such changes is large and therefore an automatic approach is preferable when possible. Algorithm 6.5.1 demonstrates this process for a CDC FORTRAN-to-FORTRAN IV conversion. This algorithm can be classified as a *two-pass replacement algorithm*.

　　　Algorithm 6.5.1 NAME_CHANGE. This algorithm replaces all seven-character identifier names by a unique six-character name. The six-character name is constructed by using the first four characters of the original name followed by $ followed by a character C (*code*), where C(1) = '0', C(2) = '1', ... C(10) = '9', C(11) = 'A', ..., C(36) = 'Z'. Prior to execution of this algorithm, all unnecessary blanks have been stripped except for a single blank after each keyword.

1. [Initiate loop to Table 7 character identifiers]
   Repeat through step 7 for all lines in program unit
   　　istart = 6
2. [Skip over comments]
   If line is comment then go to (7)
3. [Go directly to (6) for executable section]
   If line is in executable section
   　　then go to (6)
4. [Go directly to (6) for continued line]
   If ¬B1 in column 6
   　　then go to (6)
5. [Locate blank after keyword in nonexecutable statements]
   istart = position of first blank after column 7
6. [Scan for seven character identifiers]
   Do for i = istart to 65
   　　if pattern = ¬Z1.V7.¬Z1
   　　　　then if length of element 2 = 7
   　　　　and element 2 not in Table 1
   　　　　　　then add element 2 to Table 1.

7. [Terminate loop]
    Continue
8. [Initiate replacement loop]
    Do through step 9 for i=1 to number_members_Table_1
    Code = 1
9. [Create replacement and store in Table 2]
    Replacement = substr (member(i) of T1,1,4).'$'.C(code)
    If replacement not in Table 2
    *   then member(i) of Table 2 = replacement*
    *   else code = code + 1*
    *   if code > 36 then go to (error-exit)*
    *   else go to (9)*
10. [Initiate second-pass loop]
    Repeat through step 12 for all lines of program unit
    If line is comment then go to (12)
11. [Search for seven character identifiers in Table 1]
    Do i = 6 to 65
    *   if pattern = ⌐Z1.T1.⌐Z1*
    *   then replace element 2 with*
    *   equivalent Table 2 member.*
12. [Terminate second-pass loop]
    Continue
13. [Terminate algorithm]
    Exit

[Example before conversion]

```
        SUBROUTINE XYZ(LONGNAM,LONG,LONGNAN)
    C ALL 7 CHAR NAMES MUST BE SHORTENED
        DIMENSION LONGNAN(1),LONG(1)
        COMMON VAR1234,VAR1235(10),A,B,C
        LONG(LONGNAM)=A*VAR1234
        LONGNAN(LONGNAM)=VAR1235(LONG)+C
        END
```

[Example after conversion]

```
        SUBROUTINE XYZ(LONG$0),LONG,LONG$1)
    C ALL 7 CHAR NAMES MUST BE SHORTENED
        DIMENSION LONG$1(1),LONG(1)
        COMMON VAR1$0,VAR1$1(10),A,B,C
        LONG(LONG$0)=A*VAR1$0
        LONG$1(LONG$0)=VAR1$1(LONG)+C
        END
```

There are several interesting points to note about this algorithm:

1. The FORTRAN syntax makes it preferable to treat the non-executable and executable statements separately. There are some seven-character keywords in the nonexecutable statement section (e.g., INTEGER, COMPLEX); however, all keywords in the executable statement section are less than seven characters (e.g., READ, WRITE, FORMAT, IF, etc.). The difference in treatment is noted in steps 3 and 5.

2. The replacement member for Table 3 can be one of 36 different possibilities (i.e., ending with either 0,1,..., A,..., Z). If a unique name is not found within these 36 attempts (a highly unlikely situation), the algorithm branches to an error_exit (see step 9). *A good algorithm should include treatment of all exceptional cases* even though the probability of their occurrence is small.

3. One problem *not* covered by this algorithm is the possibility of using a seven-character keyword as an identifier name (which is allowed in FORTRAN). If this highly unlikely situation occurs, the keyword will be replaced in step 11; however, compilation of the resulting program will immediately detect the error. The algorithm could be strengthened to detect this problem by comparing (just prior to step 8) all members of Table 1 to the seven-character keywords and then issuing a warning if the comparison is successful.

4. Execution of this algorithm would have to be preceded by execution of several other algorithms: one to remove unnecessary blanks (e.g., Algorithm 6.4.1) and another to insert a single blank after each keyword.

5. The first seven steps of this algorithm are programmed in the CONVERT language in Section 7.7.

6.6 MISSING FEATURES

The usefulness of a particular programming language is often measured by the various *features* included in the language. Even for languages that have been standardized (e.g., COBOL and FORTRAN), computer manufacturers often add special features to their versions of the language. For example, Table 1.2 (of Section 1.2) includes an analysis of language extensions to a variety of FORTRAN compilers.

Special features can simplify the task of programming; however, if the programs must eventually be converted, the use of special features can complicate the task of the conversion team. If a particular feature has an equivalent form in the target environment, the problem can often be corrected by a simple syntactical change. When the special feature has no equivalent form in the target environment, ingenuity is required to find an *algorithmic solution* to the problem of *mapping the missing feature into the target environment.* The alternative to an algorithmic solution is to reprogram the offending sections of codes (which can be extremely costly if the feature is used extensively throughout the code).

The typical methods for mapping missing features include:

1. *Replace the feature by a call to a subprogram* and then deal with the problem in the subprogram.
2. *Modify the target compiler* to accommodate the feature. (This alternative is usually impossible without the cooperation of the compiler supplier, and even if cooperation is offered, the proposed timetable is often unacceptable.)
3. *Find an algorithmic method for avoiding use of the missing feature.*

I was once asked to write a converter for a BASIC-to-BASIC conversion. We encountered a missing feature of such crucial importance that the project was almost canceled. The problem involved treatment of *size errors* (i.e., attempts to print numbers that are too large for the given FORMAT). In the original environment, the following style of coding was typical:

```
200  NUMBER IS ###    TOTAL IS ###.##
220  PRINT USING 200,N,T1
```

If, for example, N=20 and T1=37.10, the resulting printed line would be

```
NUMBER IS 20   TOTAL IS   37.10
```

This is a fairly standard BASIC feature. The *special feature* appeared at first glance to be minor. If either N or T1 was too large for the given FORMAT (or IMAGE in BASIC terminology), *'s were printed instead of numbers. For example, if N = 84 and T1 = 1842.00, the resulting printed line would be

```
NUMBER IS   84   TOTAL IS ******
```

The generation of *'s when a size error is encountered saves the programmer a massive headache. For the particular applications being converted, these size errors occurred quite frequently. Each program produced reports going on for many pages. Most pages included one or two size errors (which were perfectly acceptable to the end user of the reports).

The *missing feature* in this case was the treatment of size errors. The target BASIC included a comparable form for the PRINT USING command. However, when a size error was encountered, an error message was printed and then execution was terminated! There was no way to override this action and attempts to convince the compiler supplier to alter the compiler were unsuccessful. One possible solution which was given serious consideration was to extend the IMAGES (e.g., change ###.## to ####.##). This solution was rejected due to the complexity and number of reports. Every report would have had to have been analyzed and redesigned if this solution had been adopted.

The use of a *function call* solved the problem. About 50 lines of BASIC were required to program around the problem; however, by including this code in a subprogram it was only added once per program. The PRINT USING statements were replaced by a few easily generated lines of code. The equivalent lines in the target BASIC for the example above are:

```
200  W$(1) =' NUMBER IS ###    TOTAL IS ###.##'
201  W(1) = N
202  W(2) = T1
220  W1 = FNQ(W$(1),2)
```

Each IMAGE was stored in a different member of the W$ array. In addition to the changes above, the W and W$ arrays had to be dimensioned and the FNQ function had to be defined. The following two lines of code were thus added at the top of the program:

```
010  DIM W$(Number of images),W(19)
020  DEF FNQ(W0,W3):GOSUB 90000
```

The FNQ function was appended to the end of the program.

Each program was renumbered prior to execution of this algorithm (starting with 100 and incremented by 20 per line). The maximum number of lines that could be inserted between two existing lines was therefore 19, which explains the DIMENSION used for the W array. Within FNQ, the image was examined number by number to detect size errors. If an error was detected, the IMAGE (in W0) was altered to include *'s. If the number was acceptable, the IMAGE was altered to include its value. The final line in FNQ replaced the original PRINT USING with the target BASIC equivalent. Implementation was successful and did not noticeably degrade the system performance. The details are included in Algorithm 6.6.1. *This algorithm is a two-pass replacement insertion algorithm.*

Algorithm 6.6.1 SIZE-ERROR. This algorithm replaces formatted PRINT USING statements with calls to a subroutine. Within the subroutine all potential format size errors are checked and if an error is detected, the image is altered to include *'s in place of #'s. Prior to execution of this algorithm, all lines must be renumbered starting from 100, with increments of 20 per line. Also, prior to execution all unnecessary blanks must be removed. The algorithm requires usage of several variables: W\$, W, and W0 through W9. Prior to execution of this algorithm a scan for these variables must be made and a warning issued if any of them are used. Another algorithm must be applied after execution of Algorithm 6.6.1 to change all references to replaced PRINT USING statements by a reference to the same line number less 19.

1. [Initiate first-pass loop]
   repeat through step 3 for all lines of program
2. [Table statement numbers of PRINT USING images]
   If line is L6.' PRINT USING '. L6.','.Q20
   Then if element 3 not in Table 1,
   Then insert element 3 in Table 1.
   k = position of element 3 in Table 1.
   Do i = 1 by 1 while (comma after element 3)
   Locate new element 5,
   new-line-number = element 1 – 20 + i,
   Insert line above current line:
   new-line-number W(i) = element 5,
   Strip off elements 4 and 5,
   If i > 19 then print error message.
   Replace current line by:
   element 1 W1 = FNQ(W\$(k),i)
3. [Terminate first-pass loop]
   Continue
4. [Initiate second-pass loop]
   Repeat through step 6 for all lines of program
5. [Search for lines referenced in Table 1]
   If line number is in Table 1
   Then k = member number in Table 1
   Change line to:
   line number W\$(k) = ' old image '
6. [Terminate second-pass loop]
   Continue

7. [Add DIM and DEF statements]
   n = number members in Table 1
   If n > 0
      then add two lines at top of program:

```
010   DIM W$(n),W(19)
020   DEF FNQ(W0,W3): GOSUB 90000
```

8. [Append FNQ at end of program]
   If n > 0
      Then append FNQ
9. [Terminate algorithm]
   Exit

   [Example before conversion]

```
100   B(#) IS ##.##   N = ###
120   A(#) IS ##.##
140   PRINT USING 120,I,A(I)
160   PRINT USING 100,I,B(I),N
```

   [Example after conversion]

```
010   DIM W$(2),W(19)
020   DEF FNQ(W0,W3): GOSUB 90000
100   W$(2) = ' B(#) IS ##.##   N = ###'
120   W$(1) = ' A(#) IS ##.##'
121   W(1) = I
122   W(2) = A(I)
140   W1 = FNQ(W$(1),2)
141   W(1) = I
142   W(2) = B(I)
143   W(3) = N
160   W1 = FNQ(W$(2),3)
90000 Appended FNQ subroutine
        .
        .
        .
```

6.7 COMPARISON OF CHARACTER TYPE ITEMS

The comparison of character (or literal) variables and constants can lead to a common conversion problem. The problem stems from differences in the *collating sequences* of the source and target environments. A collating sequence is determined by the bit codes used to represent character data. There are several character sets in common usage (e.g., EBCDIC, ASCII, CDC Scientific). If different character sets are used in the source and target environments, the results of character comparisons are not necessarily the same.

As an example, consider the following lines of COBOL:

```
MOVE '4' TO A.
MOVE 'J' TO B.
IF A > B THEN PERFORM C.
```

The EBCDIC character set uses 8 bits per character, and the bit sequences for the characters 4 and J are 11110100 and 11010001, respectively. Thus for EBCDIC-based systems, the comparison is successful (i.e., A > B) and C is performed. The ASCII character set uses 7 bits per character, and the bit sequences for 4 and J are 0110100 and 1001010, respectively. Thus for ASCII-based systems the comparison is unsuccessful and C is *not* performed. We see that *differences in collating sequences can cause major differences in results even for code that appears exactly the same in both environments.*

Tasks such as sorts, searches, and merges of character data usually require character comparison. Thus for these types of tasks the results are often dependent on the collating sequence. For example, consider a list sorted on the basis of three character sets (EBCDIC, ASCII, and CDC SCIENTIFIC). The results of a sample sort are included in Table 6.3 and illustrate the differences in the order of the sorted list. Fisher compared 13 common COBOL compilers and made the following observation: "There is little correlation between the internal character sets so that SORTS are unlikely to yield the same results on different machines" [6].

TABLE 6.3　List Sorted According to Three Collating Sequences

Unsorted List	Collating Sequence		
	EBCDIC Sort	ASCII Sort	CDC Scientific Sort
JA121	JAB21	4X*79	JAB21
4X=79	JA121	4X179	JA121
JAB21	X43RB	4X=79	X43RB
4X179	4X*79	JA121	4X179
X43RB	4X=79	JAB21	4X*79
4X*79	4X179	X43RB	4X=79

Source: G. Schneider, S. Weingart, and D. Perlman, *An Introduction to Programming and Problem Solving with PASCAL*, Wiley, New York, 1978, App. C.

When a collating sequence problem is noted, there are several possible lines of action:

1. *Accept the new collating sequence.* Often, the effect of the new collating sequence is merely to change the order of some lines on output reports. If the new order is acceptable to the end users of the reports, there is no need to attempt to reproduce the original order.

2. Some compilers allow *specification of collating sequence as a compiler option.* For example, ANS COBOL allows the following method for specifying collating sequence:

```
OBJECT_COMPUTER. computer name,
        COLLATING SEQUENCE IS alphabet-name.
SPECIAL NAMES.
        alphabet-name IS -------.
```

This collating sequence is applicable throughout the program, and affects character comparisons in the IF statements and the sequence of random access files [7]. It should be mentioned, however, that this approach might cause some performance degradation.

3. When the comparison of character data is crucial to the program logic, and the problem cannot be solved by simply redefining the collating sequence, *the programs can be modified in an algorithmic manner to accommodate the new collating sequence.* For example, the following PL/1 code might not satisfy a required collating sequence:

```
DCL  (A,B) CHAR(1),
     (C,D) CHAR(2),
     (E,F) BIN FIXED (31);
     .
     .
     .
LO:  IF A = B & (C>D | E = F)
     THEN    CALL XYZ:
```

The converted form that satisfies the required collating sequence might be

```
DCL  (A,B) CHAR(1),
     (C,D) CHAR (2),
     (E,F) BIN FIXED(31);
```

```
DCL  LOGIC1 BIN FIXED;
DCL  COMPARE ENTRY EXTERNAL RETURNS (BIN FIXED);
            .
            .
            .

LO:  LOGIC1 = COMPARE(C,D,'GT');
     If A = B & (LOGIC1 = 1 | E= F)
     THEN CALL XYZ;
```

The function COMPARE uses the desired collating sequence and returns 1 (i.e., true) if C is *greater than* (i.e., 'GT') D; otherwise, 0 is returned. Note that only C > D must be checked. Regardless of the collating sequence, A either equals B or it does not. The character comparisons that must be translated are >, ⌐>, >=, <, ⌐<, and <=. The operators = and ⌐= need not be translated.

An algorithm to accomplish this type of modification is of course language dependent. In general, however, any algorithm would be similar to the following:

Algorithm 6.7.1 COLLATING_SEQUENCE. This algorithm modifies character comparisons which are dependent on collating sequence. The comparisons are replaced by calls to a subprogram called COMPARE, which returns either 1 (*true*) or 0 (*false*).

1. [Initiate loop]
   Repeat through step 4 for all statements.
   $i = 1$
2. [Locate applicable comparison operators]
   Locate operators equivalent to:
   $>, ⌐>, >=, <, ⌐<,$ *and* $<=.$
   If search unsuccessful then go to [4].
3. [Check both sides of the operator]
   If either side of operator includes a character variable or constant:
   Then replace the logical expression by:
   LOGIC $i = 1$
   Insert a line above current line:
   LOGIC i = COMPARE(*left-side, right-side, code*)
   $i = i+1$
   If $i >$ *imax then imax* $= i$
   Go to [2].
4. [Terminate loop]
   Continue

5. [Insert suitable declarations]
   Insert declarations for:
   LOGIC1, LOGIC2, . . . LOGIC*imax.*
6. [Terminate algorithm]
   Exit.

This algorithm is a *single-pass insertion-replacement algorithm.* It should be emphasized that *this approach to the character comparison problem can cause serious performance degradation.* In particular, usage of a call to COMPARE in sorts, searches, and merges can be devastating if these tasks account for an important fraction of the cost of running the application. Normally, character comparisons are efficient; however, accommodation of a *nonnative collating sequence* is bound to be less efficient. The degradation can be reduced if the COMPARE subprogram is written in an efficient manner.

6.8 DATA FILES AND ACCESS METHODS

Many conversions require considerable attention to the manner in which data are stored and retrieved. Data are normally organized into files that reside on external devices outside the computer memory (e.g., tapes and disks). Many data processing applications involve heavy transmission of data to and from these external storage devices. Different languages and computer systems support a variety of file types and methods of access. The differences between the treatment of data in the source environment and the available options in the target environment can lead to some very complex conversion problems.

Most files contain *records* which are either *fixed length, variable length,* or *unspecified.* Variable-length records include information regarding the record length. Unspecified-length records can also be variable; however, the record length is determined by an end-of-record mark. A further complication arises when records are grouped together in *blocks.* Blocking of records is a very useful tool for improving the efficiency of input/output operations.

The two basic methods for accessing data files are sequential and random. *Sequential access* implies that the records are transmitted in the order in which they are physically stored in the file. *Random access* implies that the records are transmitted in a manner that does not necessarily have any relationship to storage order. Some systems accommodate a third possibility: *dynamic access.* This method allows one to switch back and forth between sequential and random access.

There are a number of alternative methods for organizing files. The best known *file organization* classifications are *sequential, direct, relative,* and *indexed.* Files that are organized sequentially can only be accessed sequentially. Direct, relative, and indexed files can be accessed randomly. These files can also be accessed sequentially, but not as efficiently as sequential files. Brown discusses the advantages and disadvantages of the various access and file organization methods [7].

When confronted with a file access or organization incompatibility, there are several alternative lines of action:

1. *Find a solution that can be accomplished at the job control level.* For example, for some batch processing applications, the need for a random access file can be eliminated by sorting the file prior to execution of the modules requiring the file.

2. *Find a solution that can be accomplished by reorganization or redefinition of the data.* It is often easier to recreate data files (using software tools) than to modify the program source code.

3. *Find an algorithmic method for modifying the program source code.* If such a method can be developed, the changes can then be made automatically.

4. *Reprogram the offending modules of the application to utilize the available options in the target environment.* This alternative is usually the most time consuming and costly.

When a simple solution (i.e., alternative 1 or 2 in the list above) is unobtainable, one seeks an algorithmic solution. Once again, the preferred strategy is to concentrate the changes in a subprogram and make only minor changes in the source code. As an example, consider a COBOL conversion from a mainframe to a minicomputer. Let us assume that the treatment of index-sequential input on the minicomputer is very inefficient and that we must find an algorithmic method for improving the situation.

One approach is to save recent records in a buffer, and search the buffer before searching the disk file for the needed record. Such a change would improve performance if a small fraction of the records were required most of the time. (This situation is typical in order-entry systems when a few items account for the bulk of all orders.) Let us assume that the offending lines of codes are similar to the following:

```
MOVE ITEM TO PRODUCT_KEY.
READ PRODUCT_FILE INTO PRODUCT_INFO.
```

Earlier in the FILE_CONTROL section, PRODUCT_FILE would have been specified as ACCESS IS RANDOM. The change after conversion might be

```
MOVE ITEM TO PRODUCT_KEY.
MOVE 'PRODUCT_FILE' TO FILE_KEY.
CALL 'RANDOM_READ' USING FILE_KEY, PRODUCT_KEY, PRODUCT_INFO.
```

All the READ logic is included in the subroutine RANDOM_READ. Since files cannot be shared between a main program and a subroutine, references to PRODUCT_FILE in the ENVIRONMENT and DATA DIVISIONS must be removed from the main program. Suitable file descriptions (perhaps modified according to the needs of the target environment) must be included in the RANDOM_READ subroutine.

This solution is described in Algorithm 6.8.1. The actual details are of course system dependent. However, changes from one system to another would be concentrated primarily in the RANDOM_READ subroutine. The algorithm is a *single-pass replacement algorithm*.

Algorithm 6.8.1 RANDOM_READ. This algorithm modifies COBOL source code so that all random reads of input files are executed in a subroutine called RANDOM_READ. The subroutine uses three parameters: the name of the file, the appropriate key for the random access, and the data field to which the record is moved. A similar algorithm is required for random writes to output files. This algorithm assumes that no alternative keys are used in the source COBOL. It is also assumed that a previous algorithm has been used to reformat the Procedure Division so that each statement starts on a separate line and unnecessary multiple blanks have been stripped from the program.

1. [Examine INPUT_OUTPUT SECTION for random access files]
   For each SELECT determine if access is random and if so add file-name to Table 1 and the appropriate key to Table 2.

2. [Initiate loops for all lines of Procedure Division]
   Repeat through step 4 for all lines of Procedure Division.

3. [Search for random reads]
   If line is 'READ '. T1. ' INTO '. V30
   then replace line with:
   MOVE 'element2' TO FILE_KEY.
   CALL 'RANDOM_READ' USING FILE_KEY,
   ELEMENT 2, ELEMENT 4.*
   Note: Element 2 is Table 2 member*
   corresponding to Element 2.

4. [Terminate loop]
   Continue

5. [Remove file references]

For all files tabled in T1 remove references from Environment and Data Division. Save the information for inclusion in RANDOM_READ.

6. [Terminate algorithm]
   Exit

The RANDOM_READ subroutines could be written in a manner that permits usage by several programs. All relevant files would have to be included; however, the subroutine could be designed so that only the referenced files are opened. Alternatively, a separate RANDOM_READ subroutine could be written for each program using random reads. The logic included in the subroutine could then be optimized for each program. (For example, the number of records held in the buffer, the parameters used to select which record is replaced once the buffer has been filled, and so on, could be varied from program to program.)

6.9 SUMMARY

In this chapter we have developed algorithmic approaches to the solution of a number of common conversion problems. The individual algorithms are examples that might or might not be applicable to a given situation. It should be emphasized that there are many other topics of general interest which were not included in this chapter (e.g., problems associated with data attributes and problems associated with variable-length character strings). Since the emphasis is on examples, no attempt has been made to cover all areas that are amenable to an algorithmic type solution.

It should be mentioned that some conversion problems defy an algorithmic solution. For such cases the usual approach is to redesign and then reprogram the system (or offending modules). For example, some data base applications just cannot be moved from one DBMS (data base management system) to another in an algorithmic manner. If the logical organization of the two DBMSs are radically different, redesign of the application is usually inevitable.

Some types of conversion problems can be treated algorithmically but are often handled through reprogramming. For example, it is possible to apply automatic means to convert Assembler code to a higher-level language. (Note the Assembler-to-COBOL converters listed in Table 1.7.) Nevertheless, many conversion teams faced with this type of problem elect to reprogram rather than automate the conversion. Even if one chooses to reprogram such applications, an algorithmic approach can be used to scan the source code. The results of the scan can be summarized in a manner that contributes to the task of reprogramming.

REFERENCES

1. Tremblay, J. P., and R. C. Bunt, *An Introduction to Computer Science, an Algorithmic Approach*, McGraw-Hill, New York, 1979.
2. Knuth, D. E., "Ancient Babylonian Algorithms," *Communications of the ACM*, Vol. 15, p. 671, July 1972.
3. Gries, D., "ALGOL Language Summary," ACM SIGPLAN History of Programming Languages Conference, *SIGPLAN Notices*, Vol. 13, No. 8, p. 1, August 1978.
4. Aho, A., J. Hopcroft, and J. Ullman, *The Design and Analysis of Computer Algorithms*, Addison-Wesley, Reading, Mass., 1974.
5. *CONVERT Instruction Manual*, Version 3.0, O.L.I. Systems, Inc., 421 7th Avenue, NY, NY 10001, August 1981.
6. Fisher, D. L., "Portable COBOL: Facts and Fiction," *Proceedings of the ON-LINE Conf. on Pragmatic Programming and Sensible Software.* Chameleon Press, 1978, pp. 39-69.
7. Brown, G., *Advanced ANS COBOL with Structured Programming*, Wiley-Interscience, New York 1977.

7

A Conversion Language [1]

7.1 INTRODUCTION

The number of people in the conversion business actually involved in the development of converters is relatively small. Typically, conversion software is purchased or leased. When the required software is unobtainable, the usual approach is to commission development by an organization with experience in this area. Nevertheless, occasions do arise when it becomes necessary to consider development of converters in-house.

In Chapter 6 we discussed *conversion algorithms*. In this chapter the emphasis is on *transforming these algorithms into useful software*. The types of tasks performed in converters are quite different from what one normally encounters in other software development projects. A variety of features are required that are not available in most general-purpose procedural languages. The purpose of this chapter is to discuss features that are useful in developing sophisticated converters.

There are two basic strategies for providing the necessary features required to program converters:

1. Use a *general-purpose procedural language plus a library of useful routines*. Dataware, for example, uses this approach with ANS COBOL as the source language [1].

[1] The material on the CONVERT language has been prepared with permission of O.L.I. Systems, Inc., 421 7th Avenue, N.Y. 10001.

2. Use a *special-purpose language that has been developed for writing converters*. Several conversion languages are available, including CONVERT [2-4], LEX [5], and TACOS [6]. Several other program and data conversion systems are described in the Conversion Products/Aids Survey of the FCSC [7].

Selection of either of these alternatives requires some understanding of the desired features. One can then compare the competing systems and either choose one or embark on the development of a custom-tailored in-house system.

The major advantage of *using a general-purpose procedural language* (with a library of conversion-oriented routines) is that it is a *relatively easy matter to find programmers* to write the converters. In addition, the use of a common language *allows some degree of portability*. It is not always a simple matter to obtain a library of conversion routines; however, companies viewing the development of conversion software as an ongoing activity are sometimes willing to invest the effort in building such a library.

Use of a special-purpose conversion language is usually advantageous from the point of view *of useful features*. Tasks that are common to converters can be built into the language in a natural manner. Thus the user does not have to invest the effort in building a library of routines. The main disadvantage of this approach is the difficulty in locating programmers with a knowledge of the language. One must therefore provide a training program to teach the programming staff how to use the new tool. Another disadvantage associated with special-purpose languages is that they might be restricted to specific hardware configurations due to compiler and/or interpreter limitations.

In this chapter the subject is discussed from the point of view of one special-purpose conversion language: CONVERT [2-4]. The features currently available in this language are the result of six years of development work on more than 50 different converters. The converters range from special-purpose data converters to large interlanguage converters such as FORTRAN IV to PL/1. The wide variety of conversion problems encountered in this work required a number of improvements and added features that were unavailable in the original release of the language in September 1976.

Even though I designed CONVERT, I am not advocating its use for all situations. The only currently available interpreter is written in PL/1 and therefore must be run on a system that supports PL/1. Furthermore, since converters written in this language perform conversions in-core, a large memory (or virtual memory) is required (normally between 512K and 1024K bytes). Nevertheless, the language provides the necessary features for converter development and therefore a discussion of these features satisfies the pedagogical objectives of this chapter.

7.2 LANGUAGE ARCHITECTURE

Most converters are based on some variation of the flowchart shown in Figure 7.1. The CONVERT converters use essentially this scheme (with the addition of a few "bells and whistles"). The major files required in a conversion are shown in Figure 7.2. Some auxiliary files can also be used to support various services that might be required. (For example, the XFILE can be used to add entire blocks of code through the APPEND command.)

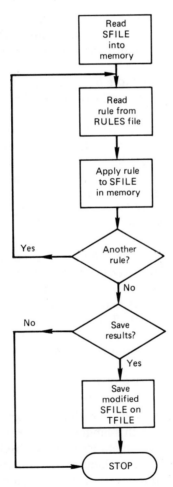

Figure 7.1 Simplified schematic flowchart for a converter. SFILE is the source file to be converted, TFILE is the target file, and RULES is the file containing the rules of conversion. In real converters additional files and features may be required.

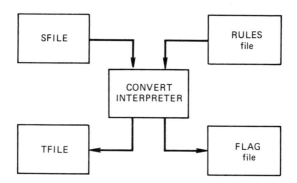

Figure 7.2 Major input and output files in a CONVERT converter. The SFILE is the source file to be converted, the TFILE is the target file, the RULES file contains the rules of conversion, and the FLAG file is a file of messages that help the user to complete any required manual steps in the conversion.

CONVERT performs conversions essentially in-core. A *work area* is allocated *in-core* and the source file (called SFILE) or a portion of the SFILE is read into the work area as shown in Figure 7.3. The work area can be allocated so that each line of the SFILE can "grow" and the number of lines can increase. Each line can have associated numeric and nonnumeric information tagged on to the line. The numeric information is stored in tables called K tables and the nonnumeric information in the H tables. The number of tables can be specified by the user by assigning values to NUMKTAB and NUMHTAB; however, if these parameters are not specified, the default values are one. *The information stored in these tables remains with the associated line in the work area even as lines are inserted and deleted.*

The K and H tables are perhaps the prime examples of *extremely important features which were completely overlooked in the original design of the language.* (Version 1.0 of the language was available in September 1976, but these features were only added in Version 2.1, which was available in January 1979.) For any multipass conversion algorithm, these tables provide a simple method for *tagging* a line. For example, after breaking a program down so that each statement starts on a separate line, a useful strategy is to tag each line according to the statement type. If we choose Table K1 for this purpose, then perhaps K1=1 represents a comment line, K1=2 is a DO statement, K1=3 is an IF statement, and so on. A subsequent rule associated with IF statements would then only require a scan of Table K1 to locate lines with K1=3. I have designed converters which use more than 10 of these tables to store a wide variety of information and have seen converters written using many more tables.

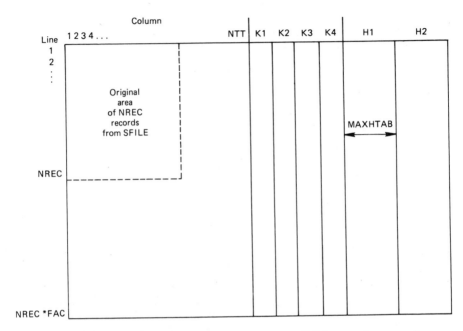

Figure 7.3 Typical layout of the work area. NREC records are read into the work area from the SFILE. The individual lines can grow to a maximum of NTT characters and the maximum number of lines can grow to NREC*FAC. Both NTT and FAC can be set to any desired value. For this example, the available number of K (i.e., numeric) tables (NUMKTAB) is four and H (i.e., nonnumeric) tables (NUMHTAB) is two. The maximum number of characters of members in the H tables is MAXHTAB, which can be set to any desired value. NUMKTAB and NUMHTAB can also be set to any desired value.

CONVERT has been designed to *consider files consisting of a series of lines, and each line is a string of characters (or bytes).* For most program conversions, this model is adequate. However, on occasion, conversion software must operate on the *bit* level. Examples of such software can be found in some data converters. *In this chapter we limit our attention to byte-level converters.*

Another important architectural feature of CONVERT is that all *core allocations are made dynamically according to a series of parameters.* Each parameter is either assigned a default value or its value can be specified as a part of the conversion *set of rules.* For example, in Figure 7.3, we note five parameters that can be specified: NTT, FAC, NUMKTAB, NUMHTAB, and MAXHTAB. The original number of lines NREC must always be inputted. The advantage of being able to specify parameters is that the converter design is not affected by artificial limits. For example, if we always set NUMKTAB to 10 and this value could not be changed, then all converters would have to be designed using a maximum of 10 numeric K tables. Dynamic allocation allows the user to allocate core in any desired configuration. The only limitation is the total core requested and this can be a large amount if one is running the conversion in a virtual memory environment.

7.3 PATTERN RECOGNITION AND SEARCHING

The *ability to recognize a pattern of characters is absolutely essential in conversion software.* Very few general-purpose procedural languages include a high-level pattern recognition capability. One language that does treat pattern recognition in a sophisticated manner is SNOBOL4 [8]. SNOBOL4 is best suited for applications that are nonnumeric in nature: the manipulation of symbolic expressions, the analysis of text, and the processing of structures. The CONVERT language uses some SNOBOL4 ideas and some concepts based on problems associated with conversion software. The CONVERT pattern recognition scheme is defined in Section 6.2. In the chapter all discussions of pattern recognition are based on this scheme.

Once we have a method for defining a pattern, our next task is to define a method for searching for the pattern (or patterns). Do we wish to search every line for the pattern or only some lines? Should the search start at the beginning of a line and proceed to the end, or should it be limited? Are we looking for one occurrence of the pattern or several? Once we have found the pattern on a given line, do we continue our search on the following lines? Do we search the file from beginning to end, or is some other order preferable?

The CONVERT solution to the pattern searching problem utilizes two commands which in many ways are similar: TEST and LOCATE. The TEST command is more general than LOCATE and the result of a TEST (i.e., *success* or *failure*) influences the subsequent processing of the line. Only one TEST can be included in a rule, but many LOCATEs can be used.

The syntax of the TEST command is [4]

TEST *(Parameter specifications: Pattern (or patterns))*

To make TEST a powerful and general-purpose command, more than a dozen parameters may be specified, However, to simplify usage, if a parameter is not specified, its value is automatically set to a default value. As an example of TEST, consider the following:

TEST(CS=7 CF=7 : 'IF'·P100·L5·',',·L5·B1)

This TEST command is used in Algorithm 6.3.1 to search for usage of two-branch logical IF statements in CDC FORTRAN to FORTRAN IV conversions. The search starts and ends at column 7 of the line. (The parameters CS and CF are *Column Start* and *Column Finish.*) This search is valid if all lines have been aligned to column 7 and all unnecessary blanks have been stripped from the lines. If CS and CF are not specified, the TEST would start at column 1 and proceed to the end of the line for all lines of the file. All other parameters assume their default values.

We can list the features required for a high-level pattern recognition and searching capability. Any conversion language should include these or comparable features:

1. A *powerful pattern definition scheme* which allows complex patterns to be developed by concatenation of simple elements. The elements should be based on the needs of conversion software (see Section 6.2).

2. *Searching commands* which allow a simple definition of how to search for the required patterns. Some of the features needed include:
   a. The ability to limit the search to specific columns and lines.
   b. The ability to set parameters symbolically (e..g, CS=R1, where R1 is a parameter than can vary from line to line).
   c. A repetition factor so that the search can be repeated on any given line (e.g., REP=10).
   d. The ability to define a search in a "backward" direction (e.g., CS=80 CF=1).
   e. The ability to define a set of patterns and then search for them in a variety of different ways (e.g., all patterns in the given order, all patterns in any order, any of the patterns, or all patterns in the given order but only separated by "definable" delimiters).
   f. The ability to abort a search on the occurrence of a specific event.

These are the main features required to allow the programmer to specify the patterns and searches required in high-quality conversion software. Examples of usage of some of these features are included in the following sections.

7.4 CONTROLLING LOGICAL FLOW

Most *general-purpose procedural languages* require the programmer to specify the "logical flow" of each program or subprogram included in an application system. Typically, one is provided with such commands as DO, IF, CALL, and GO TO to control flow. More recently, modern programming has placed emphasis on reducing the use of GO TO by employing such commands as IF–THEN–ELSE and CASE. Nevertheless, it is still quite apparent that many semantical errors occur as a result of the programmer's need to specify flow.

Problem-oriented languages can help alleviate the task of defining flow by providing the user with a simple framework in which to specify commands. The flow can be organized on the basis of *keywords*. This approach can be quite successful if a relatively small number of paths are required to define the program logical flow. Conversion software is an example of the type of application falling into this category. Typically, a *rule* requires a *search* and then some sort of *action* if the search is successful. Alternatively, if the search is unsuccessful, an alternative action might be required. In reality, life is never so simple. Nevertheless, the required number of paths is small enough so that about a dozen keywords are enough to cover most situations. The CONVERT language uses this concept [4].

We can illustrate the use of keywords by a simple example. Assume that we have a search (i.e., TEST) for a pattern. If the search is successful, we THEN perform three commands (C1, C2, and C3). However, if the search FAILs, we must perform two different commands (C4 and C5). Using the keyword concept, our rule might appear as follows:

```
            TEST( · · · )
            THEN C1
                 C2
                 C3
            FAIL C4
                 C5
```

This scheme is similar to the IF–THEN–ELSE concept, which has been with us since the early days of ALGOL. The only difference is that by default *this scheme is applied to all lines* of the file. Using a procedural language with IF–THEN–ELSE we would still have to specify a DO LOOP to process all lines. As we add additional keywords, we start to see the advantages of the concept. For example, assume that we *don't* want to apply the TEST to comment lines. We would need a keyword that allows us to specify commands which are performed *prior* to the TEST command: for example, BEGIN. If one command (C6) is required to abort processing of comment lines, our rule would be altered as follows:

```
            TEST ( · · · )
            THEN C1
                 C2
```

```
            C3
       FAIL C4
            C5
       BEGIN C6
```

The same task performed using a procedural language might be similar to the following:

```
DO I = 1 TO NUM-LINES;
   IF LINE(I) not a comment THEN DO;
      IF    TEST ( • • • • ) THEN DO;
            C1
            C2
            C3
      END;
      ELSE    DO;
            C4
            C5
      END;
   END;
END;
```

It should be emphasized that the simplicity that one can obtain *using keywords in a problem-oriented language is attractive only if the logical flow is well defined and the major paths through the program are applicable in a majority of situations.* This certainly describes the situation in conversion software.

In CONVERT, 11 *keywords* are used. All keywords apply to all commands that follow the keyword to the end of the rule or to the next keyword. The following are a general group of keywords:

INITIAL The *initial* commands are performed prior to processing the rule on line 1.

BEGIN The *begin* commands are performed prior to TEST on each line.

PASS The *pass* commands are performed after a successful TEST.

FAIL The *fail* commands are performed after an unsuccessful TEST.

AFTER The *after* commands are performed if a TEST on a given line is initially successful but then fails on a subsequent repetition.

FINAL The *final* commands are performed after processing has been completed for all lines or after an EXIT command has been issued.

The remaining keywords are related to *qualifiers*. Every TEST can be qualified by subsequent "checks" for patterns or other conditions. A qualifier can be classified as *necessary, sufficient,* or *reject.* A TEST is either rejected or not rejected depending on the results of the qualifiers.

THEN The *then* commands are performed if a TEST is successful and is not rejected by the qualifiers. (THEN is like PASS if there are no qualifiers.)

FIRST The *first* commands are performed prior to the *then* commands but only for the first repetition of a TEST.

ELSE The *else* commands are performed if a TEST is successful but then rejected by a qualifier.

QUAL*n* The QUAL*n* (where *n* is replaced by a number) commands are performed if a TEST is rejected by the *n*th qualifier.

BOTH The *both* commands are performed after all *then, else,* and *qualn* commands.

Additional logical paths can be defined and thus new keywords can be "coined." However, experience has shown that almost all situations encountered in conversion software are covered by these *keywords.*

Within a keyword grouping of commands one often needs to alter the flow from a simple sequential scheme. The CONVERT solution includes the following features:

1. An IF parameter can make any command *conditional.*
2. A JUMP command can cause a *jump* to any other command in the keyword group.
3. An ADVANCE command aborts processing of the keyword group and proceeds to the next line (starting with the BEGIN commands if any are included).
4. An EXIT command aborts processing of an entire rule, but before proceeding to the next rule, all *final* commands are processed.
5. A GOTO command causes a branch to another rule but not necessarily the following rule in the RULES file.

These features plus the keywords described above provide sufficient flexibility in defining logical flow in conversion software. One should note, however, that use of a large number of commands in a keyword group with many JUMPs and ADVANCEs makes the logic difficult to follow. Use of a larger number of smaller rules is the recommended style of programming which improves readability and maintainability of the resulting software. Use of K and H tables is also very helpful in simplifying logic.

7.5 EXCLUDE: A PATTERN RECOGNITION FEATURE

In Section 4.2.1 a simple example was shown in which a file is to be organized on the basis of a single statement per line. The algorithm requires that lines are to be broken at semicolons but *not* semicolons within literals. Problems of this sort abound in conversion software and one requires a general-purpose feature for handling these problems. The CONVERT solution to this problem is the EXCLUDE command.

The EXCLUDE command *excludes* portions of a line from pattern searches *without* altering the contents of the line. Three strings can be defined in exclude: EX1, EX2, and EX3. All portions of a line between EX1 and EX2 are replaced by EX3 but only during the search. If EX2 appears before EX1, all characters from column 1 to EX2 are replaced by EX3. If EX1 is present but not EX2, the exclusion starts from EX1 and terminates at the end of the line. No attempt is made to continue the exclusion on to the next line. However, the programmer merely has to insert an EX1 string at the beginning of the next line to ensure that the exclusion continues from line to line if necessary. The default definition of EX1 and EX2 is a single-quote character and the default definition of EX3 is a blank character.

As an example, consider our search for semicolons but not within literals. The *pattern* search is merely

```
        TEST (' ; ')     EXCLUDE
```

None of the *exclude* parameters needs to be specified because the *default values* of EX1, EX2, and EX3 are acceptable. If we want to also *exclude* semicolons within parentheses, we merely have to add a second EXCLUDE command:

```
        TEST (' ; ')     EXCLUDE
                EXCLUDE(EX1 ='(' EX2=')')
```

If we also want to *exclude* semicolons within PL/1 comments (i.e., from /* to */), we add a third EXCLUDE:

```
        TEST (' ; ')     EXCLUDE
                EXCLUDE(EX1=' (' EX2=')')
                EXCLUDE(EX1='/*' EX2='*/')
```

Another useful feature is to be able to define the exclude *level*. For example, consider the following search:

TEST('INSIDE')
EXCLUDE(L=2 EX1=' (' EX2=')')

The parameter L=2 excludes regions on a line inside *two* levels of parentheses. Thus on the following line:

PARENS ((INSIDE LEVEL2) INSIDE LEVEL 1) OUTSIDE

our search will find only the second occurrence of the word INSIDE.

The ability to define EX3 is necessary because sometimes we are searching for blanks. If, for example, we wish to *exclude* literals from a blank stripping process, the following EXCLUDE command could be used:

EXCLUDE(EX3='*')

During the search for blanks, all regions within quotes would be replaced by asterisks.

The EXCLUDE feature is extremely powerful and can vastly reduce the complexity of defining a pattern and associated search. In the original definition and prototype of CONVERT, we neglected to provide an EXCLUDE command. After several months of usage of this early version of the language, we recognized the need for such a command. The implementation of the command led to a dramatic improvement in our ability to write conversion rules. In retrospect, I find it difficult to understand why it took us so long to realize the need for the EXCLUDE command!

7.6 CHANGING A LINE

A typical conversion rule is initiated by a pattern search on a line and is followed by some action. Often the action is to "change" the line in some manner. Experience with CONVERT has led to a variety of useful commands for changing lines (or portions of lines):

ALIGN
BREAK
COMBINE
DELETE

INSERT

REPLACE

REVERSE

TRANSLATE

Each of these commands can be modified by parameters so that almost
any desired change can be accommodated. For example, the command

REPLACE(EO=5 : 'GO TO ')

means that *element 5* is replaced by the string 'GO   TO   '. (EO means
element only.) For this case element 5 would refer to the fifth element
of the pattern defined in the TEST command (or the first LOCATE
command if there is no TEST in the rule).

We can illustrate how a combination of these commands can be
used to perform a useful task by referring to Algorithm 6.3.1. This
algorithm describes the conversion of *CDC two-branch logical IF* statements to an acceptable FORTRAN IV form. The rule might be programmed as follows:

TEST (CF=1 : C6·'IF'·P100·L5·', '·L5·B1)
THEN REPLACE(EO=5 : 'GO TO ')
BREAK (E=5 CS=7)
INSERT(E=4 : ' GO TO ')

After element 5 (i.e., the comma) has been *replaced* by 'GO TO', the
line is *broken* at this point and the new line is started at column 7
(columns 1 through 6 of the new line are thus filled with blanks). The
final action is to *insert* the string ' GO TO ' just before element 4 (i.e.,
E=4).

A careful examination of Algorithm 6.3.1 reveals that the rule is
not complete because we should apply the TEST only to *noncomment*
lines. Using the ADVANCE command mentioned in Section 7.4, we can
easily accomplish this objective by adding the following line to the rule:

BEGIN ADVANCE(IF(CH1·EQ·'C'))

The *begin* commands are processed *prior* to TEST. Thus if character 1
of the line (i.e., CH1) is the letter C (i.e., a comment line), the AD-
VANCE aborts processing of the rule on the current line and proceeds
to the next line.

7.7 USAGE OF TABLES

In Section 7.2 we discussed usage of the K and H tables for tagging lines. In many conversion problems we have need for general-purpose tables (called T tables) which have no direct connection with a particular line. As an example of the use of T tables, consider Algorithm 6.5.1. The purpose of the algorithm is to change seven-character names to unique six-character names. (Many conversions require some form of name changes for identifiers.) In the algorithm all long names are stored in Table 1 (i.e., T1). A unique shorter version of each name is first derived and then stored in Table 2 (i.e., T2).

The CONVERT commands for performing necessary operations with tables include the following:

COMBINE
LOOKUP
PRINT
READ
REVERSE
SCRATCH
TABLE
TRUNCATE

Each of these commands can be suitably modified by parameters to accomplish a wide variety of tasks.

To illustrate usage of some of these commands, let us consider a modified version of the first seven steps of Algorithm 6.5.1. We will store in T1 all seven-character names that are located between columns 7 and 72 of FORTRAN programs except for names in comments and literals. If some seven-character FORTRAN *keywords* (e.g., INTEGER and COMPLEX) are also stored in the table, we can remove them in a subsequent rule (prior to creating the *replacement* table). A rule to accomplish this task is the following:

TEST(REP=40 CS=R2 CF=65 LOCK=1 : ¬Z1·V7·¬Z1)

EXCLUDE

REJECT (IF(CA2·LT·7))

INITIAL   SCRATCH(M=1 LINE=0)

```
BEGIN      ADVANCE(IF(CH1·EQ·'C'))

           SET(R=2 M=6)

THEN       STRING(M=1 EO=2)

           LOOKUP(M=1 R=1 : S1)

           TABLE(IF=1 M=1 : S1)

BOTH       SET(R=2 M=FC1)
```

The first command processed by this rule is the *initial* command SCRATCH. Table 1 (i.e., M=1) is *scratched*, so initially, there are *no members* in this table. The modifier LINE=0 means that all members are removed from the table. (LINE=3, for example, would mean that the third member is removed.)

The first *begin* command ADVANCE(IF(CH1·EQ·'C')) means that if the letter C is noted in column 1 (i.e., a comment line), then we immediately advance to the next line. This command is processed *prior* to the TEST. If the line is not a comment line, then the value of register 2 (i.e., R=2) is *set* to six (i.e., M=6). Register 2 (i.e., R2) is used in the TEST command.

The TEST command in this rule is more complex than the TESTs we have discussed in previous sections. The search is repeated up to 40 times (i.e., REP=40) starting from column R2 and terminating at column 65. The value of R2 is 6 for the first repetition and is then set to the value of the final character in the pattern (i.e., FC1) for each subsequent repetition. The parameter LOCK (i.e., LOCK=1) ensures that the search for subsequent repetitions starts from column CS and not from the default position of one column beyond the located pattern. The terminal value of the search is 65 because beyond this point no pattern can include a seven-character second element which terminates at or before column 72. The pattern for this TEST includes a nonalphanumeric character (i.e., ¬Z1) followed by a one- to seven-character variable (i.e., V7) and terminated with another nonalphanumeric character. The EXCLUDE command blanks out all literals from the search.

The need for LOCK and register 2 is best explained using the following simple example:

COMMON VAR1234,VAR5678

The first pattern we would locate is ' COMMON '. If we start the second repetition of this search at the blank following COMMON, we locate the pattern ' VAR1324,'. However, if we start our search at one column beyond the first pattern (i.e., at the V), we locate the pattern ',VAR5678 '.

The TEST is *rejected* if the number of characters in the second element of the pattern (i.e., CA2) is less than seven. (The parameter CA2 is one of a number of parameters automatically set as a result of the TEST search.) Rejection of the TEST means that the commands following the keyword THEN are not processed for the particular repetition. However, the command following BOTH is processed if the TEST is successful regardless of the value of CA2. This SET command sets the value of register 2 (i.e., R=2) to the column number of the final character of the pattern (i.e., FC1).

When the TEST is *successful* and *not rejected*, the commands following the keyword THEN are processed. First, string 1 (i.e., M=1) is created from element 2 (i.e., EO=2) of the TEST pattern. Then the LOOKUP command searches Table 1 (i.e., M=1) for string 1 (i.e., S1). The result of LOOKUP is stored in register 1 (i.e., R=1). If S1 is not found, then register 1 is set to zero; otherwise, it is set to the line in Table 1 that is equal to S1. The IF parameter in the TABLE command makes this command *conditional*. It means that the command should be performed only if register 1 (i.e.,IF=1) is zero. If this is true, then string 1 (i.e., S1) is added to Table 1 (i.e., M=1).

This rule uses three important *table processing commands:* SCRATCH, LOOKUP, and TABLE. From an examination of this rule one can begin to see the level of complexity that must be considered in writing conversion software. The need for a powerful table processing capability becomes more and more obvious as one begins to treat serious conversion problems.

7.8 SYMBOLIC PARAMETERS

In a general-purpose procedural language, an immense variety of variables can be used in a virtually unlimited manner. The user is provided with some rules for naming variables (see Table 6.2, for example), and then the variables can be used as required. In a problem-oriented language, it is sometimes possible to *eliminate the need for user-defined variables*. However, we still need some method for setting values symbolically. The CONVERT language uses a concept of *symbolic parameters* which adds great flexibility to the language.

The modifiers of a command can be set *directly* (e.g., CS=6) or *symbolically* (e.g., CS=R2). In this example, R2 is a *symbolic parameter* and means the value of register 2. A number of symbolic parameters are automatically set each time a pattern search is made. For example, a TEST for the pattern

$$C6 \cdot 'IF' \cdot P100 \cdot L5 \cdot ', ' \cdot L5 \cdot B1$$

was discussed in Section 7.6. The symbolic parameters set as a result of this search are:

IC1   Position of the initial character of pattern 1 (i.e., the TEST pattern).

FC1   Position of the final character of pattern 1.

LEN1 Length of pattern 1.

CAi   Number of characters in string A (i.e., the TEST string), element i. For this case CA1, CA2, . . ., CA7 are all set.

PAi   Starting position of element i of string A. For this case PA1, PA2, . . ., PA7 are all set.

VAi   The numerical value of element i of string A. For this case only VA4 and VA6 are set. These are the only numeric elements.

Similar information is also available for patterns included in LOCATE commands. The TEST pattern (or patterns) are always numbered first followed by the LOCATE patterns in their order of appearance in the rule. For example, consider the following:

```
TEST('IF')
    THEN LOCATE(CS=FC1  :  'GOTO  '·L5)
        etc.
```

This rule searches for the string 'IF' on every line. If the search is successful, *THEN* another search is initiated starting from the end of the TEST pattern (i.e., FC1). The second search is for a string 'GOTO ' followed by a numeric label of one to five characters. The numerical value of this label is stored in VB2, the number of characters in the label is CB2, and the starting position of the label is PB2. The GOTO string starts in IC2 (or PB1).

A number of other symbolic parameters are available. However, little purpose is served in exhaustively discussing these parameters. The interesting point to note is that use of symbolic parameters can simplify the logic associated with a particular rule. Automatic setting of parameters is a task that is easy to accommodate in a problem-oriented language where the total number of interesting parameters is relatively limited.

7.9 OTHER FEATURES

Several other features included in CONVERT have general applicability to conversion software and should therefore be mentioned.

1. *Interfacing with other languages.* Some tasks that one might require in a particular conversion are best handled within the framework of a general-purpose procedural language. CONVERT provides a simple interface to an external PL/1 procedure through the CALL command. The entire work area, the T tables, and other useful parameters, strings, and tables are all passed as parameters to a PL/1 procedure called PL1LINK. The user can write his own version of PL1LINK and can include CALLs from PL1LINK to other programs, and thus the full power of PL/1 (or for that matter any language or software package that can be called from a PL/1 program) is available within the framework of a CONVERT program. Typical applications of this feature are the generation of reports and the use of clever sorting routines.

2. *Changing parameters.* In Section 7.2 it was mentioned that core is dynamically allocated based on a number of parameters that can be changed if the default values are unacceptable. The concept of changing parameters is not limited to parameters affecting core allocation. For example, the choice of all characters used in CONVERT programs can be changed from rule to rule. A problem sometimes encountered in conversions is that a particular symbol used in the CONVERT program must also be used in a particular rule. The use of ! (the exclamation mark) to delimit CONVERT comments illustrates this point. If we must write a rule that requires some usage of this character, the simplest solution is to change the comment delimiter to another symbol.

3. *Rule timing.* Bitter experience has shown that it is quite possible to write very inefficient converters. Usually, if we can locate the cause of the inefficiency, major improvements can be made. A parameter called TIME was added to CONVERT to facilitate gathering of data related to CPU usage. The default value of TIME is zero (no timing information) and can be increased to three (maximum information). When TIME=3, the following information is typically printed for each rule:

```
RULE=1 RULETIME=2.48 DEVLTIME=0.83 RUNTIME=1.65 LINERUN=0.08
RULE=2 RULETIME=8.32 DEVLTIME=1.24 RUNTIME=7.08 LINERUN=0.35
etc.
```

After all rules have been processed, the following summary information is printed:

```
DEVLTOT=13.23 RUNTOT=27.41 LINERUN=1.37
```

The value of RULETIME is the total CPU time for a rule and is the sum of DEVLTIME and RUNTIME. These values of time can be outputted in any desired units. The value of DEVLTIME is the time required to interpret the rule and RUNTIME is the actual processing time. The value of LINERUN is RUNTIME/NREC (where NREC is the number of records originally read into the work area from the SFILE). The values of DEVLTOT and RUNTOT are the totals for DEVLTIME and RUNTIME summed over all rules.

Assuming that the time to convert a program is linearly dependent upon NREC, we can estimate T_C, the total CPU time for conversion:

$$T_C \cong DEVLTOT + NREC * LINERUN$$

This linear relationship tends to *underestimate* T_C when NREC is much greater than the number of records in the test file used to measure the parameters. As NREC increases, the value of DEVLTOT becomes less important; therefore, attempts to improve efficiency are usually concentrated on reducing LINERUN for the individual rules. Considering our example above, we see that LINERUN for rule 2 (i.e., 0.35) represents 25.5% of the total for the entire set of rules. Therefore, we would certainly examine this rule to see if we could improve its speed. Alternatively, rule 1 has only a minor effect on T_C.

4. *Interactive features.* The development of converters is best performed in an interactive environment. (The same is true for all program development projects!) CONVERT was designed to exploit the potential of interactive development. For example, the programmer can easily obtain a variety of *intermediate results* which are extremely helpful for debugging rules. There are a variety of *display* and *restart* features which simplify the programming process.

7.10 A COMPLETE CONVERSION RULE

The following example is a complete rule written in the CONVERT language. This rule comes from a Xerox SIGMA Extended FORTRAN to FORTRAN IV converter [9]. The rule converts DO loop arguments that are arithmetic expressions and modifies the statements if the third parameter is a negative constant or a variable. This rule is one of the longer and more complicated rules included in the SIGMA converter and should give the reader some insight into the complexities involved in developing conversion software.

This rule accomplishes all conversion tasks associated with the DO statements. In SIGMA FORTRAN, DO parameters may be arithmetic expressions but these are not permitted in standard FORTRAN IV. Also, standard FORTRAN IV does not permit a negative increment (i.e., the third parameter may not be negative), however, this is valid in SIGMA FORTRAN. Both of these problems are illustrated in the following line of valid SIGMA FORTRAN code:

```
20   DO 100 I= L+M*N, 17, J2
```

The first parameter (i.e., L+M*N) is an arithmetic expression and the third parameter (i.e., J2) is a variable which might have a negative value. The converted form of this DO loop is the following:

```
20   I$1=IABS(J2)
     I$2=IABS(L+M*N-(17))+IABS(L+M*N)
     I$3=IABS(L+M*N)
     I=L+M*N-(J2)
     DO 100 I1$=I$3,I$2,I$1
     I=I+(J2)
```

Note that the converted code transforms the single line above to six lines of new code.

The following CONVERT rule will perform the above conversion if unnecessary blanks have been stripped from the line and the line has been properly tagged by setting the value of K1 to one. Prior to execution of this rule, blank stripping and tagging are accomplished in other rules.

```
!** DO LOOPS WITH VARIABLE (PERHAPS NEGATIVE) PARAMETERS (PAGE 30) *400*!
TEST(CS=7 CF=7 RULE=400 : 'DO'.L5.V31.'='U100.','.U100.Y1.U100.' ')
     EXCLUDE(EX1=' (' EX2=')' EX3='*')    Y=( ,)
     X=(0123456789ABCDEFGHIJKLMNOPQRSTUVWXYZ$)
     REJECT SUBSTR(EO=8 : ',')
     INITIAL SET(R=5 M=1) !RIGHT SIDE VARIABLE INDEX!
          SET(R=6 M=1) !LEFT   SIDE VARIABLE INDEX!
     BEGIN ADVANCE(IF(K1.NE.1))  SET(R=3)
     QUAL1 LOCATE(CS=PA8 CF=PA8 : ','.L15.' ')
          SET(IF=1 R=3 M=-1)
     BOTH LOCATE(CS=PA5 CF=PA5 : X31.',')    SET(IF=1 R=1 M=-1)
          LOCATE(CS=PA7 CF=PA7 R=2 : X31.Y1)  SET(IF=2 R=2 M=-1)
          EVALUATE(R4=MIN(R1,R2,R3))  JUMP(LAB=300 : IF(R4.GE.0))
               !IF R4 IS GE TO ZERO THEN NOTHING NEEDS REPLACING!
          STR(M=1 I1=1 C2=6) REP(C2=5 : '    ')  JUMP(LAB=100 : IF(R3.LT.0))
     !NO VARIABLE THIRD PARAMETER!    JUMP(LAB=50 : IF(R2.GE.0))
          STR(M=2 EO=7) INS(L=-1 : S1.'I$'.R5.'='.S2) REP(EO=7 : 'I$'.R5)
          STRING(M=1 : '    ')  INC(R=5)  CONTINUE(LAB=50)
```

```
    JUMP(LAB=300 : IF(R1.GE.0))  STRING(M=2 EO=5)
    INSERT(L=-1 : S1.'I$'.R5.'='.S2) REP(EO=5 : 'I$'.R5)
    INCREASE(R=5) JUMP(LAB=300)
  ! THREE PARAMETER SECTION!    STRING(LAB=100 M=2 EO=9)
    INS(L=-1 : S1.'I$'.R5.'=IABS('.S2.')') REP(EO=9 : 'I$'.R5)
    INCREASE(R=5) STRING(M=3 EO=5) STRING(M=4 EO=7)
    INSERT(L=-1 CS=7 : 'I$'.R5.'=IABS('.S3.'-('.S4.'))+IABS('.S3.')')
    REP(EO=7 : 'I$'.R5)  INC(R=5)  JUMP(LAB=150 : IF(R1.EQ.0))
    INSERT(L=-1 CS=7 : 'I$'.R5.'=IABS('.S3.')')
    REPLACE(EO=5 : '$'.R5)    INCREASE(R=5)
    STR(LAB=150 M=1 EO=3) INS(L=-1 CS=7 : S1.'='.S3.'=('.S2.')')
    REPLACE(EO=3 : 'I'.R6.'$')    INCREASE(R=6)
    INSERT(L=1 CS=7 : S1.'='.S1.'+('.S2.')')
    INSERT(LAB=300 E=3 : '  ') INSERT(E=2 : '  ')
:::::::::::::::::::::::::::::::::::::::::::::::::::::::::::::::::::::
```

The following before and after examples illustrate several features of this rule:

```
        Before:
          100   DO1I=1,2
          150   DO2J=L1,L2,-1
          160   DO10K1=I*2+3,KKK
          200   DO12K=A(1,1)
          300   DO123K12345=I*J*K,L*M/N

        After:
          100   DO 1 I=1,2
          150   I$1=IABS(-1)
                I$2=IABS(L1-(L2))+IABS(L1)
                I$3=IABS(L1)
                J=L1-(-1)
                DO 2 I1$=I$3,I$2,I$1
                J=J+(-1)
          160   I$4=I*2+3
                DO 10 KI=I$4,KKK
          200   DO12K=A(1,1)
          300   I$5=L*M/N
                I$6=I*J*K
                DO 123 K12345=I$6,I$5
```

1. The simple DO (i.e., line 100) is hardly modified. The rule only puts blanks before and after the numeric label 1.
2. The second DO (i.e., line 150) has a negative increment so it is converted according to the algorithm described above.

3. The third DO (i.e., line 160) has only one arithmetic expression so only this expression is converted on a separate line.
4. Line 200 is not a DO line so the rule does not affect this line.
5. Line 300 is a DO with two arithmetic expressions and both are converted.

This rule contains an element type not included in Table 6.1. R type elements were added in Version 3.0 and are illustrated in the following command:

REPLACE(EO=9 : 'I$'.R5)

This command causes element 9 of the TEST pattern to be replaced by the string 'I$' followed by the value of register 5.

An interesting feature is the use of K tables. For example, note the commands

BEGIN ADVANCE(IF(K1.NE.1))

If K1 is not equal to one, the program advances to the next line without attempting the TEST. In this manner pattern searches are avoided for all but the true DO lines.

The pattern search specified in the TEST command is quite general and will identify DO lines with either two or three parameters. The interesting element to note is element 8 (i.e., Y1). The Y element is user-defined and is specified on the line after the TEST as either a blank or a comma (i.e., Y=(,)). If element 8 is a comma then there are three DO parameters, otherwise there are only two parameters. Note the use of the EXCLUDE command that masks out all regions on the line within parentheses. Without the EXCLUDE, line 200 would have been originally identified as a DO line because of the comma separating the array indices (i.e., A(1,1)).

7.11 SUMMARY

In this chapter we have discussed features available in CONVERT, a language designed for the development of software converters. Other conversion languages and systems have similar features. It would be a difficult task indeed to develop a sophisticated converter without many of the tools described in the preceding sections. Thus before undertaking a converter development project, it is worthwhile to investigate the possibility of obtaining a conversion software development system.

REFERENCES

1. Dinkel, R., Dataware, private communication, 1980.
2. Wolberg, J. R., and M. Rafal, "CONVERT—A Language for Program and Data File Conversions," *Software—Practice and Experience*, Vol. 8, pp. 187-198, 1978.
3. Wolberg, J. R., and M. Rafal, "Using CONVERT to Transform Source Code," *Software—Practice and Experience*, Vol. 9, pp. 881-890, 1979.
4. *CONVERT Instruction Manual*, Version 3.0, O.L.I. Systems, Inc., 421 7th Avenue, NY 10001, August 1981.
5. Lesk, M. E., and E. Schmidt, *LEX—Lexical Analyzer Generator*, Bell Labs, Murray Hill, NJ.
6. *TACOS—Tool for Automatic Conversion of Operational Software*, Proprietary Software Systems, Inc., Los Angeles, Calif.
7. *Conversion Products/Aids Survey*, Federal Conversion Support Center, Falls Church, Va., August 1980.
8. Griswold, R. E., and M. Griswold, *A SNOBOL4 Primer*, Prentice-Hall, Englewood Cliffs, NJ, 1973.
9. SIGMA Converter, O.L.I. Systems, Inc., 421 7th Avenue, NY 10001.

Name and Organization Index

ACM, 18
Aho, A. J., 177
American Standards Association, 6, 17
Anderson, G. E., 134, 142, 157
Apple Computers, 24
Applied Data Research, 151, 152
Atari, 24

Bates, R. M., 157
Boehm, B., 30, 59, 60
Brandon, D. H., 48
Brillinger, P. C., 22
Brooks, F., 60, 63, 65, 75
Brown, G. D., 28, 103, 107, 145, 169, 203, 206
Brown, P. J., 6, 13
Bunt, R. C., 133, 176, 185
Burroughs, 12, 18, 30, 41, 162, 194
Buschbach, T., 59, 76
Business Week, 61

CAP—SOGETI, 13
Capex Corp., 146
CDC, 10, 12, 19, 21, 30, 106, 144, 161, 185, 186, 187, 194, 202, 222
Cohen, D. J., 22
Commodore Computers, 24
Computer Associates, 131
Computer Decisions, 151
Computerworld, 151
Coopers and Lybrand, 139, 141, 142, 143

CRAY, 106
C-S Computer Systems, 25

DASD, 25, 161
Datamation, 12, 13, 60, 66, 71, 151
Datapro, 11, 151
Dataware, 25, 56, 57, 163, 210
DEC, 12, 106
Deutsch, M., 173
Dijkstra, E., 133
Dinkel, R., 163, 210

EEC, 11, 13
Esterling, B., 65, 66

Federal Conversion Support Center, 59, 151, 211
Felix, C. P., 43, 44, 45, 46
Fenton, J. S., 6, 7, 18
Ferrari, D., 106, 109
F International Ltd., 72, 73
Fisher, D. L., 18, 202
F. Lenker and Assoc., 26
Frank, W., 133

GE, 30, 194
Gepner, H. L., 12
Gilb, T., 109
Goldstine, H., 15
Gries, D., 176

233

Subject Index